APPLIED DRAMA

Theatre and Performance Practices

General Editors: Graham Ley and Jane Milling

Published

Christopher Baugh   *Theatre, Performance and Technology (2ed)*
Greg Giesekam   *Staging the Screen*
Deirdre Heddon   *Autobiography in Performance*
Deirdre Heddon and Jane Milling   *Devising Performance*
Helen Nicholson   *Applied Drama (2ed)*
Cathy Turner and Synne K. Behrndt   *Dramaturgy and Performance*
Michael Wilson   *Storytelling and Theatre*
Philip B. Zarrilli, Jerri Daboo and Rebecca Loukes
     Acting – Psychophysical Phenomenon and Process

Forthcoming

Mark Evans   *Performance, Movement and the Body*
Jason Price   *Popular Theatre*
Kerrie Schaefer   *Communities, Performance and Practice*

Theatre and Performance Practices Series
Series Standing Order ISBN 978–1–403–98735–8   hardcover
Series Standing Order ISBN 978–1–403–98736–5   paperback
(*outside North America only*)

You can receive future titles in this series as they are published by placing a standing order. Please contact your bookseller or, in the case of difficulty, write to us at the address below with your name and address, the title of the series and the ISBN quoted above. Customer Services Department, Macmillan Distribution Ltd, Houndmills, Basingstoke, Hampshire, RG21 6XS, UK

Applied Drama

The Gift of Theatre
Second edition

H<small>ELEN</small> N<small>ICHOLSON</small>

palgrave
macmillan

First published 2005
Second edition published 2014 by
PALGRAVE MACMILLAN

Palgrave Macmillan in the UK is an imprint of Macmillan Publishers Limited, registered in England, company number 785998, of Houndmills, Basingstoke, Hampshire RG21 6XS.

Palgrave Macmillan in the US is a division of St Martin's Press LLC, 175 Fifth Avenue, New York, NY 10010.

Palgrave Macmillan is the global academic imprint of the above companies and has companies and representatives throughout the world.

Palgrave® and Macmillan® are registered trademarks in the United States, the United Kingdom, Europe and other countries.

ISBN 978–1–137–00396–6   hardback
ISBN 978–1–137–00395–9   paperback

This book is printed on paper suitable for recycling and made from fully managed and sustained forest sources. Logging, pulping and manufacturing processes are expected to conform to the environmental regulations of the country of origin.

A catalogue record for this book is available from the British Library.

A catalog record for this book is available from the Library of Congress.

Typeset by MPS Limited, Chennai, India.

Printed in China.

Contents

List of Figures

Acknowledgements

As research in applied drama is sensitive to the contexts in which the practice takes place, there are inevitably many people to thank. First, formal acknowledgements are due to Bloodaxe Books, for permission to reproduce Jackie Kay's poem 'In My Country' which was first published in *Other Lovers* (1993). Parts of Chapter 5 were recycled from a previous publication, 'The Performance of Memory' in *Drama Australia*, 27: 2 (2003), and I am pleased to acknowledge their permission to include aspects of the article in this book. The AHRB gave me an award for research leave which enabled me to complete the first edition of this book in 2003. I am also grateful to series editors Jane Milling and Graham Ley who invited me to contribute to this series, and to Kate Haines and Jenni Burnell at Palgrave who have worked with me on different editions of the book with much tact, enthusiasm and insight.

I am especially indebted to my colleagues at Royal Holloway, University of London and to those on the editorial boards of *RiDE: The Journal of Applied Theatre and Performance,* all of whom continue to inspire and challenge me. Particular thanks are due to colleagues and friends Louise Keyworth, Sally Mackey, Jenny Hughes, Nadine Holdsworth, Steve Bottoms, Wan-Jung Wang, Baz Kershaw and James Thompson, all of whom shared their practice, insights and ideas with much generosity and good humour. The last thanks go to my mother, who first taught me to love the arts and showed me the value of community. This book is dedicated to the memory of her many gifts.

Arts & Humanities
Research Council

General Editors' Preface

This series sets out to explore key performance practices encountered in modern and contemporary theatre. Talking to students and scholars in seminar rooms and studios, and to practitioners in rehearsal, it became clear that there were widely used modes of practice that had received very little critical and analytical attention. In response, we offer these critical, research-based studies which draw on international fieldwork to produce fresh insight into a range of performance processes. Authors, who are specialists in their fields, have set each mode of practice in its social, political and aesthetic context. The series charts both a history of the development of modes of performance process and an assessment of their significance in contemporary culture.

Each volume is accessibly written, and gives a clear and pithy analysis of the historical and cultural development of a mode of practice. As well as offering readers a sense of the breadth of the field, the authors have also given key examples and performance illustrations. In different ways each book in the series asks readers to look again at processes and practices of theatre-making that seem obvious and self-evident, and to examine why and how they have developed as they have, and what their ideological content is. Ultimately the series aims to ask, what are the choices and responsibilities facing performance-makers today?

Graham Ley and Jane Milling

General Editor's Preface

Graham Ley and Jane Milling

1 An Introduction to Applied Drama, Theatre and Performance

Radical Directions: Bombsites, Theatres and Playgrounds

This book begins in the bar of the Theatre Royal, Stratford East in London, where I am eating a plate of rice and peas. The Caribbean menu not only reflects the local community, it also signals the theatre's commitment to providing a welcoming atmosphere and offering opportunities for people who live nearby to develop their creativity. There is a band setting up in the bar for an open-mic session, and a group of young performance poets are gathering in the foyer, somewhat nervously, waiting to go on stage. Their performance marks the culmination of a project called *Poet's Manifesto*, where young people were invited to create poetry that reflected their experiences about living in the area.[1] There is a buzz about the building, it feels alive. It is March 2013, and I am conscious that this area of London was recently the centre of global attention when the London 2012 Olympics were staged less than half a mile away, and yet there is still a need for the theatre to create opportunities for local people to be seen and heard.

The Theatre Royal, Stratford East is perhaps best known for its connection with Joan Littlewood (1919–2002), a socialist theatre director who did much to shake up the British theatre establishment in the mid-twentieth century. In her autobiography, Littlewood tells a story about the plans for *The Fun Palace*, an ambitious and visionary project which aimed to create a 'playground of learning' in the deprived East

End of London during the 1960s. Her article in *New Scientist* describes an acting area which would, Littlewood writes, 'afford the therapy of theatre to everyone'. For shop and factory workers, participation in theatre would counteract the daily boredom of unsatisfying working lives. People would be able to escape their drab routines and find psychological pleasure in enacting aspects of their own lives through which, she hoped, they would develop a 'critical awareness of reality' which might lead to their engagement in social research.[2] In practice, *The Fun Palace* never materialised. Plans were quashed by bureaucratic councillors who were more concerned with curbing vandalism than developing entertaining approaches to lifelong learning. Littlewood was undaunted. In 1967 she declared herself 'finished with putting on plays'[3] and turned her attention to creating children's playgrounds on old bombsites. Her ambitious project spread, and was in these playful, green spaces that Littlewood encouraged young people to participate in creative activities, and developed a programme of community events that were designed to foster social cohesion. When she eventually returned to the Theatre Royal in the mid-1970s, it was with these young people in tow. The theatre had been repeatedly looted by thieves whom the local authorities described as 'young savages' and 'unsavoury elements', but she invited these young people into the safe space of the theatre, encouraging them to tell their own stories behind the security of locked doors. By 1975, Littlewood remarked caustically, 'our savages' were organising festivals for themselves.[4]

It is an optimistic story, bearing witness to the power of drama to affect social and personal change. It is also a story which is familiar to those who work in community and participatory arts – it has been told and retold many times, about many different people, in many different social contexts. What this story identifies is the relationship between theatre practice, social efficacy, citizenship and community-building.[5] Joan Littlewood saw no distinction between these modes of cultural practice – they were part of the same political project. By working with young people and community participants, and listening to their stories, she enabled them to find their own forms of artistic, cultural and theatrical expression.

There is a symbolism about creating a playground on a bombsite that resonates with this book. Choosing to begin this book close to a former bombsite and the 2012 Olympic Stadium, over my Caribbean supper in Littlewood's theatre, seems fitting; it is an appropriate place to reflect on the value and values of drama, theatre and performance that take place in community settings and in educational contexts. This book is about theatre-making that is applied to different and sometimes rather unglamorous places – on the streets, in city farms, in gardens and bombsites or, for example, in care homes for the elderly, hostels for the homeless, schools or prisons – led by practitioners who have experience in creating drama with community participants. Socially engaged theatre takes place both inside and outside theatre buildings, and there is a neat reciprocity between contemporary theatre-makers' interest in creating interactive art or immersive theatre in found spaces – disused factories, empty swimming pools, vacated shops, and so on – and the institutional spaces such as prisons, schools and hospitals that are often the settings for applied theatre. The performance I am waiting to see at the Theatre Royal, Stratford East straddles these divisions, where the theatre still provides a space for young people to explore ideas and represent stories that matter to them.

The social turn in contemporary theatre, eloquently analysed by Shannon Jackson,[6] is redefining what it means to be a participant, blurring the boundaries between artist and audience, producer and creator. Beyond the affluent West and in postcolonial societies, there is growing awareness of the cultural potency of indigenous forms of performance in sustaining community participation and a sense of belonging in an increasingly globalised world. In this introductory chapter I shall begin to consider how applied theatre is integral to this cultural landscape, and how it is related to some of the histories and practices of community-based and educational theatre. I hope to raise questions which will be addressed later in the book, and to map some of the debates and discussions which permeate the field.

What is Applied Drama/ Theatre/ Performance?

The terms 'applied drama', 'applied theatre' and 'applied performance' emerged in universities, and gained currency during the 1990s, as students, academics, theatre practitioners and policy-makers used them as a kind of shorthand to describe forms of dramatic activity that are specifically intended to benefit individuals, communities and societies. The term seems to have emerged haphazardly and took hold quickly, suggesting that it filled a gap in the lexicon. Its popularity implies a willingness to question whether there are family resemblances between the different practices and ways of working applied to community settings, and an interest in investigating their shared concerns and common principles. Theatre practitioners have been working in educational, therapeutic and community settings for many years, but the emergence of the terms 'applied drama', 'applied theatre', and sometimes 'applied performance' signals a renewed interest in the professionalisation of these fields, and in reviewing common theoretical and political concerns which accompany their various practices.

One of the themes that is shared by different aspects of applied drama/theatre/performance is, as Judith Ackroyd pointed out, a focus on its intentionality, specifically an aspiration to use drama to improve the lives of individuals and create better societies. Ackroyd (2000) was one of the first to suggest that applied theatre is an 'umbrella term' used to describe many different forms of educational and community-based theatre – including theatre education, reminiscence theatre, theatre for development, theatre in hospitals – each of which has its own theories, debates and highly specialised practices which are often rather different from each other. She includes both process-orientated and performative practices in her description of applied theatre, and helpfully sums up the common beliefs of many different practitioners in the field:

> They share a belief in the power of the theatre form to address something beyond the form itself. So one group use theatre in order to promote positive social processes within a particular community, whilst others employ it in order to promote an understanding of human resource issues among corporate employees. .... The intentions of course vary. They could be to inform, to cleanse, to unify, to instruct, to raise awareness.[7]

The idea that theatre has the potential to 'address something beyond the form itself' suggests that applied theatre is primarily concerned with developing new possibilities for everyday living rather than separating theatre-going from other aspects of life. What are considered to be 'positive social processes' or what values are to be understood by newly empowered 'corporate employees' do, of course, change over time and are variously construed in different local and global contexts.

In the ten years since writing the first edition of this book, I have observed that the term 'applied theatre' has been described in multiple ways. During the first decade of the twenty-first century, the new name revived debate about the values and principles associated with participatory forms of theatre-making. Three books with similar titles opened discussions between 2003 and 2005 (Taylor, 2003; Thompson, 2003; Nicholson, 2005), followed by two edited collections in 2009 (Prentki and Preston; Prendergast and Saxton), with Nicola Shaughnessy's book,

Applying Performance, contributing to the field in 2012. Distinctions between applied *drama*, applied *theatre* and applied *performance* are moot. Philip Taylor, an academic and practitioner working in New York, defines differences between applied drama, which he sees process-based, and applied theatre, which he describes as performance-based.[8] Shaughnessy's emphasis on performance intends to capture a twenty-first-century shift in thinking away from a 'theatre-dominated paradigm to a performance-centred one'.[9] Differences in nuance and terminology mark, perhaps, both the research interests of the authors, and its flexibility and porousness.

Despite differences of inflection, the terms 'applied drama', 'applied theatre' and 'applied performance' are often used quite flexibly and interchangeably, with 'applied theatre' emerging as the term most regularly used. In many of the theatre practices discussed in this book there is a reluctance to make a neat separation between process- and performance-based work, and I have found that many artists and theatre-makers acknowledge a productive consonance between the two. Not only does this raise questions about how 'performance' might be defined in the field, it also suggests that the terms 'applied drama' and 'applied theatre' are often used quite flexibly and interchangeably. Plumping for both terms in the title of this book signals an attempt to recognise the importance of all forms of theatre practice and performance as they are applied to specific contexts and different audiences. In this second edition of the book, however, I have used the shorthand 'applied theatre' rather than 'applied drama', simply because this has become most widely used. In all its many definitions, it is striking that the debate most regularly revisited is the relationship between artistry and instrumentalism that has long been a concern across different forms of educational and community-based performance. For James Thompson, it is the instrumentalism rather than intentionality that defines applied theatre, which he sees as 'solely concentrated on effects – identifiable outcomes, messages or effects'.[10] By 2009, Thompson had called, somewhat polemically, for 'the end of applied theatre' on the basis that it had paid insufficient attention to the affective and aesthetic aspects of performance.

Although I share Thompson's sentiments about excessive instrumentality, I am not convinced that theatre-makers have favoured narrow outcomes over innovation in theatre form or performance aesthetics. Of course, there are some practitioners who repeat formulaic games or apply the same drama exercises to different settings. Some theatre-makers call themselves 'applied theatre practitioners' who are proficient in something called 'applied theatre' and use 'applied theatre techniques' as if the term referred to a particular genre of theatre or to a recognisable set of participatory performance practices. There may be advantages for newly professionalised practitioners to define their labour and to claim specialist forms of knowledge, but there is also a risk that its practices become too restrictive and formulaic to foster creativity and that practitioners cease to apply their artistic vision to the work. For ease of reference in this book, I have decided to call theatre-makers, artists and workshop leaders 'practitioners' and those who take part 'participants'. This is not intended to be hierarchical but simply to use this terminology to suggest the divisions of labour which I have observed in practice. Unlike Thompson, I have never consider applied theatre to be solely concerned with effect; on the contrary, I have been privileged to witness the work of practitioners who bring innovative and beautiful forms of theatre-making to challenging and complex settings. Affect and effect may share a poetic aurality in the English language, but they are not binary opposites, and witnessing many theatrical experiences has convinced me that inspired and inspiring theatre often makes the most difference to people's lives and environments. As Elspeth Probyn notes, 'affects have specific effects; it makes no sense to talk about them outside this understanding'.[11]

James Thompson rightly points out that if definitions of applied theatre are too loose and open-ended they cease to serve any useful purpose.[12] My own view is that applied theatre is most useful as a term when it is used to conceptualise theatre-making in educational, therapeutic or community settings rather than to define specific methodologies, dramatic strategies or ways of working. As a term, I think applied theatre is most pertinent when it is used to open intellectual, ethical and political questions about socially engaged theatre practice, when it asks challenging questions and provides critical frames for reflection. Just as practice in applied theatre is often multi-agency, bringing together theatre-makers with, for example, experienced NGOs, health professionals and local community leaders, research in applied theatre draws on different branches of philosophy and the social sciences, notably cultural studies, cultural geography, education, psychology, sociology and anthropology, as well as contributing to research in drama, theatre and performance studies. In other words, applied theatre is academically interdisciplinary, and artistically it takes account of many different approaches to theatre-making and performance.

In many ways I am ambivalent about categorising any artistic practice as 'applied theatre', and I would be very concerned if the convenience of this collective noun reduced a rich diversity of theories and artistic practices to a single homogeneous discourse. As I pointed out in 2005, the application of drama to different institutional or community settings illuminates fundamental questions about the role and significance of *all* theatre practice to society, and about how theatre-making articulates and challenges contemporary concerns. For me, therefore, interesting debate lies not in whether different forms of performance practice are labelled as 'drama', 'theatre' or 'performance', nor in creating strict definitions of what applied theatre might be, but in raising questions about what is meant by the word 'applied', to what or whom drama and theatre might be applied, and for what reasons, and whose artistic, social and political values the application of theatre-making serves and represents.

Pure and Applied Theatre

One way to begin to address questions about the roles and functions of applied theatre is to analyse how it relates to, and contrasts with, other cognate disciplines and artistic practices. It is interesting that other academic disciplines which customarily use the preface 'applied' often contrast it with 'pure'. In mathematics, for example, pure mathematics is abstract and theoretical, whereas applied mathematics is concerned with using theoretical models to solve practical problems. Most practitioners working in applied theatre are motivated by individual or social change and there is, therefore, a similar interest in the relationship between production and reception, and in the balance between the usefulness of the work and its intrinsic artistic qualities.

As I have already argued, the term 'applied theatre' is problematic if it is seen to stand in opposition to drama/theatre/performance as an art form, particularly if this implies that the aesthetics or its production values are unimportant. Bjørn Rasmussen, speaking at the inauguration of the Centre for Applied Theatre Education and Research in Brisbane, was concerned with different places occupied by applied theatre and 'not-applied' theatre in the cultural hierarchy.

> I never found the expression 'applied' drama or theatre quite sound, because I always found it somewhat downgrading, implying that the applied stuff is second best, not quite as genuine as the essence... I thought the concept of 'applied' amplified a low status position in the power play.[13]

Although it is interesting to note in this context that applied science has a higher status in the academy than pure science, Rasmussen is surely right to point out that creating a new set of binary oppositions between 'applied' and 'not-applied' drama risks emphasising the utilitarianism of applied theatre at the expense of its artistic and aesthetic qualities. All forms of drama and theatre practice, he argues, rely on aesthetic engagement for their power and effectiveness, and applied theatre is no exception. There is, however, another element which I would add to Rasmussen's analysis – the values attributed to the ideal of the 'pure' aesthetic.

Pierre Bourdieu's sociological study of the 'pure' aesthetic as mark of the 'distinction' of taste offers a useful analysis of the social inequalities associated with the arts. Bourdieu argued that since the eighteenth century, the aesthetic has been regarded as personally and socially transformative, with the consequence that the arts came to be thought of as a new faith, imitative in some ways of religion.[14] This elision of goodness and beauty did not, however, have the effect of democratising either aesthetic appreciation or artistic practice. On the contrary, the distinction of taste was thought to depend on highly cultivated individuals who possessed hearts and minds which were sufficiently pure, disinterested and unencumbered by everyday matters to make aesthetic judgements. Artists became increasingly sanctified and professionalised, with the Romantics claiming for themselves a special kind of disposition, and unique powers of perception and imagination. This meant, Bourdieu concluded, that aesthetic judgements acquired a social distinction which contributed to a specific form of political economy in which the bourgeois dispositions of artists and intellectuals were valued as the moral guardians of a liberal polity. Bourdieu described this as the 'politics of purity', where standards of taste became divided along class lines, and the aesthetic sense became increasingly harnessed to – and believed to legitimate – dominant class and hegemonic values.

This returns the debate to questions of power and cultural production, where the ideals of artistic production and of aesthetic appreciation have acquired symbolic capital. In relation to applied theatre, Bourdieu's sociological account of the politics of purity has particular resonance. Practitioners in applied theatre have often distanced themselves from 'mainstream' theatre practices and spaces, which have been considered as the preserve of the middle class. Writing in 1997, drama educator Jonothan Neelands, for example, recalls this iniquitous tradition when he describes the 'restrictive art of theatre' as a 'literary and private aesthetic'.[15] Baz Kershaw has also written movingly of his early encounters with Western theatre culture, from which he felt excluded by virtue of his class background. Drawing on Bourdieu's idea of theatre as 'a miracle of predestination', Kershaw describes mainstream theatre as not as a space for free speech and creativity, but as 'a social engine that helps to drive an unfair system of privilege'.[16] In this configuration, theatre becomes a place of bourgeois self-righteousness, only really available to traditionally educated, middle-class audiences who passively consume hegemonic values. For Bourdieu, this uncritical readership of 'high art' was historically linked to the *detachment* and disinterestedness associated with contemplation of aesthetic 'purity' whereas, by contrast, popular taste was linked to *involvement* and participation in the arts. He argued that displays of enthusiasm by spectators have been treated with suspicion in the academy; entertainment which appealed to 'collective participation' rather than 'formal exploration' has been thought to be inferior.[17]

Thirty or more years on from Bourdieu's analysis of class divisions in the arts, the academy has a far wider recognition of popular theatre forms. His analysis of the social implications of judgements of taste has also been rightly criticised for being too fixed around stable notions of class. Western theatre practitioners and their audiences have also enjoyed a long tradition of social criticism, and there is ample evidence that theatre can be a place where it is possible to imagine the world to be different. This involves new aesthetic strategies and forms of theatre; as Brecht understood, new artistic methods are needed to represent changing social circumstances.

> Methods become exhausted; stimuli no longer work. New problems appear and demand new methods. Reality changes; in order to represent it, modes of representation must change. Nothing comes of nothing; the new comes from the old, but that is why it is new. The oppressors do not work in the same way in every epoch. They cannot be defined in the same fixed fashion at all times.[18]

As an audience member, I find it difficult to imagine more disturbing and moving theatrical experiences than seeing Edward Bond's *Saved* (1965), Caryl Churchill's *Far Away* (2000) or debbie tucker green's *Random* (2008), all of which were first performed in London's Royal Court Theatre – a radical theatre, but nonetheless a conventional performance space. None of these plays would be considered to be 'applied' theatre, but all offer a powerful social critique in new theatrical languages. In setting an agenda for the political efficacy of theatre, the playwright Tony Kushner has argued that art is not simply concerned with passively reproducing cultural values, but it may also be actively engaged with cultural and social change.

> Art is not merely contemplation, it is also action, and all action changes the world, at least a little.[19]

For many contemporary practitioners in applied theatre, this negotiation between action and contemplation is important, particularly as it might be argued that participation has become the new virtue in some aspects of contemporary theatre-making. It is an approach to theatre-making that relies on time, involvement and affective engagement, and it is these values that have particular significance to applied theatre.

Nothing Comes of Nothing: Where Did Applied Theatre Come From?

Contemporary practitioners and debates in applied theatre are indebted to their radical predecessors in twentieth-century theatre, and to pioneering educationalists who aimed to democratise processes of learning. This century witnessed many international artistic movements that sought to integrate art and life, spanning various manifestations: the European avant-garde, the counter-cultural Happenings of the 1960s and different forms of popular, protest and street theatre. In this brief introduction, I want to draw attention to three interrelated theatre movements that made particularly significant contributions to twenty-first-century applied theatre: theatres of the political Left, which have been variously described as political or alternative; drama and theatre in education, and community or grassroots theatre. Taken together, they offer a powerful legacy which links social and personal change to dramatic practice, and articulate a commitment to using theatre to break down social hierarchies and divisions. What these traditions share is an interest in working in clearly defined contexts, with and for specific participants and publics, and in furthering objectives which are artistic, and also educational, social and political. Although differently inflected, contemporary practitioners in applied theatre are in some way indebted to these complementary histories.

The history of political, radical and alternative theatres has allied theatre to cultural activism. Although political action has long been associated with theatre, their relationship was energetically reconfigured during the twentieth century. The century saw an explosion of artistic practices designed to rally political activism through performance-making, and the development of processes of working which questioned the rigid divisions of labour and social hierarchies in commercial theatre and beyond it. At the centre of many debates which contributed to the political and artistic changes which began in the 1920s with the Workers' Theatre Movements and lasted for much of the century were questions about the social purpose of theatre, and its political philosophy. Throughout the changing political landscapes of the twentieth century, theatre held an enduring appeal to social and political activists, and particularly to those in civil rights movements. Theatre offered an immediate and visible platform for public debate, for the performance of protest, and was thought to be a powerful way to reach the hearts and minds of its intended audiences. Often linking political protest with popular culture, these were forms of theatre which generally aimed to encourage social action and grassroots mobilisation.[20] Although in many instances the politics and aesthetics of activist theatre have changed, the application of theatre to social problems and to direct action is indebted to this performative tradition.

There are two strands of pedagogy which have influenced applied theatre; one derives from the Brazilian Marxist educator Paulo Freire, and the other from European models of progressive education. Freire, whose work is discussed in more detail in Chapter 3, was committed to overturning traditional teaching methods based on the hierarchical transmission of knowledge, and advocated approaches to learning which placed the learner (rather than the teacher) at the centre of the pedagogic process. Freire was particularly concerned with adult literacy, and his work had a profound influence on August Boal, the theatre director. Boal was a powerful figure in applied theatre until his death in 2009, and remains a strong and influential presence, perhaps particularly in the USA, where his work is widely advocated.[21] Progressive education shared a similar interest in learning by doing, and drama and theatre in education were thought particularly well placed to contribute to child-centred approaches to learning, which became embedded in many educational practices in during the 1960s.[22] One of the legacies of this educational movement is the use of dramatic play and improvisation, often in role, as a learning medium. In contemporary practice, these two pedagogical strands are often interwoven, and have led to questions about where knowledge is situated and whose cultural experiences are reproduced in theatre-making. The legacy of both these movements has subjected the negotiation between power, learning and knowledge to critical scrutiny.

Community theatre (sometimes also called grassroots theatre) has been variously articulated and construed in different parts of the world. There are connections with both theatre pedagogies and radical people's theatre, and it is characterised by the participation of community members in creating a piece of theatre which has special resonance for that community. This is a different tradition from amateur theatre, where companies usually perform plays that have been commercially successful; as Eugene van Erven has pointed out, community theatre has tended to emphasise the dramatic potential of local or personal stories.[23] His documentation of community theatre took him to many different parts of the world to see how communities have engaged in various forms of theatre-making. Jan Cohen-Cruz similarly emphasised the localism in her study of community-based theatre in the USA, where she documents many different methodologies that are designed to integrate life and art.[24] The influential British practitioner Ann Jellicoe famously denied that her work in community theatre had an explicit political agenda, but there is nonetheless a concern for social inclusivity and community-building through the process of making theatre. As I discuss in Chapter 5, the concept of community in itself is controversial and problematic, and community theatre is not exempt from debates about who is included or excluded from specific community groupings. Whatever its limits and limitations, however, community-based theatre remains an important form of artistic communication which continues to influence applied theatre.

There is considerable overlap between these different traditions and, historically, there has been a strong tradition of robust debate and collaboration between practitioners across these different fields. One of the central legacies of these three cultural practices that permeate the broad field of applied theatre is an emphasis on activity and involvement rather than passivity and uncritical consumerism. Participation became the orthodoxy, with an emphasis on process-based work designed to encourage maximum involvement. The political implications of this principle have come under increasing pressure since the appearance of the first edition of this book in 2005, and the work of Jacques Rancière has precipitated widespread debate about its inherent assumptions. In her lively critique of the politics of participatory arts, Claire Bishop sums up his influence in terms that invoke the history of the field:

> [H]e has undertaken important work in debunking some of the binaries upon which the discourse of politicised art has relied: individual/ collective, author/ spectator, active/passive, real life/ art.[25]

Although much contemporary practice that is associated with applied theatre has not lost or forgotten its radical intentions, the assumption that active, collective participation is necessarily oppositional to capitalism has been subject to critical scrutiny in the twenty-first century. There is, of course, no guarantee that collaborative, process-based art-making is inherently radical, particularly in an era of increased and affective audience participation in everything from TV talent shows to immersive performances in old cellars. This shifting aesthetic register in contemporary performance marks, as Adrian Heathfield has pointed out, a move from 'the optic to the haptic, from the distant to the immersive, from the static relation to the interactive'.[26] This renewed interest in all forms of participation blurs distinctions between market-led theatre and applied theatre as artists move between different modes of practice. Furthermore, well-funded research projects and scholarly books have ensured the respectability of applied theatre in the academy, and although funding for practice is tough, particularly in times of austerity and global financial crises, many people in the charitable and cultural sectors remain committed to applying theatre to learning and social engagement.

In this climate, the shift in terminology to 'applied theatre' is significant, I think, because it does not announce its political allegiances, community commitments or educational intent as clearly as many forms of politically committed theatre-making that were developed in the last century. From this point of view, it is significant that the emergence of applied theatre as a field of study and praxis coincided with a period in the 1990s described by Baz Kershaw as a 'new world disorder' and by Zygmunt Bauman as 'an age of uncertainty'. In this period of social change, political theorists and cultural critics have been renegotiating and re-envisaging Western democratic traditions following the collapse of Cold War dualisms and the subsequent fragmentation of the political Left.[27] The social and material circumstances in which Joan Littlewood came to regard theatre practice as an antidote to social injustice may have changed, and the impulses that motivated such work have become subject to radical review.

Places, Publics and Participants

For applied theatre, a sense of political uncertainty and economic instability has strong practical implications. Practitioners often work with people in the most vulnerable of situations, and frequently see the casualties of this new world disorder at first hand – working with, for example, refugees, asylum seekers, the displaced and the homeless. Others may be involved with 'empowering' members of an increasingly mobile and globalised workforce by encouraging active decision-making and affective involvement in work processes. Globalising processes are of central importance to applied theatre, not least because they threaten to erode local, national and regional cultures through the spread of homogeneous transnational corporations. Equally significant is the impact of migration – one of the contemporary consequences of globalisation – which has forged new social identities in which members of diasporic communities feel simultaneously connected to different places. The effects of climate change are felt across the world with devastating floods and other ecological disasters, a chain of events that has prompted some artists to campaign against flying for art. The stable identities associated with belonging to a bounded place are reimagined and reconfigured as it is recognised that many people have multiple cultural affiliations, and that relationships between the local and the global are always complexly interconnected.

The conceptual metaphors associated with social change within this new world disorder emphasise the politics of (dis)location – difference, alterity, mapping, hybridity, liminality, borders and margins – all of which draw critical attention to the way place and space articulate diverse cultural and political meanings. Place has been reconceptualised, not as a rooted or fixed localism, but as a fluid social process which both reflects and shapes identities. The geographer Doreen Massey describes this in political terms, calling for 'a relational politics for a relational space'.[28] This focus on the spatial metaphors in relation to identity is important to applied theatre, particularly as theatre is often applied to specific settings, contexts and publics that are troubled. There is often a messiness about work in applied theatre, focusing on interrogating what Victor Turner has called the 'contamination' of context, which makes the 'flaws, hesitations, personal factors, incomplete, elliptical, context-dependent, situational proponents of performance' visible.[29] Applied theatre is, in Turner's terms, always contaminated by context, and is intended to be sufficiently fluid to address the concerns of local audiences and participants. This accepts that practices in applied theatre are *both* intimately connected with the social and cultural contexts in which they take place *and* symbolise experience of diasporic spaces.

The metaphor of social and personal change which I have found most appropriate for the interplay between place and identity, thought and action, in applied theatre is not one of transformation but of transportation. Richard Schechner has offered a distinction between these two aspects of performance practice. Transformation, he argues, affects a permanent change which is often, but not always, associated with ritual. In such cases (as in marriage or a bar mitzvah ceremony, for example) transformation is intended to be lasting, and the outcome is immediate, predetermined and predictable. It is led by experienced social actors whose expertise affords them the necessary status to lead the performative event or to initiate the ceremonial rites. Transportation is less fixed – performers are 'taken somewhere', actors are even temporarily transformed, but they are returned more or less to their starting places at the end of the drama or performance. Over time, this process does not preclude more permanent transformations because, Schechner argues, as 'a series of transportation performances can achieve a transformation'.[30]

Although I recognise the power of theatre-making to touch people's lives, I remain rather uneasy about using the term transformation to describe the process of change afforded by practising drama. This is partly because I feel uncomfortable about making such grand claims for the effects and effectiveness of my own work as a practitioner, but also because it raises bigger political questions. If applied theatre is socially transformative, is it explicit what kind of society is envisioned? If the motive is individual or personal transformation, is this something which is done *to* the participants, *with* them, or *by* them? Whose values and interests does the transformation serve? Seen in this light, the idea of transportation suggests greater scope for creativity and unpredictability than that of transformation. Should transformation occur, it is a gradual and cumulative process, the result of learning and negotiation with others, a progressive act of self-creation. In the process of transportation, the outcomes are clearly focused but not fixed, and change may take place gradually, a collaborative and sustained process between participants and often in partnership with other supportive agencies. Transportation is a durational process of becoming rather than being, about travelling into another world, often fictional, which offers both new ways of seeing and different ways of looking at the familiar. As British theatre director Tim Etchells has said, performance is about 'going into another world and coming back with gifts'.[31]

Making a Difference

At the heart of this book there lies a struggle, an attempt to straddle what the political philosopher Chantal Mouffe describes as an 'irreducible tension between equality and liberty'[32] between the push and pull of an overarching ideal of a radical, just and inclusive democracy for all and a respect for local cultures and circumstances. Making a difference has many different discursive registers, and is often fraught with contradictions and pitfalls for even the most well-meaning theatre-maker. The subtitle of this book, 'The Gift of Theatre', provides me with a political metaphor to articulate some of these tensions. It would be naïve to imagine that gifts and gift-giving are always positive experiences,[33] and the metaphor of the gift offers one way to begin to think through the ethical complexities associated with applied theatre.

The application of gift theory to applied theatre is a way of acknowledging the positive attributes of empathy, generosity and care for others which characterises much good practice. Yet it is significant that applied theatre emerged in a period of cultural change in which the long tradition that the arts have inherently redemptive and transformative qualities has been troubled by new insights into the cultural production and representation of knowledge. Theatre is not a universal panacea, and it is here that the gift theory is particularly helpful. The gift may be well received, but it also carries fewer positive associations with self-interest, sometimes perpetuating system of debt and social obligations that can be oppressive or unwelcome. Mart Osteen describes this ambiguity in the following terms:

> Gift practices tell conflicting narratives: on the one hand, they expound a narrative of transfer and exchange, of hierarchy, aspiration, and freedom from history; and on the other, they retell a narrative of continuity with nature and the past, a story of human inter-connectedness.[34]

I find this instructive when thinking through the values of applied theatre. The gift of theatre may be well-intentioned and generously given, but it may be experienced as an expression of hierarchy, an imposition of values that are not to be shared. This metaphor offers a conceptual vocabulary to articulate this paradox and urges continual vigilance about whose values and whose notion of goodness and the good life the practice serves. Because gift-giving is a complex and asymmetrical combination of intentionality, affect and emotion, it is always a risk.

In writing this book, I have tried to acknowledge that theoretical insights – from gift theory and elsewhere – have a performative dynamic. One of the principles that underpins this book is that critical and creative practices are not separate processes or modes of thought, with one based on action and the other on reflection. They are interdependent and constantly in flux. It seems to me that applied theatre and theoretical debate often share similar aims – to imagine the world to be different. I am reminded here of bell hooks, who argues passionately for a way of thinking about theory as social production. She describes how she saw in theory a 'location for healing', a way of looking at the world differently, a focus for asking risky questions.[35] Neither thought nor action is without a conceptual foundation, hooks claims, however implicit, and theory can be just as creative as more obvious forms of practical action. I have considerable sympathy with hooks's view. There are times when I have found myself defending both critical and creative practices on the grounds that they are related and mutually sustaining. Theory finds a point of connection between 'why' questions (such as why is drama important in educational and community contexts?) and 'how' questions (as in how do people structure and organise their practice?). At other times I want to use the flexibility of practice to test out or illuminate theoretical ideas. Both become integral to the drama, as a practical embodiment of theory. Gilles Deleuze, in conversation with Michel Foucault, has identified the relationship between theory and practice:

> At one time, a practice was considered an application of theory, a consequence; at other times, it had an opposite sense and it was thought to inspire theory, to be indispensable for future theoretical forms. ... The relationships between theory and practice are far more partial and fragmentary... . Practice is a set of relays from one theoretical point to another, and theory is a relay from one practice to another. No theory can develop without eventually encountering a wall, and practice is necessary for piercing this wall.[36]

From the point of view of applied theatre, I find this way of thinking extremely helpful. Without theory, I have found that even the most reflexive practice gets stuck and becomes repetitive, and theory can be bafflingly abstract without practice. Rather than rooting debate in a modernist polarity between theory and practice, there can be a more fluid continuum between the two. Deleuze describes this continuum as 'theoretical action' and 'practical action' and this gives theory a performative function.[37]

The political metaphor of the gift offers to mediate between theoretical concepts and practical action by challenging the assumption that theatre practice, however well intentioned or participatory, is always welcome or well received. This is the second edition of one of the first books to examine applied theatre; my task then was to trouble the rhetoric that accepted that theatre is inherently transformative or empowering, and to define and introduce a newly articulated discursive field. It is a testament to the strength of this aspect of cultural practice that knowledge has accumulated over time, and I am indebted to the new research and practice that has emerged. My aim in this second edition is not to unravel the structure or focus of the earlier edition, nor to respond to every debate that has challenged me to think differently in the intervening years. Rather, my aim is to revisit and refresh my responses to the questions I asked in 2005 – all of which remain pertinent a decade later. What are the implications of globalisation for applied theatre? What ideas of humanity, identity and selfhood are assumed by drama practitioners working in educational and community contexts? What is meant by community? Given its libertarian history and its interest in democratic action and universal human rights, how might practitioners in applied theatre negotiate different world-views in their work? How might artists contribute to communities and institutional settings that are characterised by plurality and cultural dissonance? This book offers an investigation into these complex practical and theoretical questions. What is new in the second edition of this book is an increasing alertness to the complex ecology in which applied theatre takes place, and the ways in which posthumanist debates prompt us to consider how the environment in which theatre-making takes place exerts its affective presence. These concerns are ethical and political, and woven throughout the book.

The book is structured in three parts. Part I raises questions about citizenship and pedagogy, addressed in two separate chapters, and this analysis of two of the central concepts which underpin practice in applied theatre offers a framework for subsequent discussions. Taken together, these chapters locate the central arguments of this book – that applied theatre is fortified by a robust understanding of the politics of cultural difference, in which questions of citizenship, pedagogy and praxis are neither individualised nor privatised, but acknowledged as both a positive attribute of contemporary society and as a site of struggle. Chapter 2 examines different models and practices of citizenship, and suggests that drama has a part to play in encouraging participants to *act* as citizens. In this chapter I shall consider issues of participation, asking why and how participation in theatre-making has become associated with democracy. Chapter 3 explores the challenges presented by globalisation to pedagogies and praxis in applied theatre. It builds on the discussion of citizenship by investigating the potential for relationships between pedagogy, praxis and performance, arguing that there is continual need to exercise vigilance over how learning is defined, how effectiveness is understood, and how knowledge is constructed in applied theatre.

Part II offers a discussion of narrative. The two chapters in this section are built on the premise that practice in applied theatre is poised at the intersection of different narratives – of selfhood, community, culture – which means that the narratives of fictional and lived experience are in continual negotiation. Chapter 4 offers an investigation of how fictional narratives might impact on creating narratives of selfhood. These debates were originally raised in 2005, and are strengthened by the 'affective turn' in applied theatre in the last decade. This chapter addresses questions of affective identification, and demonstrates how ideas of embodiment and reflexivity are revitalised and strengthened by this intellectual movement. Chapter 5 questions ideas of community and place, and explores how making dramatic narratives based on lived experience might contribute to the process of community-building.

Part III examines theories of creativity and social justice. Chapter 6 examines different ways of thinking about the relationship between creativity and social intervention, and Chapter 7 pays specific attention to the implications of furthering a human rights agenda in and through dramatic practice. The final chapter returns to the idea of the gift, asking questions about how this political metaphor might serve as an ethical basis for practice in applied theatre.

Throughout this book I have chosen examples of practice which illuminate and challenge some of the theoretical issues raised. The examples are eclectic rather than representational, and there is no attempt to provide a survey of practice, which is so rich and varied that it would be impossible to do it justice in a book of this length. Researching applied theatre raises many ethical questions, both in terms of research methodologies and in the representation of the voices of the participants. It is perhaps paradoxical that applied theatre, arguably the most democratic of theatre practices, often takes place in private spaces and places where vulnerable participants can feel safe. It is not the role of the researcher to invade this privacy, nor to abuse the participants' trust, and this sensitivity to context has meant that I have relied on three major sources – reflection on my own work as an insider in the process, as is customary in our field; on analysing the work of practitioners with whom I have developed sustained professional relationships; and on accounts of practice that have already been published or made public through performance or video documentation. The methodology has included participant observation, and often interviews or discussion with participants, but my critics will no doubt note that I have not presented case studies which include a detailed analysis of the participants' voices; even what might be called 'my' practice actually belongs to the participants just as much as me and, unless I have their permission, I have not discussed it here.

My aim in this book is not, primarily, to offer a fixed and detailed description of what applied theatre *is* in all its various different guises, but to raise questions about what it might be *for*, and what its values might be. Applied theatre is perhaps most helpfully regarded not as a separate academic discipline nor as a specific set of dramatic methods but as a discursive practice – as a way of conceptualising and interpreting theatrical and cultural practices that are motivated by the desire to make a difference to the world. This book raises some theoretical, political and ethical issues that might be applied to different situations and practices. In the ten years since writing the first edition of this book, this sub-discipline of theatre and performance studies has been enriched and enlivened by robust dialogue and generous debate. Inevitably there are ways of thinking about this field that I find more persuasive than others, and where I see things differently I hope to contribute to discussions with respect. It is on these terms, and in this spirit, that I invite you to share some of my experiences and thoughts, however partial and incomplete the story may be.

Part I
Participation and Praxis

2 The Practice of Citizenship

Theatre as Citizenship

The vision of a theatre which unites thought, feeling and action remains a powerful symbol of social democracy. The idea that the arts have the potential to illuminate contemporary concerns, articulate dissent and offer personal solace is deeply embedded in the popular imagination, and is seen by many as an essential attribute of a liberal polity. Theatre, as the most public of art forms, has a particular part to play in the collective exploration of ideas, values and feelings – as a space and place in which society might be reshaped through the imagination. The North American director Peter Sellars describes this impulse in theatre-making as 'a question of civil rights rather than public relations', which contributes to the process of building democratic communities and encouraging active, participant citizenship.[1] This focus on creating a society of equals through artistic practice means that applied theatre, with its particular emphasis on the social, personal and political significance of dramatic practice, is part of a wider cultural ambition. Applied theatre may be one of the most recent names for community-based, educational and interventionist approaches to theatre-making, but it belongs to a much longer tradition of cultural efficacy.

The problem with asserting that applied theatre is related to citizenship is that the concept of citizenship is highly contested – even in Western democracies – and its interpretation in practice belongs to different ideological traditions, commitments and disputes. Theorists who have followed Marx have been sceptical about ideas of citizenship, arguing that social freedom is gained through equal access to the means of production, and the liberal ideal of the free and independent citizen simply disguised the real conflicts and inequalities lying in the economic structures of society.[2] Questions of what citizenship might mean in the post-Cold War era have been further compounded by contemporary concerns with balancing social cohesion and cultural diversity in the context of economic globalisation, international agendas for human rights and pluralistic democratic societies. As a response to these changing world circumstances, there has been a recent revival of interest in citizenship, and the assumptions associated with the concept have been challenged by the proliferation of political discourses – identity politics, postcolonialism, the politics of the body, gender and sexuality, for example – which have forged a reassessment of where the margins of rights and power are drawn. One of the effects of this 'new promiscuity of the political', as Baz Kershaw has dubbed it, has been the recognition that public issues and private lives are not separate forms of social engagement, with the one focused on civic matters and the other on the domestic sphere, but complexly and intimately interwoven. What it means to be a good citizen in pluralist societies is fraught with ambiguities and contradictions, requiring a revitalised political vocabulary and renewed concept of radical citizenship.

In whatever ways it is construed, an interest in questions of citizenship remains a central tenet of many aspects of applied theatre. Citizenship education has become yet another element of formal education in the UK – as elsewhere in the Western world – and there is a well-intentioned belief that drama provides a democratic space in schools where controversial issues might be explored and consensus reached. Although I am sure this approach has its place, there is something that leaves me uneasy about linking drama to officially sanctioned versions of citizenship. The aims of citizenship education seem laudable enough – tackling apathy, stimulating debate, promoting awareness, encouraging political literacy – but it seems to me that the relationship between citizenship, theatre and performance has the potential to be rather more creative and unpredictable than this official discourse would imply. Furthermore, there are plenty of examples where institutional authority and civic action have been in tension, particularly in schools, where students have been punished for taking part in protests. When students in British schools protested publicly against the war in Iraq in 2003, for example, the headteachers' organisation treated their absence from school as truancy rather than a practical illustration of the active citizenship they were charged with promoting. This attitude has, if anything, hardened in the intervening years, during which students across the world have become increasingly politicised.[3]

In this chapter, I am interested in exploring how far a renewed concept of radical citizenship has the potential to draw attention to the many different ways in which theatre practitioners and participants construct experience and perform *as* citizens in different local, regional and global contexts. There are three strands of the citizenship debate which are particularly germane to this discussion. The first part of the chapter is concerned with an analysis of participant citizenship as well as a system of legal rights and responsibilities, and this provides a theoretical framework through which to view examples of theatre practice. With this in mind, I hope to find a way of thinking about how the passion of performance articulates with political citizenship. The second major debate is concerned with the more social and domestic aspects of citizenship, where I begin to explore how social networks built on altruism and care impact on applied theatre. This leads me to reflect on tough questions about how the good intentions of theatre practitioners working in complex settings might be interpreted. The final section begins to draw together some thoughts about an ecological citizenship, which takes account of posthumanist ideas of affective agency and social responsibility associated with new materialist debates. My discussion takes place in a world in which the traditional boundaries of nation-states have been challenged and eroded through global capitalism, prompting in turn a political climate where citizenship as a legal right is highly regulated. The debate turns on how theatre practice might articulate the interconnectedness of social networks, including the balance of power between global politics and the particularity of emotional relationships, local traditions, ecologies and beliefs. Citizenship has a strong ethical dimension, which means that challenging practice in drama always involves negotiating its various inflections.

Citizenship and Participation

Chantal Mouffe has argued that a radical, democratic citizen 'must be an active citizen, somebody who *acts* as a citizen, who conceives of herself in a collective undertaking'.[4] This conception of citizenship as participation, she suggests, is a response to the limitations of liberalism, which has reduced citizenship to a legal status. This has had the effect, Mouffe argues, of focusing on the statutory rights of the individual rather than collective forms of identification and social action. If citizenship is about *acting* as a citizen, with all the implications of performance that this phrase entails, how might practising drama encourage people to become active participant citizens?

To begin to answer this question it is helpful to understand the historical distinctions between civic, political and social citizenship, a debate which also takes account of how the public and private spheres have been differently construed and constructed. The touchstone for many sociological discussions about citizenship is the work of T.H. Marshall, whose influential essay 'Citizenship and Social Class' was published in 1949 during a particularly optimistic period in the history of the British labour movement. Marshall categorised citizenship in three distinctive stages and entitlements: civil citizenship, constructed in the eighteenth century to protect individual liberty, freedom of speech and the right to justice; political citizenship, a largely nineteenth-century phenomenon, which was concerned with the entitlement to participate in the exercise of political power; and social citizenship, which was developed in the twentieth century to provide social welfare, education and the right to a full share in the social heritage.[5] Marshall observed that citizenship became increasingly formalised during the historical period that saw the rise of capitalism, and that it represented an idealistic vision of social equality in an economic system riven with inequality.

Despite the many objections to Marshall's taxonomy, his vision of a social citizenship remains a potent symbol of policies and practices which have regarded citizenship as a collective undertaking rather than an expression of self-interest. That Marshall is now rightly accused of ignoring issues of gender and race, of creating an evolutionary model of citizenship which pays scant attention to cultural citizenship, and of ignoring the effects of economics on citizenship, is a testament to the ways in which conceptions and practices of citizenship have changed since 1949 rather than a wholesale repudiation of his utopian intent. As Nancy Fraser and Linda Gordon pointed out, there are still things to learn from his analysis, particularly in relation to the tensions he found between citizenship as a concept and citizenship in practice.[6] Marshall identified that *as a concept* citizenship is fundamentally equitable, as 'those who possess the status are equal with respect to the rights and duties with which the status is endowed'.[7] *In practice*, however, he argued that both civil and political formulations of citizenship had contributed to social and material inequalities because they emphasised the individual at the expense of the social. Whilst civil and political rights are intended to constitute a formal – and universal – legal status of the individual, social citizenship is more concerned with communitarianism, and especially with the rights and needs of the poor and socially disadvantaged.

By linking applied theatre to citizenship I am following the argument that citizenship is not simply a collection of legal rights and obligations which are not easily changed, but it is also a more fluid and pliable set of social practices. Writing from a sociological perspective, Bryan Turner has commented that the phrase 'social practices' indicates the 'dynamic social construction of citizenship', and recognises that conceptions of citizenship are contingent on their historical and cultural contexts.[8] In other words, the ways in which citizenship is practised have changed in the past and will doubtless change in the future. If citizenship is a social practice, subject to a continual process of renegotiation, it has relevance to the more ordinary and everyday activities of life as well as the bigger political issues of the day. Participant citizenship involves more than accepting one's statutory rights as an individual – however important they may be – and invites questions about the contribution we are each making to society and the process of social change. Reconciling the legality of civil citizenship with the shared responsibilities of social citizenship requires, as Chantal Mouffe has argued, a new articulation between the public and private spheres.

Mouffe is concerned to develop a theory of participant citizenship which does not regard it simply as a legal status with little impact on the everyday lives of law-abiding citizens, but as an *identity*. She argues in favour of an 'embodied citizenship' in which individuals *act* as citizens within a wider framework of personal, political and ethical associations. Borrowing an insight from psychoanalysis, she suggests that identity is constructed through multiple processes of identification which, as 'an articulation of an ensemble of subject positions', both challenge and affirm a person's sense of selfhood.[9] It is through identification with a range of identities, discourses and social relations, she argues, that individuals might recognise their allegiances with others as well as their antagonisms or differences. This acknowledgement of difference is important to Mouffe, who argues that a sense of an identity as citizens is vital for democratic politics. She also recognises, however, that political interpretations of citizenship will always be characterised by conflict and division as different communities and interest groups seek to address its exclusions and redefine its limits and parameters. This citizen is not a passive recipient of rights, but demonstrates a commitment to the ideal of citizenship by making an active contribution to creating a more equitable society. Mouffe's vision of radical democratic citizenship acknowledges that identity is built on collective forms of identification, shared principles and dependent social networks which are not simply enshrined in law, but extend to all aspects of social life.

The idea that citizenship is related to identity can, of course, be appropriated in different ways. Citizenship and identities are performative, which means that they are enacted in the habitual and domestic spaces of everyday life, as material culture, and staged, unevenly, in the performative rituals of nationhood. It is this connection between identity, nationhood and citizenship that presses political questions, particularly in an era of inequitable movement across the globe. As I pointed out in *Theatre, Education and Performance: The Map and the Story* (2011), there are implications of increased policing of national borders and differentiated access to mobility for theatre-makers, particularly when border crossing has led to deepening social division on a global scale.[10] Furthermore, nationhood has linked citizenship to disciplined performative gestures; there are ceremonies in many Western nation-states that bestow formal citizenship status, and one was adopted in the UK in 2004 following the introduction in 2002 of a citizenship test, 'Life in the UK', that aimed to test applicants' understanding of British law and cultural traditions. In her study of citizenship and pedagogy, Alison Jeffers offers an insightful analysis of the different ways in which citizenship ceremonies demand that new citizens not only demonstrate their ontological commitment to the UK, they also require that new citizens 'approach the task on a more epistemological level, to have their citizenship constructed for them by the state'.[11] A later version of the British citizenship test (2013) announces this epistemology blatantly, requiring applicants to digest the contents of a government-issued pamphlet called *The Values and Principles of the UK*.[12] These values reflect fairly bland conservative aspirations for a liberal democracy, calling for tolerance, community participation and respect for the law. But such definitions mask a more general trend in which citizenship is not only highly regulated, but the process of becoming a British citizen is also used bio-politically to enforce particular hegemonic values.

If there is, as I am suggesting, a relationship between citizenship and applied theatre, it is not because there is one definitive theory, ontology or set of epistemological practices that command universal agreement. My suggestion is that a vision of radical democratic citizenship is not based on an assumption of conformity or consensus but, following Mouffe, accepts that the realm of the political is always a site of antagonistic struggle. She is highly critical of forms of politics that seek to eliminate dissent, arguing that its emphasis on political consensus creates apathy and disaffection. A 'well-functioning democracy', she argues, 'calls for a vibrant clash of democratic political positions'.[13] It is here that she sees a political role for the arts, and in her essay 'Artistic

Activism and Antagonistic Spaces' (2007), she argues that the arts have potential to occupy a 'critical space':

> Critical art foments dissensus, that makes visible what the dominant consensus tends to obscure and obliterate. It is constituted by a manifold of artistic practices.[14]

This not only also brings together notions of citizenship as a relational form of artistic practice, it also raises questions about the social role of the arts. Theatre is one space for people to extend their horizons of experience, recognising how identities have been shaped and formulated and, by playing new roles and inhabiting alternative subject positions, finding different points of identification with others. It also suggests that theatre, as an art with 'manifold artistic practices', might take people beyond themselves and allow them to witness the world of others. Although differently represented, the idea of criticality is deeply rooted in the values of applied theatre, and this chimes particularly well with a vision of citizenship as a robust articulation of justice and relational social practice.

Performance practices that dislodge fixed and uneven boundaries between 'self' and 'other' are, in many ways, the subject of this book. It is this aspect of citizenship which, I am suggesting, has most relevance for applied theatre. It is a way of theorising citizenship which includes the visible and public acts of citizenship exercised as civic responsibility or as political protest, but it also extends to the more domestic practices of care, trust and community support.[15] These interrelated ways of acting as citizens have particular significance for applied theatre, where strong emotional bonds between participants are often created, and which also takes its responsibility for the wider social world very seriously. Of course, drama does none of these things automatically. Performance is not in itself politically radical, relationships between participants and practitioners are not automatically trusting, and theatre is not necessarily an instrument for positive change. It depends on the spirit in which they are used.

Participation, Performance and Citizenship

Political activism is motivated by passion. Theatre has a long history of articulating social dissent, and popular theatre, in particular, has been used to protest, to stimulate debate and provoke questions, thus enabling people to become emotionally engaged with political issues.

Throughout the twentieth century, activists of the political Left, influenced by the work of Meyerhold, Piscator and Brecht, found that forms of theatrical expression which were familiar to their target audiences were effective tools for social mobilisation.[16] Brecht defined the relationship between activism and popular theatre in the following terms:

> Our conception of the 'popular' refers to the people who are not only fully involved in the process of development but are actually taking it over, forcing it, deciding it. We have in mind a people that is making history and altering the world itself. We have in mind a fighting people and also a fighting conception of 'popularity'.[17]

Marxist interpretations of popular theatre, to which Brecht, of course, subscribed, would recognise only forms of expression which conform to a vision of social change based on the class struggle. More recent experiments in performance have been more ideologically eclectic, indicative of different forms of political citizenship that have gained currency since the Cold War era. Although the emphasis on the collective that informed conventional Marxism has eroded, what has remained in applied theatre is a commitment to *participation* as a route to citizenship. In this section I shall consider some of the political implications of this commitment.

The connection between theatre, citizenship and participation was predicated on the notion that spectatorship equated with passivity. This view is particularly associated with the Brazilian theatre director Augusto Boal (1931–2009), who exerted a powerful influence on socially engaged theatre in the second half of the twentieth century. His international reputation was built on his work in disadvantaged communities across the world, and his influential book *The Theatre of the Oppressed* has been widely read since its first publication in English in 1979. Boal is indebted to Brecht's analysis of the political dynamic between actors and target audiences, and he sought to develop Brecht's construction of the 'popular' by encouraging audience members to become 'spect-actors' who would take over the stage in a 'forum' – or performed debate – as part of the performance itself.[18] He applied theatre to civic citizenship; during his period of office on Rio de Janeiro's City Council from 1992 to 1996, Boal famously established a system of working which aimed to integrate political citizenship with theatre practice known as 'legislative theatre'. Gathering together special interest groups or members of particular communities, Boal aimed to encourage increased participation in the legislative process by using a range of drama strategies designed to elicit opinion about the issues of the day, stimulate political debate and find practical solutions to everyday problems. As a professional theatre practitioner and experienced political activist, Boal had significant expertise and resources to draw upon in conducting his experiments in legislative theatre. He described this process as 'making theatre as politics rather than making political theatre' and intended to use his elected power to 'transform desire into law'.[19]

The strategies Boal used to increase citizens' participation in civic politics are well documented in his book *Legislative Theatre* (1998). Boal's enthusiastic rhetoric is seductive, and it is sometimes difficult to discern how far his ambitions were realised by reading his accounts of this aspect of his work. Paul Dwyer has pointed out that although Boal was a good storyteller – clearly one of his skills as a theatre practitioner – his stories change over time, and this suggests that his summary of his political activities is inevitably partisan.[20] Yet the idea that democratic participation can be encouraged through theatre practice has endured, finding favour in less overtly politicised ways of working, where it is often seen as a way of encouraging social inclusion. Claire Bishop points out that participation became a key element in cultural policy under the British New Labour government, where 'participatory arts' were regarded as one way to address social problems (such as drug-taking, teenage pregnancy, crime, family abuse) or to encourage employability, wellbeing and so on. She argues that this approach to participation fulfils neoliberal social agendas rather than encouraging artistic experimentation and social critique:

> Participation became an important buzzword in the social inclusion discourse, but unlike its function in contemporary art (where it denotes self-realisation and collective action) for New Labour it effectively referred to the elimination of disruptive individuals.[21]

Bishop is influenced by Mouffe, who had made the case for antagonism in arts practices in her essay about the relational aesthetics of contemporary art. Turning her attention to participatory arts, Bishop is critical of working practices that prioritise collaboration and participation as virtues in themselves, thereby diminishing the focus on artistic value:

> This emphasis on process over product – or, perhaps more accurately, on process as product – is justified on the straightforward basis of inverting capitalism's predilection for the contrary. Consensual collaboration is

valued over artistic mastery and individualism, regardless of what the project sets out to do or actually achieves.[22]

This is a robust challenge, but I am drawn to Bishop's polemical analysis because it reopens some of the orthodoxies of participation associated with applied theatre to further critical scrutiny. It may rehearse the stereotype that socially engaged practice lacks artistic merit, but the practices Bishop invokes are sufficiently recognisable to invite a reconsideration of the relationship between dramatic methodologies, participation and citizenship.

The debate turns on how far participation in applied theatre equates with, or aspires towards, moral or political agreement between participants. Collective agreement was a major tenet of political theatre in the mid-twentieth century, when activist theatre was allied to the class struggle, but how far is does this ambition remain radical in the twenty-first-century 'age of uncertainty' that Bauman identified? There are, of course, different perspectives on this. Drama educator Jonothan Neelands, for example, argues that a focus on pluralist politics of place and identity that he finds in applied theatre has undermined universalist principles of equality and egalitarianism. He makes a case for theatre that is based on the 'ensemble rather than the individual' as way of ensuring that participants are provided with 'a second order identity as citizens struggling together'.[23] For Neelands, the collectivity of the ensemble inevitably equates with social freedom, a view that is based, primarily, on Hannah Arendt's liberal notion of citizenship and the common good. Though I appreciate the sentiment, my position is differently nuanced. Rather than equating plurality with generalised relativism, I am interesting in exploring, following Mouffe, whether theatre-making that takes that account of antagonistic struggle has radical potential. Mouffe argues that although Arendt considers the political potential of public spaces, Arendt follows Habermas in that she can only actually envisage public space 'in a consensual way'. In a direct reference to the ensemble, Mouffe argues that this represents a way of thinking that is politically limited. Her argument is worth quoting at length:

> The typical liberal understanding of pluralism is that we live in a world in which there are indeed many perspectives and values and that, due to empirical limitations, we will never be able to adopt them all, but that, when put together, they constitute an harmonious ensemble. This is why this type of liberalism must negate the political in its antagonistic

dimension. Indeed, one of the main tenets of this liberalism is the rationalist belief in the availability of a universal consensus based on reason. No wonder that the political constitutes its blind spot.[24]

My suggestion is not that Neelands has negated the political in his work; on the contrary, I am indebted to him for invoking a political vocabulary that applies equally to social and artistic practices. I am interested here in understanding how a radical democratic citizenship translates into many different forms of theatrical encounters and methods of performance-making, not all of which are undertaken collaboratively or as an ensemble. As Shannon Jackson points out in her discussion of criticality in theatre, 'there are numerous ways that the avowal of heteronomy can be both aesthetically precise and socially effective'.[25] There is a further debate to be had about the relationship between authorial vision and collective collaboration, and whether, for example, the dramaturgical structure of drama workshops, the social dynamics of the group and the discipline of the space operate bio-politically, positioning or coercing participants to act (or think) in particular ways.

My insistence that the term applied theatre is not used to restrict ways of performing or dramatic forms is, in part, intended to resist introducing a distinction between instrumentality and artistry. There is also a question of relying on self-reflexivity and critical reflection as the primary medium for socially-engaged theatre. This view is predicated, as Baz Kershaw has pointed out, on Brecht and Boal's perception that 'theatrical "distancing" will place audiences in a better or position to understand or "grasp" the world'.[26] This way of thinking not only privileges a particular kind of theatrical activity, it also implies that separation from the outside world is a precondition for knowing or understanding it. Taking his lead from Tim Ingold, Kershaw points out that, in ecological terms, this emphasis on human reflexivity as a means of understanding risks further separates or distances people from the material environment they inhabit. It is based on a social constructivist analysis of society, in which categorical distinctions between nature as given and culture as socially constructed are widely accepted.[27] In an era in which it has been understood that notions of citizenship must take account of environmental as well as human concerns, the distinction between natural and cultural worlds is self-evidently (and literally) unsustainable. Thinking ecologically, therefore, places questions of citizenship in a broader intellectual frame, inviting questions about the relationship between private actions and public responsibility, about values, habits and practical action.

One of the implications for this way of thinking is not only an increased interest in dramatising environmental issues, but also in the ways in which the rhythms and durational patterns of the natural world can be replicated or symbolised as art. There is sometimes an immediacy and imaginative spontaneity in the performative protests of environmental activists, who have shown that active forms of citizenship can mean spectacle, carnival and direct action as well as dramatised forms of debate.[28] These forms of collective action often link life and art; John Jordan, one of the founders of the Reclaim the Streets campaign, has described the playfulness of artist-activists who have built elaborate tree houses to halt road building, filled houses with earth to prevent demolition and held regular parties on motorways to stop the traffic.[29] Perhaps less confrontational and more durational is the concept of 'slow art', a movement that has developed to draw public attention to the ways in which global ecosystems and local environments are being destroyed. This work is designed to take time, and often invites members of the public to recognise their own place in the process of environmental change.

One particularly engaging piece of slow art called *The Arctic Gnome* was created in 2012 by Bullet Creative in partnership with Cape Farewell, an organisation that brings together artists and scientists to develop a cultural response to climate change. A large installation of white garden gnomes was assembled at the Eden Project in Cornwall, UK to represent the Arctic sea ice that is melting due to climate change. From November to January members of the public were invited to participate by taking home a gnome, in the expectation that they would make a pledge to change their daily habits in ways that would make a small difference to the planet. Over time, the installation gradually disappeared, representing the pace of environmental change as the ice melted. Gnome owners were invited to upload their pictures to a website as a performative gesture of their pledge; the rescued gnomes had their own Facebook page to document their adventures, and a Twitter account recounted the installation's slow decline.[30] It was a project that invoked a dystopic narrative, but drew attention to the relationship between the intimacy of domestic everyday life and wider ecological concerns. Rather than taming the political dynamic of citizenship, it offers potential for what Nigel Thrift describes as an affective 'politics of readiness' and Henri Lefebvre called the 'politics of small achievements'.[31]

This negotiation between the public and private spheres is related to a new political aesthetic of performance that has been well theorised by Baz Kershaw, who sees it as evidence of a newly emergent form of democratic pluralism.[32] If this is the case, the application of the playful unruliness of performance to serious political commitments will contribute to creating a dynamic and troublesome form of political citizenship which those in authority cannot easily ignore. It also operates on the level of intimacy, where it is understood that citizenship does not only include participation in public debate: it is also in the habits and unreflexive spaces of daily living that we can make a difference.

Good Intentions, Altruistic Motives

So far, my discussion has been informed by the idea that citizenship is a dynamic social practice, an identity which is constructed through networks of identification, open to change and renewal, rather than solely a legal state. An emphasis on citizenship as an embodied social practice not only implies that it is revitalised by public debate and political action, it also draws attention to the ways in which people support each other and take responsibility for other people and the environment as well as for themselves. In this section I am interested in interrogating the ways that practice in applied theatre operates at the intersection of different, and sometimes competing, agendas. In particular, I hope to find ways of thinking about the implications for organising and facilitating theatre in complex settings, and how the good intentions of those who practice in the field cohere with an active, ethical and social citizenship.

Projects in applied theatre are often organised by professional practitioners, usually with a background in theatre, and frequently working in partnership with other agencies including funding bodies (such as charities or government agencies) and in the setting of host organisations (a specified community group, a school, prison or hospital, for example). In these contexts, the values of the practitioners obviously have a major impact on the processes of working, and they are very often motivated by a desire to make a real difference to the lives of others. This is not, however, an easy role to negotiate, particularly in settings where practitioners are cultural outsiders. Writing about theatre in Bangladesh, Syed Jamil Ahmed has expressed a level of unease about the presence of 'an invisible Subject' (the practitioner) who assumes that a particular society 'needs to be transformed'.[33] Ahmed is particularly concerned with the potential imbalance of power between non-indigenous practitioners and local participants in theatre for development, but it is not uncommon for practitioners to express similar reservations about being regarded as 'cultural missionaries' when working in contexts or communities with which they are unfamiliar. There is sometimes an interpretative gap between the good intentions of the practitioners and how they are perceived by the participants which can be very troubling. And this is entirely justifiable. This uneven balance of power is not confined to more obvious negotiations between rich and poor countries, but also includes inequalities evident in settings that are in close geographical proximity. Ahmed has called into question the 'ostensibly altruistic motives' of practitioners in applied theatre, and this challenge suggests that the issue might be illuminated by a theorised understanding of the relationship between citizenship and the politics of altruism.

The history of the word 'altruism' is a useful starting point for this discussion. It was first coined by Auguste Comte, a French philosopher whose major works were written between 1830 and 1842, to mean the opposite of egoism. Comte was a positivist, which means that he was interested in developing a rationalist (rather than theological or metaphysical) systemisation of society. He believed that the highest human faculty is the intellect, and part of his project was to find ways achieving human betterment through creating a society based on rationalist principles and a clearly defined social order. In his later work, Comte became increasingly concerned with moral education, and it is at this point that altruism became integral to his social vision. He argued that altruism, rather than egoism, would bring about social harmony, because altruism would ensure that everyone would work for the common good. What is interesting, however, is that Comte linked altruism not only to public virtue, but to economic patterns of labour. In his social system, labour would not serve private enterprise but would be integral to State economics.

> [A] new system shall have taught all men that there is public utility in the humblest office of co-operation, no less truly than in the loftiest function of government. Other men would feel, if their labour were but systematised, as the private soldier feels in the discharge of his humblest duty, the dignity of public service, and the honour of a share in the action of a general economy.[34]

Comte particularly favoured the utilitarianism of industry, and his collective enterprise was based on rigid divisions of rank and status. Altruism provided a moral justification for industrial capitalism, and altruism, rather than egoism, was explicitly intended to support a hierarchical social and economic system.

The history of the concept of altruism suggests a less equitable politi-cal dynamic than more recent interpretations would imply. Altruism is generally regarded as a positive attribute of society, but it is often used rather loosely. In his discussion about the ethics of altruism, David Miller provides a definition of an altruist as 'anyone who goes to the rescue intending to help'.[35] In this description, altruism is more closely associated with the motivation of the altruist than the effects on the recipient which – like a gift – may or may not be welcome. Furthermore, Miller points out, it is more likely that altruistic gestures are offered to those whom the 'altruist' regards as deserving in some way – either morally, politically or ethically – and there is significant evidence to show that altruists are selective about who they help. In slightly different vein, Neera Badhwar argued that self-interest and altruism are not opposite poles, but interrelated. Altruistic acts are socially and psychologically beneficial to the giver, Badhwar suggests, because altruism is itself a significant part of his or her self-identity.[36] On both counts, the politics of altruism are rather ambiguous. In Miller's description, the altruist presupposes that someone needs rescu-ing for a particular reason – whether they have asked for help or not – and assumes that the recipients' lives will be enhanced as a result of this intervention. Badhwar's interpretation recognises that altruism has spe-cific benefits for the giver and that, however benign, the self-regarding motives of the altruists are always implicated in other-regarding acts.

The politics of funding can illuminate the ways in which self-interest and altruistic motives can be mutually embedded in theatre projects. David Kerr, writing with the authority of many years' experience in Malawi, points out that it is funders who drive agendas, often without detailed research, which means that the theatre is used to promote 'simplistic message formation' rather than encouraging open debate.[37] A particularly good example of the way in which the priorities of funders represent both altruism and self-interest is offered by Asma Mundrawala in her astute analysis of commissioned theatre projects in Pakistan between 2003 and 2006.[38] Mundrawala focuses on projects about forced marriages and 'honour killings' funded by the British Council and the British High Commission. British involvement derived from self-interest, as many young women who were forced into marriage in Pakistan held dual British and Pakistani citizenship. This meant that 'rescuing' women and repatriating them back to the UK was not only traumatic for the victims, it also drained government resources. Theatre companies were commissioned to raise awareness of the issues, and the large audience figures were regarded as an indicator of success. Mundrawala points out, however, that the involvement of donor agencies is not only short-term, it also fails to address deeper questions of social justice and economic sustainability. They may be 'well-intentioned causes' but they are driven by Western agendas to which local theatre activists are expected to conform. Commenting on Mundrawala's paper, Syed Jamil Ahmed comments that this form of theatre exerts 'a subtle form of manipulation' in which local NGOs will not receive funding unless they are 'willing to follow the normalising framework set by the donors'.[39] This neither promotes radical citizenship nor robust debate, leading to docile lives. What an analysis of altruism offers to this debate is another way of understanding the need to exercise vigilance, of understanding points of connection between other-regarding acts and self-interest, and recognising that they operate as a continuum rather than binary opposites. This is a salutary reminder that, when working in applied theatre, good intentions to be good citizens are not always good enough.

Part of the problem with this form of self-interestedness is that it promotes a Western view of universal human rights without understanding that social citizenship is more complexly nuanced on a local level. My suggestion is that the affective dimensions of theatre provide a good way to negotiate a productive consonance between altruism and self-interest. Placing the citizenship in the affective realm draws attention to the domestic sphere, where power relations are experienced locally and intuitively in family settings on an everyday basis. My example is provided by Anne Tanyi-Tang, who has researched how indigenous women in a region of Cameroon applied theatre to address the issues raised in their domestic lives. She described two performances devised by women in the Mundemba Sub-Division of Cameroon who used theatre 'not as a weapon' but as 'a means of appealing to men's consciences'.[40]

The first performance Tanyi-Tang witnessed was primarily directed towards civic officials who were threatening to punish many villagers for tax evasion. A group of elderly women, using popular forms of performance, demonstrated the problems they experienced in transporting cash-crops and purchasing tax coupons because of poor transport conditions and the appalling roads. They also used the performance to show the uneven division of labour in their community, with women undertaking all the farming and the domestic responsibilities whilst their husbands remained idle. Given that in this society women were not only prohibited from taking an active part in politics but also from speaking publicly in the presence of men, theatre was one of the few ways in which they could make themselves heard. The effects were significant and lasting. The officials built a road so that the women could sell their cash-crops, and this enabled local men to purchase tax coupons with less financial strain.

On a subsequent visit to the region, Tanyi-Tang witnessed women in the Christian Women's Fellowship (CWF) perform a play that was highly critical of the way in which their husbands tried to prevent their membership of this organisation. Having persuaded their menfolk to sit together wearing home-made uniforms for the event, their presence in the audience was highly visible. The play, which used the form of a Christian parable to demonstrate the inequities of domestic life, appealed to their husbands' consciences. As a result, Tanyi-Tang observed, their attitudes towards the activities of the CWF changed and they agreed to fund future activities, showing their remorse for their former selfishness by buying examples of the women's handiwork at inflated prices.

These examples illustrate the ways in which theatre provides a means whereby domestic issues might be brought into the public arena. The Cameroonian women used their experience of social citizenship to enhance their own status as civic citizens in the wider community; this effectively reverses the trajectory of Marshall's (Western) taxonomy of civic, political and social citizenship. They used theatre to raise aware-ness of their situations in ways which both showed their altruistic con-cern for the general welfare of the community as well as serving their self-interested desire for practical assistance and emotional support in their daily lives. Watching their performances led the target audience to see things from a different perspective, in turn challenging their self-interested positions, a process which enabled members of the audi-ence to behave more generously towards the women. This generosity also necessitated an improvement to their material conditions, further underlining the interdependence between the environment and the community. Altruism, as philosopher Keith Graham has identified, encourages self-development, as a process of 'broadening of horizons beyond the personal, even though as a matter of fact the person is not left behind'.[41]

One response to the complexity of working in challenging settings, particularly where practitioners are cultural outsiders, is to acknowledge the radical uncertainty of its political role. There is no easy route to equal-ity, but I still hold on to the view that practising drama has the potential to bridge ethical divisions between civic citizenship and social citizenship, and between citizenship as a legal status and the affective, interpersonal and relational dynamics of social citizenship. This observation takes me back to Mouffe's description of citizenship as a process of identifications, a 'collective undertaking' in which a plurality of identities are recognised and legitimated rather than ignored or privatised. Acknowledging that there is a reciprocal relationship between altruism and self-interest, between practitioners and participants, performances and audiences has the potential to disrupt social hierarchies and to displace individualism with forms of citizenship which are more overtly social and communitarian. At its most generous, theatre practice encourages such forms of social citizenship, a process of self-identification with others which Graham has described as 'irreducibly plural'.[42]

Ecology and Citizenship

Both drama and citizenship are creative practices, and both are concerned with the values, needs and aspirations of individuals, communities and societies. Citizenship is an evaluative term and, whilst I am not arguing for placing applied theatre at the service of citizenship education, I am suggesting that theories of citizenship offer a productive way of conceptualising the dynamic between social networks, personal relationships and altruistic practice which lies at the heart of applied theatre. The issues surrounding practice in both applied theatre and citizenship are, however, intensified by globalising pressures generated by the erosion of the nation-state, the inequities of global capitalism and the compression of space and time through digital technology. As a conclusion to this chapter, I shall focus on how a concept of ecological citizenship, as one of the effects of an increasingly networked world, might impact on thinking in applied theatre.

Ecologies of citizenship is a metaphor which suggests the complex, interdependent, interactive and often uneven relationships in the practice of citizenship between the local and global, between the human and non-human. It is a way of conceptualising a number of different themes which have emerged in this chapter – the dramaturgy of civic citizenship; citizenship and political activism; altruism and social citizenship. At its most literal, pressing concerns about environmental change raise materialist questions about how to live and act in the world (Do I drive to the shops or walk? Should I fly to work with a community across the world or go to that conference?) which place the ordinary and everyday in the context of global issues.[43] More broadly, however, ecological thought displaces the centrality of human experience by recognising that people are enmeshed in wider networks of interdependence. In their editorial for an edition of *Performance Research*, 'On Ecology', Stephen Bottoms, Aaron Franks and Paula Kramer tease out some of the implications of ecological thought for performance studies, suggesting that there is 'no fixed outside' to human experience. They suggest that performance provides a place to explore this positionality:

> Performance can broach the question of an inside/outside boundary in many ways, but whether we begin with the interiority of the subjecthood or the exteriority of relations and 'being-in-the-world', we are already in the middle, and implicated.[44]

In an article in the same issue, I suggested that theatre and performance offers a space to engage directly with the materiality of lived experience – the here-and-now of embodied creative practice – as part of a performative pedagogy.[45] As such, my contention is that theatre-making is related to notions of citizenship, not only as a way to represent moral questions or dramatise political debate, but also because we know the world in the unreflexive practices of everyday life, as enactment, embodiment and inhabitation.

This suggests that theatre might be one place to explore what J.-D. Dewsbury describes as 'the the agency of matter and its affective affordances'[46] and Jane Bennett portrays as 'affective encounters' between human and non-human 'vibrant bodies'.[47] These new materialist debates extend the affective turn in applied theatre, where affect has been theorised almost invariably in humanist terms. James Thompson, who opened this important debate, offers a politically effective concept of affect that is discussed in humanist terms, and he selects Patricia Clough's phrase 'the self-feeling of being alive' to describe affect in relation to participants' experiences of applied theatre. Nicola Shaughnessy follows Thompson's lead in her book, *Applying Performance: Live Art, Socially Engaged Theatre and Affective Practice*, where her focus lies on squarely on affect as a cognitive process and as an aspect of human play.[48] What is interesting about both these accounts of affect and applied theatre is that neither addresses the affective qualities of the non-human world and on which much affect theory is predicated. Thompson does not take up the posthumanist element of Clough's definition, where she argues that affect 'traverses the opposition between the organic and non-organic'.[49] Perhaps this emphasis on human agency in applied theatre, then, is unsurprising; the social dynamic of applied theatre is generally regarded as the product of individuals working as a group rather than as a broader ecological framework of affective sensibilities. Following Dewsbury, however, it becomes clear that 'agency is not discretely distributed between the human and the non-human; rather it mutually comes about in the immediate material constitution of any experiential encounter'.[50]

My suggestion is that an active, performative citizenship is concerned with the ethics of how people interact with each other and with their environment. It suggests that fixed boundaries between the public and private, between self and other, human and non-human, altruism and self-interest cannot be drawn. This way of thinking is based on the understanding that identity is sedimented through a multiplicity of networks, relationships and identifications – not all of them human. Artistically, this opens the way for multiple forms of expression that are alert to the affective qualities of sites and places, as well as representing ideas, thoughts and experiences. The place of performance in this construction of an active, participant citizenship lies in inhabiting different spaces and narratives and examining life from a range of perspectives. This does not only require self-reflexivity, but also involves knowing the world by becoming 'attuned to its differences and juxtapositions' as geographers Anderson and Harrison suggest,[51] and by developing habits of 'sensory attentiveness' advocated by Jane Bennett.[52] The performativity of theatre fits well with this model of citizenship, because the process invites participants to acknowledge their own vulnerabilities and limitations, and recognise that dependency on a network of affective relations is emotionally, culturally and politically productive. In this sense, acting as citizens involves recognising the unpredictability of context, the messiness of emotional relationships, the affective engagement in the material world, and the political significance of dialogue as well as more abstract conceptions of citizenship as a collection of legal rights.

3 Pedagogies, Praxis and Performance

Mapping Pedagogies

Applied theatre has strong ties to learning. Advocates of applied theatre in its different guises have regarded its participatory, dialogic and dialectic qualities as effective and democratic ways to learn in many formal and informal educational contexts. This interest in the processes of learning is generally described as *pedagogy*, a term which, as feminist educationalist Patti Lather points out, focuses attention on 'the condition and means through which knowledge is produced'.[1] Of course it has long been recognised that the production of knowledge is highly complex, and emancipatory models of education have, for a century or more, emphasised the centrality of the learner in the pedagogic process. Pedagogies designed to encourage interactivity and collaboration have been seen to be in direct opposition to authoritarian and didactic approaches to learning and, as a collaborative art form, drama has been particularly well placed to contribute to such an educational project. Drama and pedagogy are both *activities*, contingent on the contexts and settings in which they take place, and the process of bringing them together has been regarded as a powerful way of encouraging creativity.

Where knowledge is situated, what forms of knowledge are valued, and how knowledge is shared remain major preoccupations in the range of practices that constitute applied theatre. Moreover, as applied theatre is a global phenomenon which operates in many different cultural contexts, there is no one pedagogical method which might be universally effective, or universally appropriate. Any approach which advocates a 'one size fits all' learning policy is likely to ignore local dynamics and the concerns of particular interest groups. Nonetheless,

43

there are, if not general trends, recurring pedagogic principles in applied theatre which are both exchanged through global networks and reinterpreted in response to specific local contexts. As an artistic practice, it is generally understood that knowledge in drama is embodied, culturally located and socially distributed. This means that knowledge is produced through interaction with others, and that this reciprocity between participants generates new forms of social and cultural capital. 'Reciprocity', Lather argues, 'implies give and take, a mutual negotiation of meaning and power.'[2] Pedagogy is primarily concerned with how this negotiation and exchange might happen.

This insight leaves open the central question of what kind of knowledge and learning is associated with, or promoted by, practitioners in applied theatre. To address this methodological gap between meaning and knowledge, Lather suggests, pedagogy needs to be linked to *praxis*. Or, put another way, there is a need to bring together 'how' questions with 'why' questions in order to establish a clear rationale for practice. Lather's definition of praxis as 'the self-creative activity through which we make the world' is illuminating.[3] Applied to theatre, praxis does not denote a linear model of learning, but a cyclical process in which practice generates new insights and where, reciprocally, theoretical ideas are interrogated, created and embodied in practice. Praxis, therefore, is built on a circularity of thought, feeling and action. In this discussion I am hoping to reopen debates about the triangulation of performativity, praxis and embodied pedagogies, and to consider how this process of learning might enable participants to map new possibilities for meaning-making.

The metaphor of the map is a useful way of conceptualising the connections I am making between narratives of space, place and time in applied theatre.[4] You would follow a map in order to undertake a journey, to be transported (in Richard Schechner's terms) from one place to another. On this journey, paths might collide or your direction might change to take in new vistas and perspectives. You might encounter barriers, deadends or summits which force a change of itinerary, a new track or an unexpected route. A pinnacle might be reached, the landscape thrown into relief, and a new journey begun. A map shows that there are many different ways to reach the same vantage point, but although a map allows you to plan your route, each journey is different and the experience is unpredictable. The map is based on journeys which have already taken place, but it also offers a guide for those which have yet to start. It offers an imprint (but not a fixed an image) of the 'in-between spaces' which Homi Bhabha has characterised as a

space of emancipation.[5] A map indicates activity; it needs to be interpreted and inhabited before it can be turned into a story. It names
histories and alludes to local legends. It also suggests the affective and
aesthetic dimensions of a journey, marking places which are beautiful
and difficult, but not noting their significance nor offering clear solutions about how best to approach them or encounter the feelings they
invoke. Because applied theatre operates at the points of intersection
between culture, community, place and identity, the metaphor of the
map indicates the negotiation between local circumstances and global
realignments which is acutely relevant to its pedagogic practices.

This chapter is structured in four parts. The first section will examine
theories of praxis and pedagogy which are orientated towards emancipation, specifically focusing on the work of twentieth-century Brazilian
educator Paulo Freire and the related concepts of border or critical
pedagogies which have gained popularity in the USA and travelled to
many different parts of the world.[6] The second section takes the idea
of performative pedagogies as its starting point, and raises questions
about the political equations between efficacy and efficiency, liminality
and transgression. In the third section I shall consider the relationship
between knowledge and artistry and, in the conclusion, identify some
implications for a sensory pedagogy of place in applied theatre. Taken
together, these three central concepts of pedagogy, praxis and performativity provide an opportunity to investigate political constructions of
learning and knowledge in applied theatre, and to further a theoretical
framework with which to analyse learning in the context of uncertain
pedagogical journeys in a globalised world.

Crossing Borders: Pedagogies of Location

Dwight Conquergood has argued that the study of performance is
located at the intersection between two domains of knowledge – the
map and the story. The map is 'official, abstract and objective' whereas
the story is 'practical, embodied and popular'.[7] Using this well-known
analogy, Conquergood draws attention to the history of Western
thought that separated theory from practice, and cast rigid boundaries
between critical analysis and creativity. In this Enlightenment project,
he observes, objective scientific knowledge was privileged over local,
vernacular and community-based 'know-how', and this hierarchical
distinctions between officially sanctioned forms of knowledge and ways
of knowing which are more 'active, intimate, hands-on participation'.[8]

Pedagogies in performance studies, he suggests, can travel between these two domains of knowledge by finding points of connection between creativity, critique and citizenship and by opening up the possibilities for local stories and community participation in academic inquiry. There are obvious parallels between Conquergood's activist version of performance studies and applied theatre.

Conquergood was writing from the perspective of a twentieth-century North American academic, and his concern was to erode the boundaries between different forms of disciplinary knowledge. My own interpretation of the metaphor of the map is similarly intended to diminish the space between theory and practice, albeit in slightly different terms. Whereas Conquergood sees maps as primarily bureaucratic, my emphasis on the provisionality of maps recognises that they are also intimately connected to local history, legends and autobiographical stories, and that not all maps carry official or objective information (as the visual representations of journeys of Aboriginal Dreamtime in Australia clearly illustrate). But Conquergood's analysis of the political status of maps and, by extension, to the politics of location helpfully illuminates the pedagogical debate. He points out that maps become 'crisscrossed by transnational narratives' as people migrate, and that stories are transported and exchanged as diasporic populations travel across official borders either voluntarily or through economic or political necessity. Crossing borders is, of course, a political act where some people are excluded, searched and interrogated, whereas others can travel easily and freely. Borders indicate the interplay of movement and fixity, and this has repercussions for the meanings attached to places. He described the local as a 'leaky, contingent construction', and location is 'imagined as an itinerary rather than a fixed point'.[9] If this is the case, it means that in many contexts across the world is it impossible to talk about the 'local' without some implied reference to the global. This is both a literal physical experience and a metaphor for pedagogy. There are two ways of looking at this. A bounded sense of place may offer a secure basis from which to speak, to defend local, communitarian or territorial interests. Alternatively, borders are a way of keeping people in their place, of excluding others, or of ensuring that people living within its territories maintain their power or continue to be marginalised. Either way, politically and pedagogically, location is about the exercise of power.

The renegotiation of cultural geographies has been recognised in educational and cultural discourse, where spatial metaphors such as 'border crossing' (Giroux, 1994) and 'speaking from the margins' (Spivak, 1987) suggest the complex signification of movement and location in global cultural dynamics. If applied theatre appears most at home in the borderlands, it is because it is envisioned as a flexible and radical alternative to forms of pedagogy perceived to be instruments of disciplinary authority and social control. The Brazilian educator Paulo Freire, whose work *Pedagogy of the Oppressed* (1970) continues to inspire practitioners in applied theatre, extended the idea that pedagogy could act as resistance to political oppression. Freire followed Marx by arguing for active models of pedagogy in which authoritarian approaches to learning are inverted, and where learners are encouraged to share their ideas in dialogue with others. He was critical of what he described as 'banking education', in which students listen to, receive and memorise information given to them by teachers. Freire observed that this experience of powerlessness led people to internalise their oppressors' view of them as 'sick, lazy, and unproductive', an identity which he suggested might be challenged through problem-posing pedagogies.[10] In classic Marxist terms, this process of '*concientizacao*', or critical consciousness, is an approach to learning which Freire sees as leading to collective engagement in the class struggle.

In practice, Freire's political pedagogy was primarily concerned with developing adult literacy. It was important to Freire that illiterate adults learnt to read and write in order that they might take an active part in social democracy, and his progressive pedagogy was a means to achieving this end. He stressed the relationship between language, thought and human agency, describing literacy as 'word-and-action' rather than 'mere vocabulary'.[11] For Freire, literacy is 'an act of knowing', and he encouraged learners to assume 'the role of creative subjects' as part of the process of becoming literate. In order to facilitate this learning, teachers were urged to respect participants' existing cultural knowledge and experiences, but also to encourage them to develop new ways of thinking. Increased powers of literacy not only extend learners' confidence as thinkers and speakers, Freire argued, they also lead them to new conceptual horizons. In terms which are reminiscent of Wittgenstein's famous dictum 'the limits of my language are the limits of my world', Freire recognised that it is through language that people develop a capacity for 'critical knowing' in which education is a creative process of 'constant problematising'.[12] It is this relationship between creative participation and critical reflection which has become central to pedagogies in applied theatre.

There are numerous examples of practice in applied theatre which have been inspired by Freire, not least because of his profound influence on Brazilian theatre director Augusto Boal. The example I have chosen to illustrate Freire's political pedagogy is not Boalian, but an adaptation of active learning strategies devised by the charity Action Aid to encourage adult literacy in the developing world. The technique, known as 'Reflect', takes the local environment as a basis for learning, rather than prescribed literacy 'primers'. Local 'literacy circles' begin with participants representing their experiences graphically, drawing maps, charts and diagrams of places and events which are important to them in locally available materials such as leaves, sticks and beans or rice. Constructing these graphics encourages stories to emerge and discussions to take place, a creative process on which the facilitators build when the group is ready to move into making their own written texts. The process enables participants to use their own local knowledge as a starting point for literacy development, inviting them to generate a vocabulary around a theme or a place which is significant to them. Reading and writing activities are developed from this starting point, a strategy which places the experiences of the learner at the centre of the pedagogical process. They are also designed to encourage dialogue and exchange, and to foster networks of care and support both within local communities and beyond.

I have found in my own practice that 'Reflect' strategies lend themselves well to dramatic exploration, as participants represent aspects of their autobiographies in symbolic form. For example, at the beginning of the devising process a group of young refugees were asked to map their experiences, placing the symbol of a paper heart on the place in the world where they felt most at home, and then tearing it into small pieces and replacing the segments on the map to show all the places in the world where they felt that had left parts of themselves. This action – and many others in which participants similarly charted their experiences visually and physically – prompted reflection on stories of enforced migration and diaspora. Working through this process enabled them to use a range of languages to tell their stories; their first languages as well as learning English, and to move easily into the symbolic, embodied and visual languages of drama. Another group of young people in a London school found that representing their home-places as a map revealed diasporic narratives about immigration that had been handed down across generations. Writing an imagined SMS message to their grandparents provided a powerful starting point for a performance. In common with Freire's approach to adult literacy, these dramatic pedagogies provided a supportive context for participants to extend their ability to communicate. As its name suggests, this pedagogic strategy encourages reflection on lived experience, but the process also offers the participants control over what they want to say and what they wish to withhold.[13]

'Reflect' is Freirean in that it connects thought and action, an essential attribute of his praxis. The process also values the vernacular, and the existing knowledge of the participants is central to the learning process. Where strategies such as 'Reflect' often depart from a strict Freirean pedagogy, however, is in their politics. Freire's praxis is indebted to Karl Marx's politicisation of the term, a term which has its conceptual roots in Hegelian philosophy.[14] Praxis, in Marxist discourse, is not just any relationship between theory and practice, but a creative and politically interventionist strategy, consistently orientated towards socialism. For Marxists, including Freire, praxis is regarded as an active process of critical engagement with experience aimed at disrupting established power relations, on both a material and intellectual level. Praxis was an important revolutionary strategy, appropriated by twentieth-century theatre activists who aimed to disturb the complacency of naturalised bourgeois sensibilities by awakening the masses to the reality of their oppression. For Freire, whose Marxist pedagogy adhered to well-defined battle-lines between oppressed and oppressor, good and evil, self and other, praxis actively involves the oppressed in critical dialogue about their material circumstances as part of their struggle for liberation. Like many of his contemporaries, Freire assumed that 'authentic praxis' based on 'true reflection' on a 'concrete situation' would automatically lead to Marxist politics.[15]

In considering how Freirean pedagogies have influenced contemporary educational debates, US applied theatre practitioner and academic Sharon Grady has pointed out that the critical pedagogies of Henry Giroux and Peter McLaren reproduce a neo-Marxist politics of education. Does following these theories in applied theatre make practitioners into 'accidental Marxists', she asks? The question is apposite. Freirean-inspired critical pedagogy is a transgressive pedagogy in which, Grady suggests, 'teachers are asked to be revolutionary agents' whose role is to 'empower' their students to work against (or transgress) the hegemonic forces of capitalism.[16] It assumes, as I have pointed out, that there is a critical vantage point from which a transparent 'reality' might be clearly visible. Furthermore, the emphasis on borders, margins and liminality in applied theatre as a leitmotif for its pedagogical practices is based on the assumption that if learning shifts from the traditional centre to the radical margins, and surveys the world from the shifting perspective of the borderlands, it will be emancipatory. When allied to the transgressive politics of theatre-makers such as Brecht, Piscator and

Boal, this way of thinking about learning has provided practitioners in applied theatre with a powerful political agenda.

There has been, however, a paradigm shift in Western artistic practices from transgressive to resistant politics as the political certainties of orthodox Marxism were eroded. In his analysis of this change in the intellectual and cultural climate, Hal Foster argued that transgressive politics was derived from the modernist avant-garde, where it was assumed that art-making made it possible to stand outside, transcend or transgress contemporary social realities in order to critique them. Resistant politics, by contrast, recognises that all knowledge is contextually bound. It accepts that, although power is unevenly distributed, the idea that there are clearly identifiable social structures which might be transgressed is no longer an adequate representation of the complexities of capital in the era of globalisation and its porous political borders. The role of the political artist in this context, he suggests, is to challenge dominant representations by investigating 'the processes and apparatuses which control them'.[17] This leaves a political conundrum. According to Foster, all cultural action and production – including drama and theatre – is contingent on context, and although political art is resistant to dominant cultural formations it is, by implication, also parasitic on them. This gives rise to a central and problematic question, which Baz Kershaw has identified: 'how can performance, in being always implicated in the dominant, avoid replicating the values of the dominant?'[18] For applied theatre, Kershaw's question is central to formulating a new conceptualisation of praxis which both recognises and challenges its contextual limits.

What is at stake here is a redefinition of art's relationship to politics. In his illuminating book about collaborative art, Grant Kester points out that modernist artists promoted detachment and critical outsidership as a route to liberty, claiming that art provides a privileged position from which to analyse social injustice:

> This detachment is necessary because art is constantly in danger of being subsumed to the condition of consumer culture, propaganda, or 'entertainment' (cultural forms predicated on immersion rather than a recondite critical distance).[19]

This way of thinking, which has deep roots in the history of Western thought, found expression in the twentieth century avant-garde, where art became tasked with 'transgressing existing categories of thought, action and creativity' and required to 'constantly challenge fixed boundaries and identities'.[20] Despite an interest in collaboratively produced art, practitioners in applied theatre often advocate critical distance, and my own interest in unfixing identity and place has often borrowed from this tradition. Yet the idea that art provides a privileged or critical vantage-point that will necessarily lead to emancipation or uncover the 'truths' of the human condition is now regarded as hopelessly simplistic. What is needed, I contend, is an understanding that knowing the world depends on a multiplicity of human and non-human relations, represented both through critical reflection and enacted in everyday life as embodied practice.

Spatial metaphors for politics and pedagogy signify the impact of globalisation on contemporary thought, and images of borders and margins are often intended to suggest an interest in disrupting dominant regimes of knowledge. But this risks romanticising outsidership and forgets that borders are arbitrary constructions that represent specific narratives and require policing. According to educationalists Richard Edwards and Robin Usher, this emphasis on spatiality draws attention to the 'place' of the learner, to how and where knowledge is located and performed:

> As location is simultaneously a dislocation from other positions, pedagogy therefore becomes a process of constant engagement, negotiation and encounter… . Here, what is central is not the fixed position (a state of being) but the active and open state of becoming.[21]

These dynamic learning processes require open-handed guardianship of the ethical borders of applied theatre, and continual vigilance about where its political limits might be drawn. Praxis is informed, therefore, by the creative and contingent mapping of different narratives – cultural, personal, social, political, artistic – and learning is negotiated and choreographed as encounters between the artistic practices of drama and theatre and the vernacular know-how of the participants. These radical pedagogic processes are always recognised as incomplete, continually orientated towards 'an open state of becoming', and are also *performative* pedagogies.

Performative Pedagogies: Efficacy or Efficiency?

The idea that pedagogy is a performative encounter, rather than a meeting of fixed positions, turns attention to how constructions of performance in different disciplinary fields might illuminate learning in applied theatre. This concern is amplified by the fact that drama is in itself a performative act, even when the work does not lead to a conventional theatrical performance. In all its manifestations, questions of power and knowledge have been central to discussions about the politics of performance, and surface in many different guises. The two interpretations of performance I am particularly interested in exploring in relation to pedagogy in applied theatre derive from performance *studies*, which analyses performance as cultural practice, and from performance *management*, which was generated in the corporate sector and is concerned with accountability and achievement. The differences between the two uses of the term appear difficult to reconcile. Broadly speaking, performance studies looks to the margins, to local cultural practices, the dispossessed and the diasporic, whilst performance management looks to the global, to standardisation, homogenisation and to uniformity. One is associated with efficacy, the other with efficiency. They seem to emphasise very different, and incompatible, ways of articulating the performance of knowledge and power.

On the face of it, pedagogical approaches to applied theatre have little to do with the language of performance management and are closely allied to performance studies. In performance studies, the emphasis on marginality has introduced a vocabulary of playfulness to describe practitioners and practice. Dwight Conquergood emphasises the relationship between performance studies, play and the politics of location:

> Performance privileges threshold-crossing, shape shifting, and boundary-violating figures, such as shamans, tricksters and jokers, who value the carnivalesque over the canonical, the transformative over the normative, the mobile over the monumental.[22]

There is, however, a risk that this very emphasis on marginality becomes domesticated and forms a new orthodoxy. In response to pedagogical questions about social exclusion and inclusion, Jon McKenzie's analysis of performance studies is illuminating. McKenzie argued that in performance studies liminality has become the norm and the dominant conceptual model. It is an interest in transgression and performance efficacy, he suggests, that defines performance studies and thus an emphasis on marginality lies, paradoxically, at the centre of the discipline. As a further challenge, McKenzie invokes Victor Turner's anthropological research to show how liminal performances which begin as transgressive rituals aimed at disrupting social norms often mutate over time, and eventually become conservative reinforcements of the status quo.[23] A good example of this is the Notting Hill Carnival, which is held annually in London.

It began in 1964 as a resistant protest against racism and an assertion of Caribbean culture and, although the carnival itself maintains some of its radical roots, by 2002 carnival performers were also content to lead the Queen's Golden Jubilee procession staged (and commodified) as a show of the kind of national unity described by Michael Billig as 'banal'.[24] The emphasis on marginality in applied theatre has not, by and large, taken account of the potential slippage of liminality into conservatism, nor how quickly theatre practices and pedagogies once regarded as 'alternative' become absorbed into the mainstream.

Whatever the cracks and fissures of transgressive pedagogies, practitioners in applied theatre have maintained a continual commitment to the democratisation of learning. Performance management seems diametrically opposed to this. If performance studies has emphasised the liminal, focusing on performative practices which are 'in between' spaces and times where social conventions are challenged, models of management have focused on the norms, standards and elements of performance which signify achievement or competence. The political differences between the two disciplines seem huge, and the relationship between power and knowledge inverted. Applied theatre, with its interest in border pedagogies, decentralisation and deterritorialisation of knowledge, seems distant from the discourses of efficiency associated with management studies. Performance management has, however, introduced a new language into commerce and industry, emphasising the importance of creativity and intuition in the workplace. Employees and managers are both expected to be flexible and adaptable, to take initiative, operate as part of a team and be affectively engaged in their work. Jon McKenzie has offered a summary of the paradigm shift from manager/ employee roles based on models of people as machinery to those based on systems theory.[25]

This way of thinking about workplace relations has a remarkable resonance with the language of the kind of participant pedagogies with which applied theatre has been associated. Substitute the word teacher, practitioner or facilitator for manager, participant or student for employee, and these lists would not look out of place in many drama education or applied theatre texts, where they might serve to summarise the differences between traditional and radical pedagogies. Performance management's drive for effectiveness, efficiency and productivity has appropriated Freire's argument that an oppressive society naturalises characteristics such as laziness and ignorance, and turned them into a system which supports global capitalism. By inverting the dialectic, this approach to management seeks to ensure

The Changing Role of Management

From	To
Risk-taking avoided	Innovation encouraged
Directive	Participative
Control of people	Enabling control of product
Inform if need to know	Inform if want to know
Commitment to boss	Commitment to purpose
Competitive	Collaborative

The Changing Role of Employees

From	To
Dependent	Empowered
Passive	Assertive
Childlike	Mature
Cynical	Optimistic
Competitive	Co-operative
Distrustful	Trusting
Ignorant	Informed
Unskilled	Skilled
Assumed lazy	Motivated

FIGURE 1 THE CHANGING ROLES OF MANAGEMENT AND EMPLOYEES

greater commitment from 'human resources', a process which is in turn expected to lead to greater commercial profit.

Performance management is based on the ideal of an active subjectivity, where employees are created who have people skills, the ability to adapt to new situations, and are committed to self-improvement. Seen in this way, some of the 'unfixed' qualities of performance, valued in performance studies and in applied theatre, are also evident in performance management. Chantal Mouffe further argues that global capitalism has appropriated the strategies of counter-cultural artists:

> The aesthetic strategies of the counter-culture: the search for authenticity, the ideal of self-management, the anti-hierarchical exigency, are now used in order to promote the conditions required by the current mode of capitalist regulation, replacing the disciplinary framework characteristic of the Fordist period.[26]

Designer employees or active, participant citizens? In one interpretation, following Foucault, performance management means that the self becomes an enterprise, representing yet another attempt to 'govern the soul' through creating self-regulating citizens.[27] An alternative reading is that this kind of reflexive modernisation is more benign, creating increasingly flexible and egalitarian work practices. However construed, applied theatre cannot escape this debate. For some working in applied theatre, performance management has made corporate commissions a palatable option and drama programmes aimed at team-building, creative thinking or customer service have proliferated. One aspect of this work that is particularly intriguing is that many companies use the dramatic strategies of Augusto Boal, a central element of his *Theatre of the Oppressed*, despite the fact that the aim is to maximise corporate efficiency and economic competitiveness. In an article in *Personnel Today*, an on-line trade journal for human resource managers, this connection is made explicit:

> Drama techniques, if used appropriately, are ideal for experiential training, using the skills of an actor to foster trust, build collaboration and allow risk-taking... . At its simplest, drama-based training uses actors or theatrical techniques to illustrate a particular outcome. This approach can involve a relatively conventional presentation to a large group of people – such as on a health and safety catastrophe. Or it can involve more intimate groups of delegates using the Forum Theatre methods pioneered by Augusto Boal in the early 1970s.[28]

These drama-led training programmes expect to engage employees on an affective level, with the assumption that the training will inspire greater personal commitment and thus lead to higher productivity levels. This is designed to encourage affective labour, defined by Hardt and Negri as labour that 'produces a feeling of ease, well-being, satisfaction, excitement or passion'.[29] Similarly, I have observed that theatre workshops on promoting equality and diversity often emphasise staff recruitment and retention rather than any political or moral reasons for creating an equitable working environment.

Both performance management and applied theatre are allied to performative pedagogies, as in each case learning is embodied and understanding is shown in practical situations. Both have an expectation that skills and insights learnt in rehearsals or workshops will be transferable into other situations and contexts. Kester points out that this way of thinking emerged in the Enlightenment, and invokes a separation between 'real life' and the creative space that has become subsumed into contemporary justifications for the arts. The assumption here is, in Kester's words that '[t]he work of art trains us for social interactions that we aren't yet prepared for in real life'.[30] Writing from the perspective of education studies, Edwards and Usher have also identified this instrumental trend, further suggesting that learning is not valued for its own sake, but for its usefulness or efficacy:

> [T]he performativity of knowledge can take different forms because of its location in different social practices. This means that its efficacy may vary. For instance, it can enhance self-knowledge and lifestyle through personal development opportunities made available through the consumer market. In critical practices, it can be a pedagogy of performance which moves beyond a Western form of rationality and its preoccupation with the written word (the book) to embrace diverse forms of cultural learning across the globe... . [O]ther than its efficacy for realising different socially constructed aims, knowledge no longer has a single canonical referent.[31]

From the point of view of practice in drama, it is interesting that Edwards and Usher emphasise that pedagogics of performance recognise plurality, and that it takes account of forms of learning which are not confined to the written word. The central point, however, is that 'efficacy may vary', and this disrupts faith in the utopianism often ascribed to the arts. The destabilisation of canonical forms of knowledge implies that no pedagogic practices will, of themselves, generate a specific form of social change. In the language that is familiar to both applied theatre and performance management, performative pedagogies might be 'empowering' but in very different ways. What is learnt depends on how theatre is applied, on the educational aims of particular projects, the narratives of the participants and the specific social locations and cultural contexts in which the work takes place. This is both pedagogical and profoundly political, making the need for a clear rationale for practice – a praxis – even more acute.

Artistic Vision and Social Effects

One of the reasons why it is particularly important to tease out some of the implications of the different ways in which performance is understood is that this has a bearing on the objectives and agendas that sometimes govern applied theatre. Despite different motives and intentions, aspects of performance management have crept into the kinds of organisations on which applied theatre depends for its funding – such as charities, educational institutions, hospitals, prisons and voluntary organisations. Professional practitioners across the globe have become skilled in writing grant applications in which performance indicators are identified, and where evaluation is expected to measure the social outcomes and effectiveness of the project. In many ways the invokes familiar concerns about distinctions between art and instrumentalism, but this approach also raises deeper questions about the kind of conceptual vocabularies that are applied to theatre-making, and how the criteria for its evaluation are understood.

The emphasis on the social effects of theatre-making is, in part at least, a consequence of the idea that participating in theatre enables people to 'make sense' of experience, that drama is a rehearsal for life. This implies, of course, that the value of participating in theatre is evidenced in other areas of life, rather than in the moment of the practice itself. This art/life binary leads to an easy slippage into searching for quantifiable outcomes, where it is expected that the impact of the practice on 'end-users' will be measured. Claire Bishop has noted this tendency to overplay the social outcomes at the expense of its aesthetic value or artistic qualities. In arguing that this has commodified participatory arts in the creative industries, she suggests that there is a need to redress this balance by reconsidering how this work is read as *art:*

> Without finding a more nuanced set of vocabularies to address the artistic status of the work, we risk discussing these practices solely in positivist terms, that is, by focusing on demonstrable impact.[32]

The word I should like to emphasise here is 'demonstrable', as it is often the ability to *demonstrate* specific social outcomes that places creative limits on the work. My suggestion is that it is not necessarily the *effect* of theatre-making that is the problem – practitioners in applied theatre intend to make a difference – but that the discourses and practices of performance management are dictating the ways in which creative practitioners are expected to work and so are undermining their role as artists.

There are implications in this for the relationship between collective practices and authorial or artistic vision, and the knowledge and skills that practitioners bring to the work. There is a spectrum here. Some practitioners, particularly those who use a recognisable set of games and similar workshop activities, consider that bringing a strong artistic vision to the practice creates an uneven balance of power. There is a further debate about whether applied theatre projects always need to be run by theatre specialists, or whether client support groups, prison officers or the police, for example, can develop some skills in drama facilitation. Others have a clearer sense of themselves working as artists working in specific contexts. This poses interesting questions about where knowledge is situated, and what kind of knowledge is valued. Freire's dialogic pedagogy is instructive here. He based his pedagogy on an exchange of differentiated knowledge, where literacy teachers were not expected to deny their own specific expertise or pedagogical intentions, but were asked to build on the expertise and knowledge of the learners. In terms indebted to Gramsci's concept of the organic intellectual, his pedagogue is a 'knowing subject', a 'specialised educator' who does not perpetuate the symbolic capital of dominant culture, but regards education as a dynamic process of coming 'face-to-face with other knowing subjects'.[33] The North American feminist educator Elisabeth Ellsworth has described this negotiation of different forms of knowledge as a 'pedagogy of the unknowable' because it is never possible to 'know' fully the social experiences of others.[34]

The balance between the known and the unknown is particularly significant to applied theatre, where practitioners not only need skills as artists and facilitators, but also benefit from gaining an understanding of the contexts in which they are working. In order to develop their understanding of the community or institutional settings, many drama practitioners work in close partnership with related professionals such as teachers, social workers, probation officers or psychiatrists and develop inter-agency projects in which the participants themselves act as co-authors and collaborators. A good example of how authorial vision, collective collaboration and the complexities of setting were successfully negotiated was a project devised by the British artist Mark Storor called *A Tender Subject* (2012). This was a three-year project in which Storor worked for extended periods with gay prisoners and gay prison officers. It was commissioned by Artangel, a cultural organisation that produces contemporary art that is both socially engaged and artistically innovative. Speaking about *A Tender Subject*, Rachel Anderson, head of interaction at Artangel, described the company's commitment to both learning and the arts:

> Its roots are in educational practice, it articulates itself through social value and through the value of those participating in the process but it stands in a mainstream arts framework.[35]

The project culminated in a performance for the public, performed by members of Only Connect, a company of ex-offenders and young people at risk of offending, but this represented only one aspect of the work. Storor was alert to how prison life shaped the project's learning throughout its duration; he observed that the hierarchal structure and disciplined practices within prisons affected gay prison officers as well as prisoners who, over time, had become desensitised by their environment. Rather than making over-simplified judgements about prison officers as oppressors and the prisoners as the oppressed, Storor wanted to question and erode hierarchies, and find sensitive points of connection between officers and prisoners whose sexuality was shared. With the support of the organisation Gays and Lesbians in the Prison Service (GALIP), Storor developed workshops with prison officers and prisoners in three different British prisons, working separately at first, but gradually and with care bringing the two groups together. Trust emerged gradually, Storor commented, but as prison officers relinquished control of the space and everyone recognised resonances of their own stories in others that were shared, 'the presence of the officers gave them [the prisoners] absolute freedom'. Perhaps most significantly, working in drama often requires a change in institutional culture, a shift in thinking from the idea that professionals control the situation because of their expert disciplinary knowledge, to recognising that participants have specialised knowledge of their own situations and experiences which are central to the work.[36]

Storor found that prisoners protected themselves from the brutality of prison life in many complex ways, making tender moments and intimate encounters impossible. In a recorded interview, he recounted one workshop in which a prisoner said that he felt that he had left 'a suit of himself' at the door when he entered prison, and would only put it back on when released. In response, Storor and Anderson bought up all the men's suits they could find in local charity shops and asked the men to choose one that 'most spoke to them' and to customise it how they liked. The man who had sought invisibility ripped out the lining, drew things inside that had emotional meaning, and over-sewed it so that it looked to Storor 'like a heart-bypass scar'. One man, who performed his sexuality as a defensive high-camp stereotype, sewed up the sleeves, one of the legs and the breast pocket. He explained that underneath the extrovert exterior he felt hobbled, that he longed to reach out to someone but it felt too dangerous, and that he had sewed up his breast pocket to keep his heart safe. These moments of tenderness, though not directly represented in the performance, illustrate Storor's workshop methodology and his artistic vision, where working with material objects enabled the men to find metaphors that helped them to create a new affective community within the confines of prison.

This is applied theatre at its most radical and innovative, and although Storor's ability to create beautiful, complex theatre that is also defined by an ethic of care is a rare gift, there are lessons to be learnt about the balance between social agendas and aesthetic value that can be applied elsewhere. On a philosophical level, the work illustrates Jacques Rancière's perception that the aesthetic and the political are mutually embedded, eroding tired distinctions between activity/passivity, real life/art, individual/collective, author/spectator. Elizabeth Ellsworth describes this sensory pedagogy that is constructed spatially and dynamically as 'a complex moving web of interrelationalities'.[37] This is generated over time, involving the vernacular and everyday as well as specialist understanding of dramatic form and metaphor, and builds affective communities in the here-and-now of the artistic practice. Pragmatically, of course, quoting Rancière at prison officers may not help an artist's case, but there are lessons to be learnt about how practice can be framed in ways that resist simplistic divisions between social outcomes and artistic value.

Sensory Pedagogies of Place

So far I have argued that whatever the different values of the practitioners and participants, the efficacy and effectiveness of the work depends on the formulation of a praxis – the embodied synthesis of theory and practice – rather than a particular battery of drama strategies, forms or techniques. Practitioners in applied theatre use many different forms of theatre and performance in their work, and any recommendation of one particular set of dramatic practices over another would be restrictive. What makes theatre 'applied', however, rather than just 'theatre' is not only the also the pedagogical processes, but understanding the educational, institutional or community settings in which it takes place. The feeling and atmosphere of places influences learning; places have an affective power that is, itself, often pedagogical. In this final section I would like to draw together some tentative thoughts about the relationship between place, affect and pedagogy.

An affective pedagogy of place is both situational and temporal. James Thompson's elegant theorisation of the relationship between theatre, affect and social change is apposite here. He has in his sights a narrow set of lifeless, instrumentalist practices orientated towards representing and solving social problems; his argument that learning is 'an affective, felt state' serves as an important reminder that social change is produced through embodiment as well as critical engagement with social issues.[38] Thompson's primary interest lies in 'affective transactions' between people rather than other forms of environmental relationality. He follows Massumi and Gossberg (both influenced by Gilles Deleuze) in suggesting that moments of change prompted by the affect of an event (such as a performance) are sudden or abrupt, described as 'moments of rupture' (Grossberg, 1996) or a 'shock to thought' (Massumi, 2002). And although I would not doubt that social change can result from such moments of epiphany, I am also interested in another reading of Deleuze that takes account of durational time, and is less dependent on the shock or suddenness of spontaneity.

Deleuze is indebted to Henri Bergson's notion of time as habit, in which time is embodied as a durational and aesthetic encounter. It is significant that, in *Difference and Repetition* (1994), Deleuze finds points of connection between learning and theatre. In Deleuze's paradoxical terms, new insights can only emerge through repetition. He distinguishes between learning and imitation, and argues that learning takes place 'not in the relation between a representation and an action (reproduction of the Same) but in the relation between a sign and a response (encounter with the Other)'.[39] In finding a place for theatre *as* learning, Deleuze is interested in the affective dynamic of theatre, in the 'powers that act beneath the words, gestures, characters and objects represented'.[40] What I take from this elision of theatre and learning is that both depend on repetition and difference for their affective power – without repetition life would be a jumble of incomprehensible signs, but as each performance is differently experienced it allows for the possibility of risk and alterity. Theatre and learning are thus *both* constituted at the dynamic intersection between repetition and difference, an inhabited space where learning is dramatised. In other words, I am suggesting a slower pedagogic patterning that is both alive in the space of performance and accumulates, reflexively, over time.

Theatricality lends an aesthetic doubleness to this pedagogic process, framing the practices of everyday life and inviting participants to pause long enough to pay attention. My suggestion is that theatre and performance, when pedagogically attuned to the affects, practices, dispositions, senses that contribute to a sensory understanding of place can support participants in finding affective affiliations between the daily patterns of living and, to borrow Dewsbury's words, how 'we *believe* in the world' (my italics).[41] These beliefs and values are, crucially, sited and situated rather than abstractions; they are enacted and performed in places we inhabit – on the street, at work, at home, in prison or in school – in the many different sites in which applied theatre takes place. It is attentive to the movement of bodies, to memory, forgetting, sound, smell, taste – it marks the limits of me and you (or self and other). This sensory pedagogy is not intended to comprehend theatre as an indeterminate third space, but as an ambivalent space of association in which to witness consonance, dissonance and interrelationality.

Part II
Narratives and Narrativity

4 Narrative and the Gift of Storytelling

The storyteller is the figure in which the righteous man encounters himself.

Walter Benjamin, 'The Storyteller'

Changing the Story

This chapter is an exploration of some of the ways in which narrative is set and experienced in applied theatre. Throughout this book I am suggesting that applied theatre is concerned with how narratives are constructed, and how they might be deconstructed or challenged. Drama is in itself often a narrative art, and theatre-making is a good place to explore and represent narratives of selfhood, culture, place and community. There is often an oppositional quality to this work, and many practitioners in applied theatre have a particular commitment to ensuring that dominant ˌsocial narratives are disrupted. Theatre-making provides a powerful opportunity to ask questions about whose stories have been customarily told, whose have been accepted as truth, and to redress the balance by telling stories from alternative perspectives. It is this understanding that narratives can be changed which lies at the heart of practice in applied theatre.

In *The Storyteller* Walter Benjamin described the ethical implications of the change from a society built on oral narratives and shared experience to a culture in which information is received in short bursts, through images, photographs and news clips. Writing in the aftermath of the First World War, Benjamin's analysis of the social role of the storyteller ends with the claim that the storyteller is allied to goodness. The storyteller's gift, he argued, is to use experiences of life to offer practical wisdom, finding narratives and metaphors which make connections between life as it is, and life as it might be. As a Marxist, Benjamin recognised that stories play an ideological role in society, and he differentiated between stories which disrupt dominant patterns of thought, and those which perpetuate the values of the powerful. Successful storytellers for Benjamin are not those who report events or provide information, but those whose stories encourage people to share their experiences and stimulate moral discussion. This form of storytelling is a craft, which storytellers use to engage their listeners through the expressiveness of their bodies as well as with their words. Good storytelling, in Benjamin's terms, combines aesthetics and ethics, an act of generosity.[1]

However nostalgic Walter Benjamin's account of the master storyteller might be, this elision of narrative, ethics and aesthetics has continued resonance in contemporary social theory and implications for applied theatre. Narrative theory provides a good vehicle for exploring the ways in which practising drama brings about changes of understanding and generates new insights because, as Paul Ricoeur has pointed out, it is placed at 'the crossroads between the theory of action and moral theory'. 'Telling a story,' Ricoeur suggests, 'is deploying an imaginary space for thought experiments in which moral judgement operates in hypothetical mode.'[2] On this basis, working in the 'imaginary space' of drama enables participants to juxtapose different narrative perspectives, to fictionalise life as it is experienced and, conversely, to make the imaginary world of fiction tangible and 'real'. Conceptualised and practised in this way, theatre-making becomes a place to explore the ethical gap between description and prescription, hypothesis and factuality.

All stories are read and created through the lens of personal, social and cultural experience, and this means that narratives are inevitably interpreted in many different ways. Recognising that stories have multiple interpretations involves identifying the limits of one's own horizons, and an interest in seeing alternative perspectives. This approach signals an aspiration towards social equality, as Kathleen Gallagher has pointed out:

> The distinctive educative force of theatre, however – its dialectics – invites us to take up points of intersection *and* confrontation, so that our dramatic explorations do not simply calcify cultural and ethnic boundaries and limit our own and our students' abilities to affiliate with multiple cultural identities, productively manoeuvre across borders, and develop capacities for functioning in diverse situations.[3]

Gallagher is concerned to erode fixed binary divides between self and other, identity and difference, and to encourage dramatic explorations of narratives that actively interrogate and contest these boundaries. In these terms, self-creativity is an explicitly political process. It is her challenge to find ways of working in theatre that enables participants to affiliate with multiple identities which I should like to begin to explore here.

The idea that identity is a continual process of *becoming*, rather than a pre-given expression of *being*, has involved a reconsideration of the concept of narrative and its significance in everyday life. A narrative conception of selfhood recognises that identity is not constructed autonomously, but over time and in relation to others, through language and through other symbolic codes available in cultural practice. Avtar Brah summarises the argument:

> Since identity is a process, what we have is a field of discourses, matrices of meanings, narratives of self and others, and the configuration of memories which, once in circulation, provide a basis for identification.[4]

The idea that the self is a narrative, continually created and re-created through interaction with others does not, however, suggest that individuals are without agency, nor lack the ability to think or feel for themselves. In describing the self as discursively or culturally constructed, I am suggesting that identity is uniquely layered through a historical sedimentation of events and experiences over which, as individuals, we have some degree of choice. Life is not itself a coherent unity nor a linear narrative, but a 'configuration of memories' and 'matrices of meanings' which become stories as experiences are re-told, re-created, ordered and interpreted. This acknowledges that the aesthetics of self-production is built on the convergence and interplay of different narratives, and that constructing narratives of selfhood is both an ethical and a creative process.

If working in theatre is to enable participants to manoeuvre productively across borders, to borrow Gallagher's words, practitioners will be alert to how different narratives – personal, cultural, social and artistic – converge in the process. This is not, of course, confined to dramatic forms which have an obvious narrative structure – a wider description of narrative would include the games, rehearsals or drama workshops that also convey something of the messiness of reality and explore its incoherence, and to which participants bring the complexity of their experiences of life, however fictionalised and incomplete. In this chapter I will investigate the representation of 'real' issues as fictional narratives, and in Chapter 5 I shall continue the investigation of narrative by focusing more explicitly on narratives of community.

Fiction as Reality

One of the central arguments in this book is that fiction and reality, self and otherness are not in opposition or isolated from each other but, as narrative constructions, they are interrelated and mutually embedded. Autobiography often blends the fictional with the real, and over time life histories are rehearsed and become fictionalised. Conversely, fictionalised narratives found in myth and legend are integral to narratives of selfhood and community. This is particularly relevant to applied theatre, in which participants are often invited to explore matters of local interest and personal concern, and in which the divisions between fiction and reality are deliberately blurred in order to provide a safe space for participants to transform experiences into dramatic metaphor or to find points of connection which narratives presented theatrically. Changes of understanding or new ideas come about when narratives are contrasted or juxtaposed or, as Paul Ricoeur put it (with echoes of Deleuze), 'meaning emerges through the interplay of identity and difference'.[5]

One of the practices familiar to drama educators and dramatherapists is the use of both fictional and autobiographical narratives to play with alternative constructions of selfhood, to frame experiences in order to view life from alternative places and perspectives. The aims of dramatherapy and applied theatre are very different, but many forms of theatre-making in applied theatre have an interest in how fictional narratives might illuminate lived experiences. Writing about her work in prisons, Sally Stamp has offered an insightful discussion of how participants in drama education workshops often create narratives which, whilst not explicitly autobiographical, are analogous with their own situations and experiences, and they will identify strongly with plays or films which reflect aspects of their lives.[6] In dramatherapy, by contrast, as the work is intended to encourage participants to explore personal situations and feelings, members of a group will establish a contract which clearly identifies the scope and boundaries of the work, and dramatherapists are bound by professional codes of conduct.[7] This distinction is important, and I remember very clearly feeling cheated and hurt on one occasion when I had signed up to participate in a workshop for drama educators, but I was requested, unexpectedly, to explore quite personal relationships within my own family with a group of people I had met only a few minutes previously. This clearly contravenes codes of professional practice in dramatherapy and the ethics of drama education. But the boundaries between a fictional narrative and autobiography can blur very easily, and in non-therapeutic settings sometimes the narrative is taken in unexpected directions by participants, and this may touch nerves or invoke particular feelings for individual members of a group.

My assumptions about the ethical implications of constructing fictional narratives in drama workshops were tested on a visit to Sri Lanka in July 2003. I have noticed before that working in a very different context from my own makes me acutely aware of how deeply my own cultural values and experiences inform my practice, often unconsciously, and this work was no exception. As part of a small international delegation to a conference, I had been invited to run a workshop which would take place in the village of Seelamunai near Batticaloa. I would be working with a group of conference delegates – including teachers, theatre activists, youth workers and NGOs – and, as I would be working under the trees, probably the local children would join in too. I was aware that many people taking part were working with young people who have been affected or traumatised by the war. Tackling the issue of war trauma directly would obviously be both insensitive and inappropriate in a workshop of only two hours, particularly when my understanding of the context was limited. But I was interested in developing a workshop which involved constructing a fictional narrative which I intended to be sufficiently ambiguous for the participants to interpret in many different ways.

I had chosen to adapt a workshop I had developed with drama educator Andy Kempe for an in-service course for drama teachers in Wales. The narrative had been stimulated by a particularly haunting image of a little girl's dress, apparently washed up on a beach. In Wales we began the workshop with no preconceived idea about what the story of the dress might be – just that it had been found on a beach. In the three days we worked with the group of teachers, they developed a powerful story about loss, guilt and collective memory, in which the back-story of a little girl's disappearance was always present, but never discussed or explained. The work had been particularly successful, and I was interested to see what happened when it travelled. I knew that the workshop plans would need editing, and that I wanted the work to be much lighter in mood. Rather nervously, I asked James Thompson and Irene Fraser, both highly respected for their applied theatre work in

Sri Lanka, what they thought about starting by laying out a little dress on the ground, and leading various creative activities through which the group would construct their own story about the little girl who owned the dress. There was nothing in the activities to suggest that she had died or disappeared – she would simply be an imagined character. There was a pause. In the village where I would be working, they told me, children had been murdered and their bodies washed up on the lagoon. Something that seemed very remote and imaginary in Wales felt painfully close.

I had to think again. I wanted the imagined world of the dramatic narrative to provide participants with a safe space, but this workshop was primarily intended to share models of professional practice rather than explore anything more personal. I made the decision that the girl would be imagined rather than enacted, and I hoped that this ambiguity would enable the group to create the story they wanted to tell. If it were too close to reality, there would be no space for the imagination, and only one possible story – that the little girl had been murdered in the civil war. I decided to change the tense from past to future. I still used the dress, but told the group that it belonged to a girl who had grown out of it, and who was alive and well and living locally. The narrative focused on her future, beginning with a comic representation of helping a wriggling and unco-operative child struggle into a dress which was too small for her, and moving into adult gossip about her sense of mischief. But despite my intentions, I was surprised how quickly the participants chose to create her back-story, with one group turning what I had expected to be a light-hearted scene about a prank into a far more harrowing story of the beatings she had received during the war. This was the participants' choice; in response to the same activity another group devised a very witty scene complete with two children commenting on the girl's antics in scandalised tones from inside an imaginary television. Gradually, however, a picture was emerging of an unhappy child, and the group wanted to offer an explanation for what they portrayed as her bad behaviour. They did not seem interested in apportioning blame, and the atmosphere in the workshop did not seem at all tense, but I was concerned that the workshop was being taken in directions I had not anticipated and which might be inappropriate in this context. In the moment, I made the decision not to intervene and to enable the story they wished to tell to emerge. But by the end of the workshop it seemed important to think again about the future, and I put the little girl's dress back in the centre of the circle. Following their cues, I told the group that she had woken in the night with nightmares, and that, in my country, there is a tradition of singing lullabies to children if they are scared. I joined the other two British participants in singing a lullaby in English, and the other participants followed with a song in Tamil, with each person in turn making a wish for her future, the dialogue underscored by the local lullaby. In that context, this moment was almost unbearably moving. The story the group had created was of a child who had been damaged and traumatised by the violence she had experienced and seen. This had not been my intention, but this was not my story. It was theirs.

What I had not anticipated was how closely the imaginary character of the girl and the fictional narrative of the drama would reflect lived experience, and how closely the participants would identify with her situation. As a cultural outsider, and particularly as someone who has never experienced war at first hand, I was very conscious that there was a huge gap between my life and those of the participants. For example, one group had used the drama to satirise the daily routines of confronting armed guards, meeting curfews and coping with military occupation, and this was received with a hearty laughter of recognition, but to me the scene brought home the reality of living in a war zone which was far more troubling. I had been open about the fact that I was offering a workshop similar to those I run in the UK, and it was offered in the spirit of inter-cultural dialogue and exchange of practice rather than anything else; the practitioners with whom I worked were perfectly able to discern which elements were useful to them and which were not, and the children ran in and out of the workshop as they wished. The content of the story was created by the group, but I had created a narrative structure for the drama in which I had assumed that the girl's actions could be explained in terms resonant with Western models of psychology. I thought that all I had done was offer a structure for the workshop, leaving the work as open-ended as possible, but had I insidiously exported my own values and assumptions? In the workshop, the child was a trope – in Ricoeur's words, an 'imaginative space' – who became the object of the participants' sympathy, and on whom they projected their own ideas and feelings. This was integral to the narrative structure. I had learnt that Western models of psychology were ineffective with traumatised victims of war in Sri Lanka and, although it was not my intention to enter this territory, I wondered how far I had naturalised my own culturally specific ideas of the narrative construction of selfhood.

James Thompson has analysed a similar confrontation between fictional and real narratives in his work during the war in Sri Lanka, arguing that encouraging participants to see situations in the drama from multiple perspectives revealed his own ethical values. In the course of a drama about the occupation of the participants' town, he had asked a group to find imaginative sympathy with a soldier who was part of the occupying force. He described how 'he sought to complicate the single narrative' but in the process was concerned that he was 'also undermining the single-minded sense of direction that a community in struggle needs if it is to overcome virulent oppression'.[8] Similarly, my own concern with challenging fixed perceptions of identity and difference in drama, and encouraging multiple affiliations, seemed inappropriate and hollow in a context where the participants had their cultural identities systematically denied by a brutal occupying force.

On the same day as I ran my workshop, Sithmparanathan, a Tamil leader and theatre director, had argued that the liminal space of ritual is the 'theatre of liberation'. Through these local tools of cultural expression, he argued, 'deep feelings' might be released.[9] My point is that, however much a group appears to own a story to the practitioner or workshop leader, there are undoubtedly cultural assumptions – ideas of individuality, for example – hidden in the aesthetics of storytelling, embedded in different narrative genres and therefore structured into even the most open-ended workshops. Seen in this light, the narrative structures of a workshop are never innocent; they lead the participants' imaginative journey. It would be good to think that my own workshop was part of a rich intercultural dialogue and exchange, and certainly the feedback I received suggested that some of the strategies I used would be effective in work with children in the Sri Lankan context. But given the history of colonialism in Sri Lanka, I also thought that the generous participants who took part in my workshop would have been right to be suspicious of British people bearing gifts, even if they were wrapped as fictional stories in well-intentioned drama workshops.[10]

Identity and Identification

My reading of the workshop in Sri Lanka raises questions about the cultural politics of narrative, but the impact of working with narrative in drama warrants further theorising. Many forms of drama rely on the convergence of different narratives because participants bring a range of ideas and experiences to the drama. This means that, from the perspective of any one participant, there is always a triangulation between their own narratives of identity, the narratives of others, and the narratives of the drama itself, which needs to be negotiated. My suggestion is that an understanding of this negotiation between different narrative perspectives – both 'real' and fictional – might be helped by an understanding of the concept of identification. I have already raised this concept in relation to debates about citizenship, where I have suggested that citizenship is not solely a legal status, but that active citizenship is based on collective forms of social identification. There are two ways of looking at identification which seem particularly germane to debates about selfhood and social action. The first builds on the work of Freud which has influenced subsequent thinkers in the field of psychoanalysis, and the second draws on Brecht's critique of 'identification' in theatre (a term he sometimes used interchangeably with 'empathy'). I am interested in whether it is feasible that identification with different narratives offers participants in drama the opportunity to bridge the gap between self and other, identity and difference, and to mark points of contact between fiction and lived experience.

At the centre of Freud's writing about identification there is an ambivalence about how far it threatens or subsumes identity, and how far it acts as a more positive force for self-creation. His writing presents different and sometimes conflicting arguments about the relationship between identification and identity. My aim here is to use two of Freud's key texts on identification, 'On Narcissism' (1914) and 'Group Psychology and the Analysis of the Ego' (1921), to sketch some of the ways in which his thinking might be applied to drama. In his early essay 'On Narcissism' his account of the transition from self-love to love of others turns on the process of identification. Childhood, he argued, is a narcissistic phase in which identification with others is uncritical, purely mimetic, based on self-love rather than a love which recognises others as separate people. This primary identification is sometimes extended into adulthood, where love of others remains fixed at the narcissistic phase, based on an identification with an ideal and idealised other, invoking the all-consuming emotional attachments of childhood. At this point in his writings, identification was inextricably tied to narcissism or, conversely, to the other key theme in his writing, hysteria. In *The Interpretation of Dreams* (1900) Freud interestingly described the 'secondary identification' of hysterics as a theatrical metaphor. Hysterics, he argued, are able 'to suffer on behalf of a whole crowd of people and to act all the parts in the play single-handed'.[11] Taken together, these two ways of thinking suggest a double-bind; primary identification with others is associated with a narcissistic sense of self, where love of others is a regressive search for the lost narcissism of childhood, or secondary identification is a symptom and cause of an unstable identity, where the hysterics' secure sense of self is threatened by fantasies about their over-powerful effect on others. Neither version is likely to be attractive to practitioners in applied theatre.

Perhaps more productive for theatre practitioners is the revision of the concept of 'secondary identification', both by Freud in his later writings and by subsequent psychoanalytic theorists. Loosened from its negative association with hysteria, secondary identification can be very enriching. The theatrical metaphor Freud used in 1900 to describe secondary identification already signified its social dynamic, and his emphasis on identification *with regard* to another person, rather than just *with* them signified the significance of social relationships and emotional attachments between people. It is in 'Group Psychology and the Analysis of the Ego' that Freud qualified his earlier position by recognising that secondary identification allows for personal development, and that relationships with others can lead to 'new perceptions'.[12] Unlike primary identification, where individuals are unable to distinguish between themselves and others, this kind of identification has much clearer boundaries. Social relationships are entered into, and emotional attachments are formed on the basis of recognising that other people are *not* oneself, and that they have distinct identities of their own. It is from this position of self-awareness that individuals might learn to see identification not as a violation of identity, but as a potentially positive dynamic in the process of self-creativity. In this sense, identification both produces and destabilises identity.

A Freudian conception of identification, therefore, offers a way of thinking about the relationship between self and other which both recognises its potential for self-development and warns against a loss of identity. Freud was obviously analysing relationships between people, but his discussion of identification also has implications for engagement with the arts. Hélène Cixous has articulated the relationship between identity and identification in relation to reading:

> One never reads except by identification. But ... [w]hen I say identification I do not say a loss of self. I become. I inhabit. I enter. Inhabiting someone at that moment I can feel myself traversed by the person's initiatives and actions.[13]

This kind of identification relies on metaxis – a sense of being both in the world of the story and outside it. In these terms, identification with fictional narratives involves both a process of self-reflexivity and emotional engagement with others. Drama, which often invites multiple forms of identification, is potentially a very good vehicle for extending understanding of oneself in relation to others. Physical embodiment of the narratives of others can be a particularly powerful way to 'become' another temporarily or to 'inhabit' another's story. Cixous also pointed out that because the process of identification may challenge or affirm patterns of identity, there is no guarantee that it is a consoling experience. There is an ethical ambiguity here. On the one hand, although challenges to fixed patterns of identity may feel threatening, they may also lead to psychological liberation through which new social identities may be formed. On the other, there is no guarantee that identification with others, however life-changing, will be for the better, in whatever terms 'better' is construed.

In psychoanalytic terms, identification has an historical dimension, as identity is formed through a lifetime of identifying with others. The question which Freudian theories of identification fail to address, however, is concerned with its social and cultural meanings. There is a political dynamic to any discussion of self and otherness which has been particularly powerfully articulated by feminist and postcolonial theorists, whereby identification with a dominant 'self' has, historically, created a marginalised and objectified 'other'. In other words, there is no certainty that identifying with multiple narratives in drama, as elsewhere, leads to social equality. This is central to Brecht's objections to identification (and empathy) in theatre, which he regarded as essentially conservative. He argued that identifying with characters inhibits spectators' ability to contrast the circumstances of their own lives with those portrayed on stage. For Brecht, this kind of identification perpetuates a familiarity or sameness rather prompting change – in Freudian terms, it is solely narcissistic. Brecht was similarly scathing about the concept of a coherent identity or ego, which he regarded as a bourgeois myth. In these terms, the comforting elision between identification and identity had no place in Brecht's theatre. In the *Appendices to the Short Organum*, however, Brecht showed his awareness of the theatrical power of disrupting spectators' identification with characters on stage, and pragmatically suggested that this device might be used to challenge their political assumptions.

> However dogmatic it may seem to insist that self-identification with the character should be avoided in the performance, our generation can listen to this warning with advantage. However determinedly they obey it they can hardly carry it out to the letter, so the most likely result is that truly

rending contradiction between experience and portrayal, empathy and demonstration, justification and criticism, which is what is aimed at.[14]

It is clear from this that Brecht placed qualities of self-identification such as 'experience', 'empathy' and 'justification' in opposition to 'portrayal', 'demonstration' and 'criticism' – terms he associated with more radical forms of social inquiry. What Brecht does value, however, is the spectators' identification with the *performers*, and he expected that this would denaturalise and unfix any bourgeois illusions which might arise from identifying with *characters*. In an interesting passage, he explained how spectators might observe and critique their own social positions through identification with the performers:

> The performers' self-observation, as an artful and artistic act of self-alienation, stopped the spectator from losing himself in the character completely, i.e. to the point of giving up his own identity, and lend a splendid remoteness to the events. Yet the spectators' empathy was not entirely rejected. The audience identifies itself as being an observer, and accordingly develops his attitude of observing or looking on.[15]

This elision of self identity, self-observation and self-alienation suggests that, in Brecht's theatre, some forms of identification have interventionist potential. It is not Freud's 'affective identification', but a cognitive process whereby established social and cultural meanings can be recognised and historicised.

What is useful about the unlikely combination of Freud's and Brecht's conceptualisation of identification is that it focuses attention on both the affective and the cognitive, on the potential for both social change and emotional engagement. In different ways, both writers accept that identity is constructed through a sedimented history of identifications, a process which has the potential to either shore up established patterns – either social or personal – or to destabilise them. Both perspectives are informed by epistemologies based on modernist conceptions of the subject. Distancing herself from this essentialism, Teresa Brennan has pointed out that from a psychoanalytic point of view social identification with others is not in itself necessarily transformative. She conceded, however, that 'multiple identifications' with the narratives of others may produce 'a way of coming to terms with the images one receives from others', a process which 'permits different thinking'.[16] This implies that affective identification with a multiplicity of narratives in drama has the potential to wear away fixed narratives of self and other, identity and difference, and open the spaces in between where new insights might be generated.

Empathy and the Social Imagination: Plays and Players

In this section I should like to tease out some of the implications for applied theatre for identification with dramatic narratives as both performers and as members of audiences. Playing roles is experientially different from seeing plays, and the premise that breaking down theatrical illusion is socially liberating has been accepted in many different practices in applied theatre. Practices in applied theatre are frequently explicitly designed to erode divisions and hierarchies between performers and audiences – Boal's hybridised 'spect-actor' is the most obvious example. Theories of audience have, of course, moved on since Boal developed his methodology in the 1970s; yet one of the central tenets of applied theatre is that it encourages participation, and there are many ways of working which challenge the separation between performer and audience that exists in some forms of theatre. This impulse takes Brecht's exhortation for audiences to identify *with* the performers to its logical next stage, in which participants are asked to identify themselves *as* performers. It is this distinction I am interested in exploring in this section, and I want to ask some further questions about the concepts of empathy and identification in relation to the moral and social imagination.

The example I have chosen to explore these ideas comes from a play that was developed in a school. Drama education is well known for its history of encouraging engagement with social and moral issues through improvisation, but I have chosen to discuss a play, *The Unravelling* (2009) written by the playwright Fin Kennedy as a result of his residency at Mulberry School in London. The play was first performed by girls from the school at the Edinburgh Festival, where it not only held its own against professional companies, but won a coveted '*Scotsman* Fringe First', the first school ever to receive such an award. Kennedy's play was the third in a trilogy of plays produced during his period as playwright in residence, and was devised with the girls as well as written for them. Mulberry is a girls' school situated in Tower Hamlets, London, and has a student population of 98 per cent Muslim students, mostly second- or third-generation British Asian of Bangladeshi heritage. This means that the girls possess, according to Kennedy, 'a disarming mix of East and West' and have inherited the rebellious spirit of London's East End.[17] This play provides me with the opportunity to consider the empathetic responses of an audience to the play and the potential for the young people's learning as performers. Another reason for choosing this play is because it addresses the social and emotional significance of the imagination directly, which in turn raises questions about the role of traditional tales and storytelling in relationship to students' moral and social education.

The play is set in an East End fabric shop, where a seamstress sits among rolls of beautiful fabric that will eventually unravel as stories unfold. As the mannequins in the shop come to life, their stories can be told. The narrative focus of the play is a mother who runs the fabric shop and her three daughters, Eldest, Middlest and Youngest, each of whom has their own style and fashion, illustrated by their choice of fabric. The turning point in the play is when the Mother is tells her daughters that she dying and, in the manner of traditional tales, she is given until sunrise the following day to live. The daughters become serious, and it is at this point that the metaphor of the fabric shop becomes explicit:

> MOTHER: I have before sunrise before the disease takes me.
>   I have to know that this place
>   Everything I have worked for
>   And all that we have will be secure.
> ELDEST: It will.
> MIDDLEST: Of course it will.
> YOUNGEST: We'll take care of it.
> MOTHER: No.
>   It needs a guardian
>   Someone who understands that all this
>   Is more than material
>   More than cloth
>   It is the fabric of reality itself.[18]

The Mother invites each of her daughters to tell stories that will demonstrate their readiness to 'inherit the future'. The stories they tell are poetic, and each serves a moral purpose; Eldest travels into the dark world of the Underground to discover the perils of wishing for eternal life and the curse that brings. Middlest tells the story of a jeweller who stole pearls and was condemned to a life as a mermaid at the bottom of the sea, and Youngest recounts how a servant girl climbs into the sky and turns its beauty into a gift that her Queen can give to the King on their wedding day. The dramatic tension is provided by the Mother's impeding death, and as she becomes weaker and her death becomes closer she recognises that each of her daughters' stories have shown their readiness for life. At her death, the shop around them begins to dissolve and disintegrate, and the daughters become mannequins again. The narrators explain that the storytelling was not a competition for the shop, but a 'test of their readiness to leave it behind'. The play's use of a mixture of direct address, dramatic metaphor, colloquial dialogue and its East London setting invokes the lives of the girls for whom it is written and also references an older tradition of dramatic storytelling.

On one level *The Unravelling* is a good illustration of the neo-Aristotelian philosopher Alasdair MacIntyre's view that traditional tales serve a moral purpose in society. *The Unravelling* is about moral decisions, about coming to terms with death and the qualities that are needed to live a good life. MacIntyre expresses the moral importance of traditional tales in apocalyptic terms:

> Deprive children of stories and you leave them unscripted, anxious stutterers in their actions as their words. Hence there is no way to give us an understanding of any society, including our own, except through the stock of stories which constitute its initial dramatic resources... And so too of course is that moral tradition from heroic society to its medieval heirs according to which the telling of stories has a key part in educating us into the virtues.[19]

MacIntyre accepts, somewhat schematically, that lessons from stories will be assimilated into the practice of everyday life. In this, he has ignored reader-response theories which would suggest that readers (or audiences) bring their own values to textual interpretation. Furthermore, he has assumed that traditional tales generally offer examples of contemporary notions of virtue, and that in turn children will accept the moral message largely without question.[20] But *The Unravelling* opens more complex moral and ethical debates about how to live, and asks young actors and audiences to consider the choices that young people face in their daily lives and in moments of emotional hardship and crisis. When I saw the play in 2011 at the Southwark Playhouse, a London theatre, I was struck by the sense of event that surrounded the performance; teachers and parents engaged me in conversation in the bar, and girls discussed films that they had made which were playing on a series of small screens. This created a sense of community, and also suggested that this way of working was part of the school's values and ethos.

Performing the play demands empathetic responses to a complex situation, and also invites young performers to identify with people in an unfamiliar situation in ways that require imagination. In his author's note on the play, Kennedy writes that it is 'an existential fable about the power of the imagination',[21] and it is this relationship between identification, empathy and the social imagination that I wish to tease out a little further, as it has significant implications for practice in applied theatre. In an essay entitled 'The Risks of Empathy', Megan Boler cites Aristotelian ideas of pity to argue that empathy creates politically passive readers. Empathetic readings, she argued, may induce pity but not action, and she denies that the social imagination is educated into an understanding of difference or suffering through this kind of compassionate reading. Boler offered a critical reading of Martha Nussbaum's view that readers might 'know the other' and understand how others feel through empathetic engagement with their narratives. I have some sympathy with this view, and I remain sceptical about some of the grander claims that drama enables participants to know what it was like to live in specific social circumstances. I don't believe, for example, that walking around for an hour with a blindfold enables me to know what it is like to be blind, although it may give me a little understanding of some of the ways in which I rely on my sight. Boler argued that passive empathy is too comfortably pleasurable; it shores up the status quo by allowing readers to 'consume' the other, exonerating them from blame 'through the denial of power relations' which produce social injustice. A socially responsible reading, according to Boler, is based on the idea of testimony, in which readers recognise the historical specificity of the narrative rather than its universality, and in which readership is a collective process that requires 'self-reflective participation' rather than individualised empathetic consumption.[22]

Boler and Nussbaum both focused their discussion on reading literary narratives, especially novels, and it would appear that Boler's conclusion advocates the kind of collective readership and self-reflective engagement with narrative which is intrinsic to drama as a multidimensional and collaborative art form. I think it is worth probing ideas of empathy and identification a little further, for which I shall return to *The Unravelling*. The daughters' predicament would risk sentimentality without the moral dilemmas they faced; the audience has empathy for the daughters that engages their emotions, that hooks them into the narrative, but it is their identification with their failure and shortcomings that stimulates moral debate. What Boler fails to acknowledge is that empathy and identification are not always the same thing. She is right to point out that empathy can induce a comfortable passivity because it relies on an understanding that the reader is not in the same situation as the character with whom she is empathising. She does not, however, take on board that identification with others can be a rather less comfortable affair because, if Freud is to be believed, it has the potential to challenge one's own sense of identity.

If empathetic responses to theatre were left unquestioned, I would probably agree with Boal that empathy can be a 'terrible weapon' in which 'the *man* relinquishes his power to of decision to the image'[23] (his italics). But his view presupposes that the man (*sic*) is sitting passively in the audience rather than constructing the image for himself as a performer, or deconstructing the image as a critical audience member. It suggests, in other words, that empathetic responses are not offset by any other forms of social identification. I am interested in the implications of inhabiting the dramatic narrative and embodying roles which may or may not be appealing, and which may represent values, feelings and ideas which may be personally or politically challenging. Young people performing *The Unravelling*, for example, not only are implicitly invited to consider what stories they would tell that would illuminate their own dilemmas, they are also required to consider how they will encourage the audience to respond empathetically to the play's dramatic narrative. It is a way of working that invites students to consider how ideas are constructed and represented theatrically. It invokes a dialectic, described by Kathleen Gallagher as the 'points of intersection *and* confrontation', and derives from locating oneself in relation to others, through recognising the parallels and differences between one's own values, feelings and situation and those of others.

Embodied Narratives

From the point of view of practice in applied theatre, one of the central elements missing from the various analyses of narrative offered by Boler, Nusbaum and MacIntyre is a concept of the performative. Performance always unfixes and, because narratives in drama are embodied and made in collaboration with others, their meanings are always multiply layered. One of the distinguishing characteristics of applied theatre is that the focus of attention is on the experience of participants, and their ability to work together in different ways – both in and out of role – is often of central importance. Participants and practitioners will not only identify or empathise with the narratives of the drama but also with each other, and this is often seen as a powerful part of the process. This means that, as John O'Toole has pointed out, in applied theatre identity, role, acting and performance are often complexly interwoven.[24]

Theoretical debates about acting, performance and dramatic role-play have become increasingly nuanced in applied theatre, particularly as questions about the formation of social identity have impacted on performance studies. It once seemed quite straightforward to assume that acting was the job of actors and usually seen in theatres, and that performance was an event for which you could buy tickets. With these relatively uncomplicated descriptions firmly in place, dramatic role-play seemed the most flexible and democratic activity, spanning a range of activities including childhood play, spontaneous improvisation and other forms of role-taking often in fictional or fictionalised contexts.[25] Given this history, it is unsurprising that, as a methodology, working in role has had an enduring appeal for practitioners in many different aspects of applied theatre, where it has valued its apparent authenticity, flexibility and immediacy over the artificiality and staginess sometimes associated with acting and performance. This is, of course, predicated on a rather old-fashioned view of theatre and acting styles. It also is based on a deeper philosophical belief that somehow improvisation and spontaneity is more likely to reveal the 'real' self, a perception that equates authenticity with moral goodness. One challenge to this assumption has been led by philosophical readings of identity formation, where the Enlightenment ideal of the autonomous individual has given way to the idea that identity is constructed and deconstructed as a dynamic and interactive process of narration, performance and representation.[26] More specifically related to participatory theatre, Claire Bishop has argued that this way of thinking about the arts privileges the ethical over the artistic, suggesting that 'empathetic identification' is more highly valued than artistic form. Bishop's argument mirrors my own, in that she suggests that artistic form elicits particular affective responses and, as such, they are both 'crucial to the work's meaning'.[27]

There are two interrelated points which I should like to extract from this debate. The first is concerned with the implications of social interaction between participants, and the second relates theories of role and performance to practice in applied theatre. In her book *Unmarked* (1993), Peggy Phelan pointed out that social interaction in theatre is primarily a negotiation between cultural production and power. She invokes Foucault's analysis of the authority of the spectators' gaze to suggest the locus of power is not with the performers, but with the audience. Writing from a feminist perspective, she argues that dramatic narrative is often constructed according to a normative (male) perception of the spectators' desires, and this controls the theatrical exchange between audience and performer. This creates a point of view which is clear and easy to identify, but it also perpetuates specific values and perspectives which are not easily dislodged:

> Redesigning the relationship between self and other, subject and object, sound and image, man and woman, spectator and performer, is enormously difficult.[28]

My suggestion is that, although applied theatre is often explicitly concerned with analysing how images and narratives are constructed, and interrupting predictable and inequitable points of view, its practices are not exempt from this difficulty. There are, as I have already argued, cultural assumptions in the way in which drama workshops, plays and other theatre events are constructed that position audiences and participants in specific ways. Furthermore, it accepts that representing a particular ethical stance or moral and political views within a dramatic structure leads participants to adopt similar values in everyday life. This perception is not only reliant on specific theories of identity, it is also predicated on particular notions of performance.

Performance has long been a metaphor for all kinds of social behaviour, and Phelan's observations about the construction and location of power in theatre have wider implications. One of the central arguments in this chapter is that theatre is a good vehicle through which participants might experiment with different identities and test out new ways of being. Although I am sure that drama can make a contribution to the process of *becoming* by shaping autobiographies and changing social narratives, I have expressed some scepticism about some of the bigger claims that drama transforms beliefs and attitudes. This is based on the understanding that no social encounter – including drama workshops – is exempt from other social narratives and alternative perceptions of power. It is often difficult to gauge the social effects of drama immediately, and when I read that participants have expressed profound changes in attitudes I often wonder whether they have been complicit in following the 'script' of the workshop, or whether their change of heart indicates a positive but temporary identification with a kindly practitioner whose point of view may not be actually expressed, but whose values are nonetheless clearly visible to them.[29] As Teresa

Brennan points out, the affective qualities of a group encounter are often contagious:

> The origin of transmitted effects is social in that these affects do not only arise within a particular person but also come from without. They come via an interaction with other people and an environment. But they have a physiological impact.[30]

Brennan's suggestion that the affective qualities of group encounters are experienced as bodily changes has implications for the ethics of applied theatre. The process of embodying narratives in theatre may have the potential to trouble inequitable boundaries between the 'real' and the imagined, between self and other, subject and object. But its affective qualities may also serve very different moral purposes, and equally powerfully. Re-plotting these relationships draws attention to the performative, and extends applied theatre beyond an emphasis on role and situation and creating new narratives by using many rich and varied traditions of theatre-making and innovations in performance. It suggests that changing stories involves looking not just at the narratives themselves, but at how they are formed artistically and constructed as narratives, where assumptions of power are made, and whose values they represent.

5 Narratives of Community and Place

In my country
walking by the waters
down where an honest river
shakes hands with the sea,
a woman passed round me
as if I were a superstition;

or the worse dregs of her imagination,
so when she finally spoke
her words spliced into bars
of an old wheel. A segment of air.
Where do you come from?
'Here,' I said, 'Here. These parts.'
        Jackie Kay, 'In My Country', *Other Lovers* (1993)

Questions of Community

A sentimental picture of local communities as comfortable social systems has re-entered the popular imagination and has been much used by politicians in their rhetoric, with positive connotations of interpersonal warmth, shared interests and local loyalty. Jackie Kay's autobiographical poem challenges this image. Kay's experience of her 'honest' local landscape in Scotland is marred by the hurtful suspicion of those who assume that she does not belong there, and with the racist implication that she, as a black woman, is not welcomed by the 'locals'. Communities, as Iris Marion Young argues, are idealised symbolic constructions which not only bind people together, they also act as powerful means of exclusion, separating 'us' from 'them'.[1] If this is the case, the construction and shaping of local communities, a recurring theme in applied theatre, is not so much a matter of recovering or rediscovering the lost narratives of a homogeneous past, but of making a contribution to redefining their actual and symbolic boundaries in the present and for the future.

It is interesting that there has been a renewed emphasis on the ideal of community at a time when an actual sense of belonging has become increasingly problematic. Zygmunt Bauman's now well-known description of contemporary society as 'liquid' is predicated on the view that cultures of consumerism have undermined communities of belonging, and rendered relationships short-term and disposable.[2] It is tempting to believe that creating heterogeneous local communities will come to the rescue of beleaguered and fractured political economies, and community-based art has often been cast as resistance to this fragmentation of society and to the commodification of the entertainment industry, a practice that Jan Cohen-Cruz describes as a form of civic activism.[3] This impulse in applied theatre frequently revolves around the view that face-to-face encounters invite new forms of social connectivity as well as artistic engagement. Yet there are questions to be asked about what kind of communities the professional artists or theatre practitioners envision, and how far theatre projects that focus on straightforward constructions of local identity, shared histories and ideological unity are likely to reinforce the more conservative images of 'otherness' evoked in Jackie Kay's poem.

The concept of community has come under increasing critical scrutiny by cultural policy-makers, academics and community-based arts practitioners in the last ten years. This change of thinking particularly responds to the suggestion that communities, nationalities or identities that are considered fixed or immutable are likely to maintain cultural hierarchies and deepen social division. One of the most influential thinkers in this debate is the French philosopher Jean-Luc Nancy, whose book *The Inoperative Community* (1987, translated into English in 1991) has drawn attention to the politics of conventional models of community that are predicated on the mutual recognition of shared, essentialised identities. Nancy offers a critique of constructions of community, arguing that this has been based on an idealised fantasy of commonality. Rather than rejecting the concept of community as necessarily conservative, however, Nancy redefines community in terms that emphasise that identities are always open to change and renewal and, as such, communities are a 'gift to be renewed and communicated'. This is a process that, he suggests, is an 'infinite task'.[4] One of the distinctive aspects of Nancy's *inoperative* community is that he suggests that community is not created through dialogue and conversation, but through what he describes as an 'ontological sociality' that exists between people on a pre-discursive level. The ethical conditions for this inoperative community are always contingent, and it is only in the realisation of finitude (the experience of mortality) that 'being-in-common' can be recognised. Arguing that 'community is revealed in the death of others', he contends that community is not a project (operative) but always contingent:

> Community is given to us with being and as being, well in advance of our own projects, desires and undertakings. At bottom, it is impossible to lose community... Community is, in a sense, resistance itself: namely, resistance to immanence.[5]

This emphasis on intersubjectivity, resistance and alterity means, for Nancy, that community is experienced as an affective state.

Nancy's suggestion that community is a 'gift' chimes well with debates in this book, and his argument that community exists on an affective level has implications for artists working in community settings. Grant H. Kester has offered an illuminating analysis of how Nancy's theories relate to community-based arts, with a particular focus on practice in North America. He suggests that Nancy's challenge to community as a collective form of mutual identification raises significant challenges to community-based artists who assume that building a coherent (or operative) community is a project that can be achieved through artistic collaboration. Yet he also points out that Nancy follows in the tradition of the twentieth-century avant-garde in his view that the idealised myth of a homogenous community can only be broken through somatic shock, rupture or by inflicting an 'aggressive sensory derangement' that will shake people out of their comfortable subject-positions. As I have already argued in Chapter 3, learning is an accumulative process, and the idea that artistic events lead to sudden moments of epiphany or enlightenment is at best wishful thinking or, at worse, politically manipulative. Furthermore, Nancy's emphasis on self-realisation as a result of an artistic encounter or theatrical event relies on cultivating a self-reflexive attitude and, as I have already argued, this implies a sceptical distancing of oneself from the world in order to better apprehend it. Kester similarly notes that Nancy's emphasis on suddenness ignores the possibility that change accumulates over time, suggesting that 'identity is only partially transformed' though 'dialogic encounters'. He suggests that this way of thinking implies that uncertainty is preferable to predictability, and mutability is valued over social stability. Writing about the site-based work of Miwon Kwon with disadvantaged people in US cities, Kester points out that, however unintentional, it is 'hard to avoid the implication that union workers and public housing tenants do not know any better' and that she implies that it becomes 'the artist's responsibility to instil them with a properly self-reflexive attitude'.[6]

What is useful to my analysis of applied theatre is Nancy's critique of community as a stable, fixed entity. However construed, this emphasis on the porousness of community has effectively loosened the idea from its idealisation as a local and bounded set of practices and expanded the cultural field.[7] Writing from a sociological perspective, Vered Amit's analysis of conceptions and practices of community concludes that a sense of belonging is more likely to arise from informal social groups and networks rather than ephemeral but deterministic social 'categories' (such as social class, religion, race, sexuality, gender, nation, ethnicity). Amit is particularly critical of the rhetoric of diaspora and multiculturalism which invokes borderlands and marginality without acknowledging the social content of transnational movement, and the real sense of anxiety and suffering experienced by those displaced. 'The greater the claims for their revolutionary and empowering possibilities', she argues, 'the more nebulous and metaphorical these representations of categorical difference become'.[8] Amit has pointed out that the actual construction of communities always needs rather more effort than deterministic categories of identity might suggest. She argues that social practice is rather more flexible:

> [T]he most common avenues for forming a sense of fellowship, of belonging and social connection are realised through modest daily practices that are not often marked by symbolic categorical identities. These are people and identities loosely known as friends, neighbours, workmates, companions in a variety of leisure, parenting, schooling, political activities. Many of these associations are limited in time and space to particular places and activities.[9]

Amit's argument rests on the claim that social groups and networks are fluid and temporal, based on everyday interactions and associations. Put simply, people make friends, form social groups at work or develop networks because they like them and because they have experiences and interests in common at the time.

Amit's theoretical discussion of the workings of social networks offers an important reminder of the social significance of emotional bonds, a key concept in the feminist theory of the ethic of care. Although Amit recognises that relationships may strengthen or wane over time, she suggests that communities are built on personal networks forged in present situations rather than on identification with collective histories. The sense of community she invokes is dependent on temporary social bonds, rather akin to those Bauman criticises in the society he calls 'liquid'. It lacks a sense of the complexities of cultural histories, and she emphasises those social networks that are found in the immediacy of lived experience and which have short memories. By contrast, Avtar Brah takes the condition of diaspora as a basis for narratives of community rather than social networks. She argues that identity is a 'context-specific construction', an ongoing process in which a sense of self is developed in relation to those in *both* local and imagined communities of nationhood.[10] This places an emphasis on the significance of the interplay between collective and personal histories in identity formation. She argues that feelings of community may be created by those who have 'shared collective narratives', even though personal testament and collective memories may tell different stories, and these narratives may frequently unsettle or contradict each other.[11] How meanings are ascribed to these interwoven narratives of self and community becomes, therefore, not a search for an 'unmediated truth' but a more creative process of invention and speculation.

Whatever their differences of inflection, Brah and Amit share an understanding that social relations are negotiated and redefined through dynamic processes of interaction and shared experiences. In this chapter I shall interrogate different conceptualisations of community in relation to theatre projects that aim to represent and interpret personal, historical and collective narratives. Following Brah, I shall explore how imaginative interpretations of history might intervene in the future by relocating past identities in the performative present. I shall also consider, following Amit, how theatre might create a sense of belonging through the social networks and friendships fostered by working together. My interest is, primarily, in recognising the importance of affective bonds in community, experienced empathetically as part of the ontological sociality Nancy described. My suggestion is that this way of working has the potential to take account of narratives of selfhood and identification and to be open to alterity by recognising the different values and perspectives with which they are accompanied.

Communities of Location: Meeting Places

Community is intimately related to notions of place. Although there are multiple forms of community that are not place-dependent, communities of location serve as a powerful articulation of what it means to experience a sense of belonging. Lucy Lippard described the 'lure of the local' as 'the pull of the place that operates on each of us',[12] a sentiment that is widely echoed – and well theorised – by cultural geographers in relation to place. In some ways, place has become more widely discussed than questions of community in applied theatre, not least because place suggests a material presence within everyday life, whereas community is often regarded as a concept and an immaterial practice. The political geographer David Harvey describes place as a reactionary force in contemporary life which, like some conceptualisations of community, serves as a means of exclusion. More optimistic readings of place furthered by Doreen Massey and Tim Cresswell have gained currency in applied theatre, where place is regarded as progressive and open to change, yet also significant in identify-formation.[13]

Both community and place are contested terms, and perhaps it is adding the word 'community' to location that renders the concept particularly problematic; one common argument is that communities of location are often romanticised, harking back to an imagined era in which homogeneity, unity and shared values formed the basis of social interaction. A related position, developed particularly by feminists, is that localism has had the effect of keeping people in their place, of entrapping the poor and confining women to the sphere of the domestic. More positively, as Amit has pointed out, people often rely on their locality for day-to-day companionship, support, sense of security and well-being. This double-bind has been recognised by feminist theorist Elspeth Probyn, who has analysed both the potential and the limitations of communities of location. She described the local as 'only a fragmented set of possibilities' which can be restrictive if they are fixed at moment of time, but 'to take the local not as the end point, but as the start' has greater social potential.[14]

My experience of working practically in communities of locality has led me to believe that they are often rather messy and imprecise places, which means that thinking about the local as 'a fragmented set of possibilities' serves as a useful idea with which to begin this analysis of practice. The project I shall discuss was based in a city secondary school that had, for many years, provided education for young people in the local area. Schools can provide an important meeting place for local people, and significant social networks can develop from this shared meeting point. Few of us, however, escape experiencing complex and contradictory emotions when visiting schools, especially if we attended them, and this has particular implications for using schools as sites of community-based theatre. Schools are not neutral spaces. Former pupils often experience an ambiguous sense of belonging and not belonging, a strange and unsettling feeling of walking through a film set of their lives. Others may have feelings of exclusion from institutional cultures, or be constrained by self-regulation, feeling they should in some way 'behave themselves'. Empty schools, like empty theatres, are full of ghosts. Schools are not like graveyards, static monuments to past lives, but they are nonetheless haunted by expectation – memories of what generations of pupils hoped they would become. They feel like archaeological sites, restless with hundreds of shards of half-remembered stories. This means that community-based performances held in schools or other venues of local significance always have elements of the site-specific. The performance space may be transformed physically and aesthetically from ordinary school hall to theatre, but there is always the ghost of the past haunting the place. Mike Pearson and Michael Shanks described this aspect of site-specific work as a balance between 'the host and the ghost', a negotiation between the contemporary and the historical in which 'no single story is being told'.[15]

The image of hosts and ghosts is particularly relevant for theatre projects undertaken in a local context in which the 'host community' had not always been welcoming to outsiders. The dramatisation of oral histories, however, even within the relative confines of a school, ensures that private narratives enter the public domain, a process which means that contentious social 'issues' or community 'problems' are dissipated as they become associated with familiar people. This project took place in a school that had been built in the 1950s as part of the post-war comprehensive ideal, and fiercely guarded its reputation for innovation and equality. A sustained period of industrial action by the teachers, however, had soured valued local links, perhaps most aptly symbolised by the fact that we were barred from the community centre at lunchtime (unpaid lunchtime supervision was particular point of dispute), which meant that there were significant bridges to mend. The theatre project began as part of a sustained programme of community liaison intended to develop a stronger sense of belonging and self-esteem for young people, and greater involvement of local people in education. By encouraging young people to work with people of different ages and from diverse sectors of the community, we hoped to provide opportunities for young people to extend the social space which they lived and renegotiate its boundaries. Pedagogically, the project was multi-layered; it invited students to blur the boundaries between the factual and the artistic, and to consider how they negotiated questions of authority and authorship in relation to the theatrical construction of oral history.

The starting point for the devised work involved the students interviewing people they knew – their grandparents and other elderly members of the local community – about events that had shaped their lives. For many young people, learning to listen presented real challenges, and I suspect that many covered their embarrassment about the potential emotional closeness of the situation by firing questions designed to elicit information rather than encouraging more personal reflections on experience. From the interviews the students conducted, however, two distinct narratives emerged. One concerned the experiences of those who moved to England from previously colonised countries during the 1960s, with one particularly lively account from Ahmed's uncle about pompous immigration officials, lost children and bursting luggage providing clear characters and a good plot. The other story which captured the students' imagination was told by Lucy's grandmother, who had worked in the local cigarette factory during the Second World War, where flirtatious 'tobacco girls' used to put their names and addresses in cigarette packets destined to be sent to soldiers. Interestingly, both sets of stories were humorous. There appeared to be an element of self-censoring on the part of the people they interviewed which excluded more painful or difficult memories. As Portelli points out, it is often the silences and omissions in the stories which are most revealing.

[T]he most precious information may lie in what the informants *hide*, and in the fact they *do* hide it, rather than in what they *tell*.[16]

It is possible to speculate about why more painful memories were hidden. Many interviewees had family relationships with the students, and they presumably selected aspects which they deemed appropriate to the context. More intimately, some stories were illustrated by treasured possessions; small, private mementos – an aeroplane ticket, a hat, a cigarette packet, immigration papers – which symbolised particular events. They also served to focus the students' attention on the content of the narratives, as visible signs of lived experience.

The process of editing and adapting the material into theatre form presented particular challenges. How are conversations interpreted?

Whose stories are chosen for development in drama? Who controls the texts? Do the actors have the authority to fictionalise the stories? How are the narratives shaped? How is the work presented and received? Because I had not introduced the students to the idea that memories are continually revised in the retelling, they were concerned to tell the stories as 'authentically' and 'faithfully' as they could. I found this desire to *reproduce* events rather than *represent* them troubling. Some students expressed an understandable anxiety about misrepresenting the very personal stories they had been told, and responded to this by insisting on a dramatic form which was heavily dependent on naturalistic acting styles in linear and episodic dramatic structures. Their reluctance to experiment theatrically meant that their drama was limited by the confines of a form which, whilst it suited a rather simplistic re-telling of events, did not really capture the ambiguity or emotions of memory. Conceptually, this suggested that the students had a partial understanding of the ways in which personal history is constructed in memory, accepting without question that everything that had been told was literally true. They were actively resistant to alternative readings, feeling, with some justification, that they should honour personal narratives they had heard. This central dilemma – how to *both* validate the testimony of the original speaker *and* open the narratives for critical interrogation – or, in this case, creative interpretation – has been theorised by oral historians. The Personal Narratives Group sum up the debate:

> When people talk about their lives, people lie sometimes, forget a little, exaggerate, become confused, get things wrong. Yet they are revealing truths... the guiding principle could be that all autobiographical memory is true: it is up to the interpreter to discover in what sense, where, and for what purpose.[17]

The idea that there are multiple interpretations of truth in autobiographical memory suggests that a dramatic style which relies heavily on naturalistic forms of representation is politically, as well as artistically, constricting. As Peta Tait convincingly argued, to represent social experience as a 'coherently ordered, stable pattern of reality' in theatre is implicitly to accept hegemonic values.[18]

My aim in this project was not to imply that there is one, coherent historical narrative that binds people together, but to represent the plurality of experience that existed in this performative meeting place. To encourage the students to question the boundaries between the fictive and the real, I suggested that they asked to hear the stories again, this time listening particularly for *how* the speakers commented on past events, and to notice any differences in the details. The act of re-telling personal experience creates, as Joan Sangster points out, a dialectical relationship between the past and present in which the speaker does not 'relive' events, but 're-writes' them.[19] The students discovered that descriptions of past events were interwoven with new insights and explanatory comment, sometimes contextualising the moment, at other times pointing out how the events had influenced the tellers in later life. By acknowledging the similarities and differences between the past and the present, the students recognised how the storytellers situated themselves in the present whilst negotiating their relationship with the past. Observant students noticed how performative elements of the story-telling (use of voice, enactment and gesture, for example) suggested particular emotional connections with specific events; whilst the stories were not substantially different in content from the 'original', on second hearing, the interpretation and emphasis had often changed. They became aware of the rehearsed elements of autobiographical stories, where it was obvious from the 'performance' that they had been retold many times, and when the elderly people were recalling details of life events which they had not spoken about for many years.

The awareness that the tellers themselves moved between the past and the present, and between multiple 'realities' gave the students licence to break the pattern of linearity in their drama. Until that moment, the students had been searching, in Derridean terms, for the 'myth of origin', for the single, unmediated presence of truth. The process of devising became more concerned with what Derrida described as absence than presence; the artefacts, tape recordings and other ephemera used as props symbolising the missing originators of the stories. This sense of absence weighed the participants down; the objects carried the affective symbolism of lives that have been lived. Educationally, it inhibited their development as theatre practitioners as they were reluctant to experiment with dramatic form. It also prevented them from trying out ideas spontaneously; they were not representing lived experience creatively, but were engaged in a form of ventriloquising. The process felt, and was, second-hand. Furthermore, their insistence on accurate presentation of the material culture of the times, particularly in the form of props and costumes, had prevented them from asking more abstract questions about memory and the interpretation of the past in dramatic form. From the moment when they began to interrogate the stories more closely, they recognised the dialectic between past and present, and they wove this into their drama, using the comments they had heard to frame the dramatic action. This was used most interestingly by one group of students, who spoke in Urdu when representing the story of the past, and English for the contemporary commentary, fluctuating between the official and the domestic, indicating multiple identities symbolised in powerful dramatic moments.

The shift in emphasis from 'authentic' reproduction to dramatic representation moved the work from an unmediated and uncritical retelling to a popular theatrical aesthetic. By introducing montage and popular songs of the period, they succeeded in creating a dramatic atmosphere which, to borrow John McGrath's phrase, made the shows a 'good night out'. Some elderly members of the community had small walk-on parts, and were sometimes seen at different ages on excerpts of ciné film (recorded in pre-digital days), and audience members joined in the songs. The problem with the performance was the use of theatre form, which was limiting. The process of working had used standard drama education conventions designed to disrupt narrative closure (hot-seating, narration, still images, and so on), leading to moments of reflection and political comment in performance, but the effect of the devised plays was still nostalgic, celebratory and safe rather than challenging. There was also little in the form or performance style which included the artistic traditions or popular culture of elders in the South Asian families; it was almost based entirely on a Western performance aesthetic. Some of the stories recounted, albeit often humorously, major life events, and there was a risk that the difficulties became sanitised or sentimentalised in the process of retelling. Above all, the work still lacked a sense of the stories *as* memory. Despite disrupting the linearity of the narratives, the past still came across as logical, rational and ordered. The social realism of the plays led to an emphasis on the mind rather than the body, on representing material realities rather than more abstract expressions of feelings or ideas. There was no real questioning of how the future might have turned out differently, nor how the events contributed to constructing subjectivities and framing a more progressive sense of place. All autobiographical memory is fragmented and partial, and presenting neat, linear narratives in autobiographical performance is, according to Dee Heddon, to 'pretend that gaps in knowledge and memory do not exist'.[20] In other words, the dramatic style led the students to accept modernist definitions of subjectivity as essentially stable, thus missing the opportunity to consider how the performance of memory can, in itself, work creatively.

Perhaps one of the most moving aspects of the performance was how it led to dialogue between the elderly members of different ethnic communities whose previous personal contact had been limited and sometimes strained. But its weakness lay in the fact that the work did not really capture the aesthetic of memory, its instability and its contingency. Baz Kershaw has written critically of the 'performance of nostalgia' in community theatre, in which the struggles of the past are sanitised into a commodified heritage.[21] This was not quite the case in this project, and perhaps in this particular context a safe and celebratory evening of lively drama, with an engaged and integrated audience, represented good progress. It was not dissimilar to Bruce McConachie's experience of directing grassroots theatre in Williamsburg, USA, where he attempted to change the community's attitude to race. Although the project had many successes, his verdict on the performance was ambiguous:

> Local citizens probably felt better about themselves and their community when they joined in on the final chorus. I would like to be able to say that several spectators came to me afterwards and admitted that Christian faith, individualistic capitalism... could not create our ideal community of the future, but of course that did not happen.[22]

In this intergenerational community project I was similarly left with a sense that something was missing. In this case I wondered if there might have been more effective collaboration, and if a more resistant pedagogy would involve all participants discussing how the stories were represented and the cultural politics of form. The community the theatre invoked remained, on one level, a nostalgic vision of a past world that Jean-Luc Nancy described as mythic.

The process of retelling autobiographical stories exhumed them, relocating them in space and time and breaking down distinctions between the real and the imaginary. As Portelli points out, the process of retelling autobiographical narratives allows 'historical, poetical and legendary narratives' to be interwoven.[23] Carolyn Steedman describes the role of remembered narratives as 'an agent of social formation', where interpretations of the past illuminate and extend people's understanding of their current place within their social world.[24] The performance did focus the participants' attention on the kind of community we were becoming, and there was evidence in the evaluations that seeing autobiographical stories performed had enabled people to gain some insights into their neighbours' actual experiences. Perhaps equally significantly, by exchanging stories about themselves some local people also became, if not close friends, friendly acquaintances.

Crafting Communities

It is a conventionally held view that all dramatic practice captures some element of the collective, in Richard Schechner's words 'a community for the time being', not least because it involves people actually meeting or working together.[25] Concepts of community have been rethought as a result of new cultural, political and economic realities in which generations of men and women have found themselves with a sense of belonging to more than one place or feeling kinship to people with whom they share styles of living or political solidarity. These descriptions are usually harnessed to ways of living in the atomised West, in which the boundaries between 'lifestyle', political commitment and shared identity often seem rather blurred. Linking community to empathetic identification with like-minded others, and to identity politics, opens up the possibility of new ways of thinking about community, but it also begs questions about how multiple identities might be narrated and understood.

Throughout this book I have followed the idea that identity is created and performed in dialogue with others and with the emotional geography of place. A deeper sense of belonging, however, derives from shared interpretations of experience. Developing this theme, communities of identity are constructed when people recognise their own experiences in others, and share an understanding of each other's values or stories. In some contexts, strong communities of identity are built by those who feel that they share common struggles: social movements, such as gay, black and feminist movements for example, in which a shared sense of collective identification is seen as politically oppositional. The term 'community' is, however, often applied rather loosely to identity politics; labels such as 'the gay community' may provide a convenient shorthand, but they can also have the effect of disguising very real differences between people, and missing the possibilities of multiple identities, such as being gay and black, for example. In other words, communities of identity are constructed on a balance between sameness and difference – on the acknowledgement that particular interpretations of experiences are somehow different from the experiences and understandings of others. Equally, however, they are also discursive categories, and thus open to change. In this section I shall focus on a play which both illustrated and troubled the participants' membership of a community of identity. It was devised and performed by three women in London, all of whom were refugees, all from different parts of the world, with very different narratives of migration.

Becoming a refugee was not an identity of choice but of necessity, and membership of the local south London refugee 'community' was forced upon them by global circumstances. Their practice raised some interesting questions about the temporality and historical contingency of communities of identity, and how dramatic interpretations of autobiographical narratives inevitably give partial accounts of lived experience.

A Woman's Place was billed as 'a play devised and performed by refugee women'.[26] This play had developed from a sustained period of work with refugee organisations, although the three actors who volunteered to take part in the project did not know each other before working together. I saw the penultimate performance of the play at The Albany in Deptford, an arts centre in one of the most deprived areas of London. Not for the first time, I was struck by the efforts made to create a sense of community through the use of the building – a whiteboard behind the box office showed that in addition to the refugee play, rooms were being used by a National Association for the Care and Resettlement of Offenders' drama group, a music group for adults with learning difficulties, and for the rehearsal of a company of black dancers. When I had booked my ticket, I had been told to arrive early for my free drink and to see an exhibition by refugee artists. Duly arriving in good time for my beer, I found that tables inside the auditorium had been arranged to encourage conversation, nightclub style. The art exhibition around the auditorium was supported by information tables offering resources for refugees in the area, and a raffle to raise funds. The play was the focal point of the evening, clearly, but it was framed by other events. This layering of the evening suggested that the amateur performers were in a sympathetic environment. What was interesting about the context of performance was that it consolidated a feeling of belonging to a welcoming community *of* refugees and gestured towards the sympathies of the host community in a country in which refugees have been vilified by a shamefully hostile press.

The play centred around the autobiographical narratives of two women, one an asylum seeker from Rwanda and another an escapee from a Cameroon prison who had recently obtained what is officially termed Indefinite Leave to Remain in the UK. Their stories were framed by French performer, Fleur, whose own story of displacement remained largely untold. Her role was, however, crucial to the structure of the drama. Through direct address she opened the performance by inviting the audience into the world of the play, offering a bridge between the rather comfortable environment of the theatre and the harrowing stories the performers had to tell. At times Fleur also acted as translator, as parts of the stories were told in Olive's and Clarice's first language of French. As their stories unfolded, the actors were supported by the strong visual aesthetic of the performance, particularly by pools of light which seemed to envelop the performers as they enacted their stories of human rights abuse, escape and eventual arrival in London. The final moments of the play drew attention the idea of 'home' as each woman in turn left the stage to take a seat in the audience, a symbol of belonging to a new local community represented by the audience, and leaving behind her status as refugee. Projected above the empty stage was a video of the women at home in London, each carrying out ordinary domestic routines. These images problematised the performers' identities as refugees by showing their multiple identities as mothers, wives, friends and active profes-sional members of society.

The theatricality of this play protected the performers by creating an aesthetic distance between them as people and their own autobiographical stories. The use of non-naturalistic acting styles, poetry and, particularly, the lighting and projections enabled the performers to represent rather than retell their autobiographies. Olive, a Rwandan Hutu who had been in London for around seven months, agreed to be interviewed by me on condition that her full name would not be included in this book for fear of recrimination. Olive explained that she found her own story so distressing that she could only perform it by imagining that she was talk-ing about someone else. She also told me that in the devising process she had edited her story significantly, selecting events that she felt capable of retelling in live performance and missing out aspects which were either too personally painful or, interestingly, which perpetuated a negative image of her country as a violent place. This begs questions about how these women constructed their role as performers, and how they negoti-ated their identities as refugees in this specifically performative context. Olive described the process in terms of behaviour, where for the duration of the performance she behaved as if she were someone else:

I am thinking that this is about someone else. My story is so sad it makes me very, very emotional if I tell it as me, so I behave like someone else. When I first started the devising I had not been in London long and I kept thinking, 'What are these white girls [the directors] asking me to do?' We were telling stories in ways I had never done before, using bits of string and maps and pictures. It is not like performances at home. I tell my story in my own words but I also tell it in new languages because I had not seen a play like this before. It was fun to learn it this way.

This short comment is particularly revealing. Olive found a number of ways to separate herself from her story, both as an actor in the performance itself and in the devising process. Not only did she try to find way of acting which made her feel safe, she also made an interesting distinction between her 'own words' and the theatrical language of the play.

How might Olive's process of enacting her identity as a refugee be understood? For both Olive and the audience the performance was complexly layered. As a performer, she knew that she was telling her own story, that she was performing herself. However, she also recognised that her performance was, in Schechner's terms, 'not me – not not me' in which it is evident that the actor is 'himself (*sic*) but he is not himself at the same time'.[27] Schechner is particularly critical of Western actors who, devoid of a 'culturally elaborate theatrical system' take refuge in individualism, relying on clichés such as 'sincerity' and 'personal truth'.[28] This takes on a particular resonance in relation to *A Woman's Place*. In many ways whole the point of the project was the interpretation and representation of lived experiences, intended both to raise awareness of the experiences of refugees and encourage the actors to explore their feelings in a safe context. Whilst in performance Olive may have been able to distance herself from her experiences, it was nonetheless a 'personal truth' which she performed. Olive's description of this process has something in common with Schechner's view of performance as 'restored behavior' in which performers 'get in touch with, recover, remember or even invent' behaviour in performance.[29] Schechner's description does not, however, take full account of the interiority of the performer, as Baz Kershaw has pointed out, nor the importance of memory.[30] Michael Balfour and Nina Woodrow, writing about the complexities and paradoxes of refugee performance, comment that artists and refugee artists often have to negotiate the 'complex terrain of aesthetic representation'. This is particularly evident where performance has multiple purposes, they suggest, and serves 'as an attempt to direct itself to the broader sociopolitical context, to seek affirmation, understanding and acceptance and/protest'.[31] That Olive relied on managing her memories whilst she was actually on stage was important to her. She needed to keep her feelings under control. By maintaining an aesthetic, linguistic and cultural distance between her stories and herself, between the exterior world and her inner feelings, Olive was able to redefine her relationship with her past and separate her identity as torture victim and refugee from her present identity as storyteller and performer. In other words, it was the act of performing herself as a refugee which also enabled her to step outside this categorisation of her identity. This was also indicated by Olive's awareness of the social purpose of the performance: 'I am also thinking it is a good story for white people to hear as they don't know the real stories of people.'[32]

The supportive context of the performance was endorsed by the presence of the local Member of Parliament who, before drawing the raffle, commented on how the play had enabled her to see refugees as individuals, with different stories and families, rather than as legal cases awaiting adjudication. For the women themselves, working on the drama symbolised a transitional moment in their identity formation, from refugee to local community member. As Avtar Brah has pointed out, identities are contingent on time and place, and might be renewed or altered. Although communities of identity extend beyond the spatial plane on which the rooted traditions of local communities depend, they also suggest an interesting social dynamic based on interaction, dialogue and shared interpretations of experiences and memories.[33] As such, although Olive, Clarice and Fleur were cast – and cast themselves – as refugees in *A Woman's Place*, taking part in the project showed that identification with particular communities can be changed in time. Their sense of belonging to a community altered as a result of working on the drama and, as Marx predicted, changes in their material circumstances enabled them to see the world differently.

A Phenomenology of Community

Vered Amit offers a sceptical account of theoretical constructions of community, arguing that they have neglected to account for actual relationships of intimacy and social bonds. Although she suggests that in principle forms of identification are 'quite portable', a sense of belonging to communities beyond the immediate experiences of everyday living often only lasts for the duration of actual emotional or familial ties, and becomes watered down over time.[34] Following Merleau-Ponty's phenomenological idea of 'being in the world', I should like to extend Amit's account of how social experiences can turn into personal intimacies and social networks and make a case for the significance of the body in feelings of community. This is intended, following Nancy, to move the discussion of community-building beyond the idea that communities are either imagined or constructed through 'face-to-face' interactions, as if the rest of the body were somehow invisible. As an illustration, my aim is to examine narratives of ageing in order to consider how the actual social experience of community involves what Merleau-Ponty described as 'body-knowing', an embodiment of personal and collective narratives.

What I am searching for here are ways of working in theatre which respect the relationship between the affective body and the various narratives of place and community through which identities are formed and reshaped. Places and experiences are not only inscribed on the body, but are integral to its material presence; our physicality and sense of being in the world are integral to the archaeology of identity, contributing to the 'historical sedimentation' of selfhood, to borrow Kate Soper's memorable phrase.[35] Elspeth Probyn sees the embodiment of locality as symptomatic of oppression:

> In conceiving of the local as a nodal point, we can begin to deconstruct its movements and its meanings. Thus, in thinking how locale is inscribed on our bodies, in our homes, and on the streets, we can begin to loosen its ideological effects.[36]

Boal extends this perspective, describing how the body becomes 'hardened by habit into a certain set of actions and reactions'.[37] Linking memory, emotion and the body, Boal claims that the habitual repetition of movement is personally and politically limiting. In certain contexts this is, of course, painfully obvious. I vividly remember a Tamil primary school teacher in Sri Lanka showing me how his body had been irrevocably scarred by the beatings he had sustained at the hands of the 'peacekeeping' Indian army who had attacked him after a school football match. Boal's use of dramatic strategies to deconstruct how experience has been etched on the body is explicitly political; his drama is about 'de-mechanising, de-structuring, dismantling' the effects of daily life.[38] Boal's objective, Philip Auslander explains, is to enable participants in the drama to liberate themselves from this physical oppression, but in the process he labours under the misapprehension that it is possible for the body to escape 'ideological encoding'.[39]

Whilst Boal's reading of the living body is an important reminder of how histories are carried physically, the idea that the body is marked by signs of oppression (rather than experience) does assume that life has been a rather negative experience. Further, one of the implications of the affective turn in applied theatre is that it presses an awareness of how identity cannot be regarded as fixed and immutable, and also that the notion of the human body as a singular, bounded entity is problematic. Communities become formed and re-formed as habitual enactments of locality, or maintained through other forms of common-place or everyday interactivity. Thinking about community as habit, collective memory, place and embodiment draws attention to the ways in which 'community is revealed in the death of others', to quote Jean-Luc Nancy.[40] Nancy's concept of 'singular plural' is apposite here, which challenges both the self-identity of an 'I' and the essentialising 'we' that he associated with conventional constructions of community.[41]

Embodied memory is significant in moving from understanding community as an essentialist myth to more fluid, intuitive and affective social connections. In a moving essay, Andrew Dawson offered an anthropological reading of the social effects of the ageing body on the practice of community in a former mining village in the north-east of England during the 1990s. Dawson found that handicrafts, poetry writing and performance played a large part in sustaining a sense of community amongst the elderly, who measured 'ageing well' according to how mental and physical decline was controlled and managed through these kinds of activities. Interestingly, Dawson points out that the traditions of artistic creativity in mining communities are indebted to the early twentieth-century modernist intellectual élite who, not unlike their successors in applied theatre, set up arts activities in miners' welfare associations as part of their social reforms.[42] By the end of the century, when mining had been decimated and the population was ageing, cabaret nights at the Old Age Pensioners' club specialised in self-parodies of old age. As an example, Dawson tells the story of Ida, Kate and Mary, female members of the OAP group 'The Evergreens', whose ironic performance of the cancan revealed incontinence pads beneath their tutus. In part this was a veiled gesture of community solidarity to the incontinent Mr M, who was under threat of expulsion from the club by officials, but it was also an example of the kind of self-deprecating humour which sometimes characterises the social capital of communities in deprived circumstances.

Perhaps most interesting in Dawson's account is his description of how good stories become appropriated over time, challenging the notion that individual and community are separate ontological entities. I can't be the only person who has appropriated a good story if it is plausible that it happened to me (now is perhaps the right time to confess that I have never actually taught a boy called Russell Sprout, although one of my friends certainly did). Passing on anecdotes is also a mark of the longevity of family relations – I could, for example, tell you quite detailed stories about 'cousin' Lizzie Berry's mince pies, baked some time during the 1920s, without knowing exactly who Lizzie was nor how I am related to her. In Dawson's account, there are two instances in which personal narratives were relocated into specific community settings. The first concerns Hilda, the source of many salacious stories about goings-on in colliery houses. As her memory deteriorated through Alzheimer's, she was prompted in her storytelling by those who knew her anecdotes well. In time, her fading memory led other members of the club to take over her stories, with Hilda prompting them. Eventually her stories became integrated into the community, and continued to be told long after her death. Another account involved Jimmy, who took Dawson to different places in the area (his allotment, the library), in order to locate his life history in places which were meaningful to him. Dawson concludes that:

> As memory fades, responsibility for the construction of narratives of self and, indeed, possession of these narratives slip inexorably from individual to community. In essence, the experience through bodily ageing of a self that transgresses the boundaries of the individual body is a matter for celebration precisely because it becomes a basis for sameness, a merging of individual selves, integral to senses of community.[43]

This relocation of the narratives of selfhood into narratives of community stretches the boundaries of the past and the future, the living and the dead. Rather than focusing on the negative aspects of old age, it finds a more secure place for personal memories in the future life of the community.

If memory is sensate, and places and experiences are imprinted on the body, it follows that the physical act of interpreting personal narratives in drama is a process which may touch old wounds or uncover consoling memories. Any drama which draws on how experience and location have been internalised and embodied is likely to feel very personal to the participants, and may be uncomfortably intrusive. More productively, the act of listening in environments of trust can create moments of friendship and intimacy, in which faceless political situations or moments of history become personalised. 'To listen', Nancy suggests, 'is to be straining towards a possible meaning, and consequently one that is not always accessible.'[44] This act of listening is a form of witnessing, and requires attentiveness. In my own practice I have found it revealing to listen to how stories were told, whether people sound comfortable or distressed, and observe how their physicality alters as their stories are told. I remember working with one elderly man in 1984, then in his eighties, whom we interviewed about his experiences in the trenches in the First World War. We could see the body visibly stiffen as he told his story, shoulders back, a military bearing which relaxed and dropped when he told stories of his demobilisation and return home. This physical response is what Jeff Friedman, whose LEGACY project recorded the oral histories of dancers in the San Francisco Bay area, calls the 'meta-gestus of re-membering'.[45] In rehearsal for the play, the boys in the cast who told the old man's story followed his physical lead, and devised an almost unbearably moving scene in which one boy read out the roll of honour on the local war memorial – many family names still evident in the cast list of the young people. The meta-gestus of remembering was referenced in performance; the old man himself mounted the stage to take over reading the roll, and together he and the boys changed the dramatic atmosphere by offering ironic comment on his homecoming in 1918.

Friedman argued that the disciplined body has encoded and embodied different forms of knowledge, all of which are forms of a cultural language. Friedman theorised his work on performed oral histories by focusing on Bourdieu's concept of habitus, a concept he uses to analyse how both oral communication and physical expression are 'embodied channels of communication' located in social practice. This way of thinking about the kinaesthetic imagination narrows the gap between the cognitive and corporeal, and offers a way of historicising the body by constructing a shared sense of social identity and agency. It does not, however, fully address the realities of living with an ageing body, nor challenge discourses of deterioration with which ageing is often accompanied in the West; both my grandmother and my father experienced an overwhelming sense of social uselessness as their bodies changed with age. Although there is no doubt that the marks of lived experience are carried in the body, I am very sure that the elderly people I have worked with would have not taken at all kindly to even the remotest suggestion that drama would liberate them from the embodiment of their oppressions, nor is the Boalian principle that a lost humanity will be restored by freeing the body from social inscriptions at all appropriate in this context.[46]

The idea that the body is a site of cultural inscription is familiar, but can the body be theorised, not just through the iterability of its enculturated languages, but through its history and genealogy? In his essay 'Nietzsche, Genealogy, History' Michel Foucault links the idea of genealogy to the body. He challenges Nietzsche's notion of *Herkunft*, a term by which he describes the 'stock or descent' of a person, such as blood ties, tradition and as indications of race and social type, a way of thinking about ancestry which he describes as Nietzsche's 'dangerous legacy'. Nonetheless, Foucault acknowledges that, unlike the idea of soul or selfhood which suggest integration and unification, *Herkunft* implies discontinuity and lost events rather than integrity and wholeness. In a distancing himself from the political pitfalls of an essentialist reading of identity, Foucault argues that 'genealogy does not resemble the evolution of a species and does not map the destiny of a people'.[47] By attaching the idea of genealogy and descent to the body, Foucault acknowledged that the body both is imprinted by experience – which he calls the 'stigmata of past experience' – and by the immediacy of 'feelings, desires, errors'. As such, he argues, the body is a site of conflict between the past and the present.

> The body is an inscribed surface of events (traced by language and dissolved by ideas), the locus of a dissociated self (adopting the illusion of a substantial unity), and a volume in perpetual disintegration. Genealogy, as an analysis of descent, is thus situated within the articulation of the body and history. Its task is to expose a body totally imprinted by history and the process of history's destruction of the body.[48]

This theoretical discussion of genealogy adds to the discussion about the body in community-based theatre by suggesting that history is imprinted on the body, not only as a readable system of linguistic signs, but as a rather more blurred and contested site, as a layered and sedimented repository of the past which articulates with the present. As a genealogy, our bodies store the imprint of previous generations, but also point to the discontinuities between one generation and another.

What I find problematic about Foucault's analysis of genealogy is his emphasis on the deterioration of the body, which remains curiously unproblematised. For Foucault (as for Nietzsche), history is destructive to the body, and as cultural values are inscribed on its surface, it inevitably suffers and deteriorates. In relation to applied theatre that involves people of different ages, this has two interrelated problems. First, I have felt that it risks implying to young people that although old people's bodies might be a bit decrepit older people had some great stories to tell if only they listened carefully. Secondly, I have found that negative perceptions of the deteriorating body were readily challenged through practice. As collaborator on an intergenerational project in the Hiroshima district of Japan in 2008, I remember witnessing the delicate and careful ways in which elderly people shared their craft skills with children. There was a practised dexterity evident in their bodies when they taught them, and some of their skills both in cooking and in the craft of calligraphy, putting paid to any pessimistic discourses of the inevitable deterioration of the ageing body. In very different setting, I have had the pleasure of working with a man who was experiencing advanced dementia, and living in a residential care home. He condition meant that he was now post-verbal, and we spent time planting some seeds carefully together in a plant pot, and sharing a moment of companionship and community. He had been a watchmaker by trade, and although he spoke rarely, he held the tiny seeds in the palm of his hand with all the attention to detail of his craft. His pleasure and satisfaction in the job was clear, and he took pride in ensuring that each speck of soil was dusted from the table. By what criteria might these skilful people be described as deteriorating? Not only did they possess the physical skills associated with their craft, but they also showed through their embodied memory that they had learnt to use their ageing bodies gracefully.

Rather than seeing ageing in negative terms an alternative way to conceptualise the body is as an archive. This builds on Foucault's idea that the body bears 'the stigmata of past experience', but also allows for optimism by looking at how the body might be reinterpreted for the future. In his essay 'A Note on the Mystic Writing Pad', Freud conceptualised the archive as static, fixed, about recalling past 'without distortions'.[49] This conceptualisation of the archive does not look very promising. However, in *Archive Fever* Jacques Derrida offers a challenge to Freud, arguing that an archive is not about fixing the past, but always looks to the future. For Derrida, an archive is elusive, a promise which is just beyond reach.

> It [the archive] is a question of the future, the question of the future itself, of a promise and of a responsibility for tomorrow. The archive: if we want to know what that will have meant, we will only know in times to come. Perhaps.[50]

Derrida briefly applied this way of thinking to the body, in which the marks given to the body (he cites circumcision) are a sign of belonging to a society or a community. For Derrida, the archive marks the boundaries between the known and the unknown, the past and the future. To extend this idea further, the archival body is not the site of the deterioration of the individual, but a mediating presence between past experiences and future lives. In this conceptualisation, the body archives our lives performatively, where emotions, experiences and expectations are (consciously or unconsciously) recorded and to which we can, or may, return. This is particularly the case in performed oral history, where actors inhabit the stories physically and emotionally as well as cognitively and verbally. As memories are recalled they are reinterpreted, and as they are performed, they are unfixed, and may be relocated and archived in another's body. Dramatically representing their own and others' stories is, therefore, to become an archivist, a process which draws on physical memories as well as those that are linguistic and cognitive. This invites a new way of thinking about the body in space and time. Inhabiting other's stories, and archiving them in the body through performance, is not about 'preserving', 'conserving' or fixing history, but about making it a part of a dynamic of lived experience. This coheres with the phenomenology of Merleau-Ponty who focuses on the living, moving body-subject. He argues that the body continually exhibits 'expressive movement', an aesthetics of movement, and also 'body orientation', which looks forward and knows where we are going. Together, they result in *inhabitation*, a term he uses to point to the centrality of the body in perception, knowledge and understanding:

> We must therefore avoid saying that our body is *in* space, or *in* time. It *inhabits* space and time… I am not in space and time, nor do I conceive space and time; I belong to them, my body combines with them and includes them… The space and time which I inhabit are always in their different ways indeterminate horizons which contain other points of view.[51]

In this configuration, the living body both has a sense of location, of belonging, but is not constrained by time, place and space. The body has indeterminate horizons and boundaries. This means that the body is a space of possibilities, effectively dissolving the limits of subject and object, self and other and, I would add, human and non-human.

The idea that physically inhabiting community narratives in the theatrical moment opens new horizons lends an ethical dimension to practice in applied theatre. As Derrida points out, an archive signals a 'responsibility for tomorrow', and to encourage this approach to dramatic practice aims to move the participants towards a more dynamic and practical ethic of care. As an alternative to Foucault's deteriorating body, the archival body is a storehouse of narratives which are both located in the present and might travel through time, belonging to future communities. As such, narratives of community become physically imprinted on the body, as an imaginative, ethical and optimistic process of 'becoming'.

Part III
Creativity and Social Justice

6 Creativity and Social Intervention

Cultures of Creativity

Because applied theatre involves making art, it is inevitably associated with theories of creativity. The idea of creativity occupies an ambiguous place in contemporary discourse. Its close historical alliance with humanist notions of genius, originality and the visionary powers of the artistic imagination has meant that, as a concept, artistic creativity has come under critical scrutiny alongside the wider theoretical contexts from which it emerges. Scepticism about the politics of creativity is exacerbated by a new, twenty-first-century interest in creativity as a valuable commodity in knowledge-based economies, and there is a sense of unease about the social role of creativity, particularly amongst those of the political Left. Whatever political reservations and interpretations there may be about the idea of creativity, there remains a belief that it is an important element in both artistic production and in the everyday practices of living. This chapter represents an attempt to further prise open the debate, to consider the implications of debates about creativity for applied theatre and, in particular, to explore the importance of creativity to narratives of social intervention.

Although many different activities are now described as creative, most popular conceptions of creativity have their roots in the idea of the artist, a legacy of the Romantic movement. Although the 'artistic type' as isolated melancholic was not new to Romanticism, what became accepted in this period was the idea of artist as visionary who expressed, in the words of Raymond Williams, 'a higher kind of truth'. In the writing of William Blake, for example, the creative imagination emerged as a form of divine inspiration; for Coleridge the professional artist had a natural inborn genius; and Shelley famously described poets as 'the unacknowledged legislators of the world'.[1] Building on Kant's interpretation of the aesthetic faculty as the means through which moral laws are internalised, nineteenth-century Romantic artists saw themselves as instrumental to social change. This view was based on the premise that freedom and autonomy are intimately linked to democracy, and that the liberated imaginations of professional artists would give them exceptional insights and visionary powers. This way of thinking about creative practice continues to resonate in liberal societies, where social commentaries offered by artists, however anti-establishment, are often taken as a sign of a free and healthy democracy.

Sceptical readings of how creativity has been articulated in the history of Western ideas have revealed its ideological underpinnings with, for example, Marxist critics claiming that some conceptions of creativity have naturalised the bourgeois subject, and feminist thinkers arguing that the ideal of the creative genius assumed masculine norms.[2] Most enduring, however, is the twentieth-century reinterpretation of Romanticism, where it became accepted that qualities formerly associated only with the specialised artist – sensitivity, originality and imagination – are universal aspects of human nature. If, the argument goes, the imagination is the inner voice of our own benign human natures – a common Romanticist principle – we should listen to it, and allow it freedom of expression through creative practice. This way of thinking had the effect of democratising Romantic conceptions of creativity, but in the process it also naturalised and universalised a particular aspect of liberal individualism. Creativity, self-expression and freedom of the imagination have been regarded as not only positive for the individual, but also socially beneficial – an idealist view based on the liberal maxim that good citizens will create good societies.

In this chapter I shall explore how creative practice is articulated in different situations, recognising that creativity is about doing and making, about the material manipulation of form and content and that, as such, it always has a social and political dynamic. Although there have been political challenges to the ideal of the creative artist, the idea of creativity remains an important concept within applied theatre and in everyday life. There are creative breaks in social systems, as well as new forms of artistic communication, and different ways of experiencing the world can produce new forms of social action. What I am searching for here is a theory of creativity that might be applied to theatre which is not entirely individualised, but takes account of the materiality of place and the cultural contexts in which the work takes place. The chapter is structured into three main areas of discussion. The first part examines the idea of the creative individual, making connections between the idealisation of the creative artist and the newly articulated model of the creative employee. The second aspect of the argument examines creativity in relation to social change and, using Boalian practice as an example, tests out differences in materialist and idealist conceptions of creativity. The final part of the discussion is concerned with creative agency and everyday activities, and suggests that human creativity is contextually and environmentally located. Rather than searching for an ideal model of the creative process, I am hoping to place the discussion of creativity solidly in the rather messier, unpredictable and material world of dramatic practice.

Creative Individuals and the Creative Economy

Although the Romantics' idea of artistic genius has been widely refuted, their codification of the creative individual retains some contemporary resonance. Over time, Romanticist myths have been softened and democratised, and creativity has come to be regarded as a faculty of mind which might be developed through certain types of training or education. The idealisation of the intuitive artist has been largely replaced by the more general idea that creative people possess specific personal and cognitive qualities, which are variously summarised as the ability to think divergently, to be spontaneous, to be flexible, to take risks, to generate new ideas, and so on. This form of creativity is not confined to the arts and, in the post-industrial West, creative people are valued for their contribution to the economy and are regarded as essential to successful performance in an increasingly globalised market. In this conceptualisation, the creative individual is thought to possess abilities which bring about innovation in whatever field they choose to practise. In this section, using Howard Gardner's influential work as an example, I shall raise some questions about the values which have become associated with the relationship between creativity and the economy.

Howard Gardner is credited with the theory of 'multiple intelligences' which he developed during the 1970s and 1980s and has continued to revise.[3] As a cognitive psychologist, Gardner was concerned to recognise more forms of human intelligence than those measured by IQ tests. He identified many different forms of intelligence not valued in traditional forms of education, such as spatial intelligence, bodily–kinaesthetic intelligence and intrapersonal intelligence, all of which, he advocates, should be included as part of the pedagogic enterprise. His work on creativity extends these ideas, and it is in his book *Extraordinary Minds* (1997) that Gardner develops a new taxonomy of creativity. He builds on his analysis of Freud, Virginia Woolf, Mozart and Gandhi, all of whom he described as 'exceptional individuals'. He uses his case studies to codify four 'species' of creator: Masters (*sic*); Makers; Introspectors; and Influencers. Masters and Makers (Mozart and Freud, respectively) work in specific domains or areas of interest. In terms that echo descriptions of personality types found in some forms of corporate management, Introspectors and Influencers are more concerned with people, and their creative endeavours are either focused inwardly, towards their own worlds (Woolf), or orientated towards influencing others (Gandhi). There are distinct differences between these categories, Gardner claims, and different varieties of creativity are associated with particular personality traits and autobiographical influences. For example, he separates scholars from performers, arguing that the former require years of patient research to solve problems, whereas the latter need the more immediate rewards afforded by an audience. In defining the species of genius, Gardner quotes Keats's categorisation of 'the poetic character' approvingly, in which Keats claims that creative artist has transcendental powers, a form of inner freedom which completely takes him over.[4]

According to Gardner, creative people tend to adopt common processes and practices. He uses his insights into the extraordinary minds of these highly gifted individuals to make more generalised suggestions about the characteristics of the creative individual. His argument shifts, therefore, from notions of the transcendental genius to practical strategies for creative learning. It is in part his attention to effective learning processes which have led to his work finding favour with educationalists interested in creativity.[5] Creativity, for Gardner, is primarily individualised, and it is interesting that nowhere in his account of 'extraordinary minds' does he locate the subjects of his study in their social or cultural contexts, nor does he reflect on how factors other than those associated with personal life histories might influence their learning or achievements. This means that in his theories the inner workings of the mind are privileged over more social concerns of the ways that class, gender or ethnicity (for example) impact on learning. It is interesting in this context that Gardner describes drama as a form of 'bodily intelligence' which is based on close and concentrated observation of life, imitation, and emotional engagement. Nowhere in this brief account does he grapple with issues of creative collaboration, nor how ideas are generated with others, nor the more cognitive or intellectual aspects of theatre-making. There is an awareness of muscle memory and the physical elements of learning in drama, but his analysis is built on the work of actors as individuals, who learn their craft by observing others, but who develop their abilities outside the ensemble. Gardner is primarily interested in learning lessons from the work of those gifted with 'high potential in the area of bodily intelligence', citing Stanislavski, Charlie Chaplin and Woody Allen as models of excellence.[6] Marxist educators Bill Roper and David Davis have analysed Gardner's theories of multiple intelligence in relation to drama education, where they point out that he has not taken account of the social dimensions of learning. Applied to creativity, this implies that his priority is the development of a particular kind of creative individuality with the consequence, Roper and Davis suggest, that his work has had an enduring appeal for the middle classes.[7]

The relationship between class and creativity is further articulated by Richard Florida, an American economist who describes himself as a 'business guru'. Florida claims that there is a newly emerged 'creative class' which is made up of an ideal type of creative individuals who are unconventional, passionate about their work and highly paid.[8] It is important to locate Gardner's theories of creativity in this North American context. Gardner's 'Project Zero' aims to develop approaches to critical and creative thinking in education, and his 'Good Project' has the broad and utilitarian objective to identify productive relationships between the needs of society, the professional classes and their employers.[9] This is a significant development which allies creativity to current economic needs. With the demise of manufacturing industry in the West, developing a culture of creativity in the workplace is regarded as one way of encouraging employees' affective involvement in their work, their flexibility and commitment to their organisation, which is expected to lead to economic success. Michael Hardt and Antonio Negri describe this as 'immaterial labour' that dominates the post-industrial West, requiring employees to engage affectively in their work, a process in which creativity is integral to contemporary biopolitics.[10] This commodifies creativity, which becomes primarily orientated towards workplace efficiency and to successful competition within a global marketplace. Some practitioners in applied theatre have extended their brief to include corporate work or large organisations in the public sector, as I pointed out in Chapter 3, and they find their work fitting into an environment where employees are encouraged to take risks and use their initiative. Shelley's revolutionary poet seems to have become an advertising executive.

Gardner's theories of intelligence and creativity have their roots in idealist philosophies which place the primacy of mind over culture and society. By so doing, he accepts and naturalises ways of thinking about creativity which are historically contingent. Once loosened from the liberal assumption that creative practices ensure that the benign qualities of human nature are made visible, however, it becomes apparent that 'natural' creativity has very different political articulations. I have offered a more detailed analysis of the relationship between creative learning and the creative economy in my book, *Theatre, Education and Performance: The Map and the Story* (2011), where I suggest that there is a risk that creativity in education becomes harnessed to the values of global capitalism.[11] There are at least two ways of looking at this that are particularly relevant to wider debates in applied theatre. On the one hand, the idealisation of the creative individual has become harnessed to the culture of competition and individuality which characterises corporate employment, and is thus only really beneficial to the professional classes with metropolitan tastes. Alternatively, and this is a point argued by British educationalist Ken Robinson, a creative education values a wider conception of intelligence than is afforded by traditional academicism and is thus more socially inclusive.[12]

Creative Interventions

The idealisation of the creative subject is based on the liberal assumption that ideas change the world. The challenge to this idealist philosophy has traditionally come from Marxists, who have argued that society changes when material circumstances change. They regard idealism as an inadequate account of social progress because it fails to take account of how human thought and ideas are responsive to wider social and economic factors. In other words, people's ideas change when their material circumstances change, rather than the other way round. From this perspective, the idealist position is productive only of human consciousness, whereas Marxists argue that the struggle for social freedom is not to be found inwardly in ideas or the imagination, but is achieved though collective acts in which dominant and oppressive structures of power are challenged and material circumstances changed.[13]

In relation to applied theatre, there is further to go with this debate. It is rare to find either materialism or idealism in their 'pure' forms, if such a thing exists, and in practice the boundaries between these two political positions are often blurred. Creativity in the arts is complex and, although critical of the politics of individualism, many Marxist critics also acknowledge that artistic creativity is dependent on some way on the development of individual abilities.[14] It is important, especially for those practitioners whose intention is social change, to consider the relationship between idealism and materialism in relation to creative practice, as each defines different objectives for the work and asserts a different social vision. A practitioner influenced by idealist philosophies would emphasise the imagination and creative freedom of the individual, whereas materialists would be more likely to use drama to expose the social forces which govern people in different situations and to consider how theatre and performance contribute to constructing social reality. In order to examine some of the ways in which drama is mediated through these two critical lenses, I have chosen to focus on the theories and creative practices of Augusto Boal known collectively as 'theatre of the oppressed' (TO).

Depending on how you look at his work, Augusto Boal is either an inspirational and revolutionary practitioner or a Romantic idealist, and this makes his work particularly interesting. He famously described theatre in Marxist terms as a rehearsal for the revolution, and his dramatic strategies are designed to encourage 'actors and non-actors' to learn about the world. Although his theatre is orientated towards social change and experimentation, Boal has consistently argued that 'it is not the place of theatre to show the correct path' and this has led to considerable debate about his ideological positioning.[15] Richard Schechner has claimed that Boal's refusal to offer solutions to social problems places him firmly amongst the postmodernists, whereas Michael Taussig has argued that Boal is a traditional humanist because he believes that human nature has the power to transcend cultural difference.[16] As a contribution to the debate about Boal's influences and commitments, Graham Ley and Jane Milling have offered a meticulous analysis of Boal's misreadings and interpretations of Aristotle, Shakespeare, Machiavelli, Brecht and Hegel. The strength of their essay lies in detailing Boal's intellectual contradictions in his manifesto for radical theatre, *Theatre of the Oppressed* (1979), which Milling and Ley systematically examine through close readings of Boal's sources, authorities and adversaries. They point out that Boal's theatre of commitment is built on an inattentiveness to historicism in his account of theatre and to decontextualised political theory.[17] Taken together, this means that although Boal's conception of creativity is consistently orientated towards making a better society, it is sometimes unclear from his theoretical writings what kind of society is envisioned.

It is hardly surprising that, as a politician and theatre director, Boal was a better polemicist than he is an academic. My interest here is in exploring how the practices he advocates illuminate his political positioning, a debate which turns on his conceptualisation of the creative individual. Boal offered a codification of the creative subject, and his 'spect-actors' are neither exclusively actors nor spectators, but a combination of the two functions. As such, the 'spect-actor' is *both* able to look at the world *and* act in it, albeit in 'rehearsal' for life. At the end of his influential chapter 'Poetics of the Oppressed' in *Theatre of the Oppressed* (1979), Boal ascribes particular values and characteristics to the spect-actor:

> 'Spectator' is a bad word! The spectator is less of a man and it is necessary to humanise him, to restore him to his capacity of action in all its fullness. He too must be a subject, an actor on equal plane with those generally accepted as actors, who must also be spectators. All these experiments of a people's theatre have the same objectives – the liberation of the spectator, on whom theatre has imposed finished visions of the world... The spectators in the people's theatre... cannot go on being passive victims of that theatre.[18]

In this passage Boal equates his idea of the spect-actor with 'man' (*sic*) which is, for Boal, an ideal category. In terms reminiscent of Romanticism, the spect-actor possesses a vision and active imagination which have been lost to the passive spectator. The purpose of theatre, therefore, is to restore a lost humanity to the spectator, to counter his uncritical encounters with 'finished visions' of the world which have rendered him inhuman and emasculated. Once freed from social restraint through the liberating power of theatre, Boal anticipates that this renewed self-knowledge will enable individuals to act at their most creative, which he assumed would be a positive force for the good. His argument is developed in his later text, *The Rainbow of Desire* (1995), which he wrote as a response to his work in the West where he found 'new oppressions' based on psychological pressures rather than the more visible effects of poverty. Here he appears most interested in self-reflection, recommending the 'faculty for self-observation in an imaginary mirror' found in theatre which, as 'the true nature of humanity', will lead spect-actors to self-knowledge.[19] Boal ascribes special qualities of creativity, autonomy, freedom and self-knowledge to his spect-actors, and although his language and terminology are often Marxist in tone, it is on this idealist and Enlightenment construction of human nature that Boal depends for his vision of social change.

Boal does explicitly discuss the distinctions between idealist and materialist politics in his manifesto *Theatre of the Oppressed*, in which he aligns himself with the materialism of Brecht which he sees in direct opposition to the idealism of Hegel. Milling and Ley have argued that in this book Boal presented a 'primitive communism' in which he sustains sharp divisions between the passive spectator and the active actor to illuminate his perceptions of social inequality. Although Boal's version of theatrical exchange may underline his Marxist credentials, it is actually based on a selective reading of Arnold Hauser's social history of art, in which there is a more subtle reading of the dialogic relationship between performers and spectators than Boal has owned. Boal similarly rewrites Brecht's theories to serve his own political inflections, positioning his own participatory practices as having the stronger revolutionary potential.[20] For those with an interest in applying Boal's theatrical strategies to pedagogical encounters, although his interpretations of Brechtian theatre are important, it is Boal's relationship to the work of Paulo Freire which has most direct relevance. It is here that the pedagogical implications of the negotiations and tensions between materialism and idealism in Boal's work become most apparent.

Boal's relationship to the political pedagogies of Freire has been investigated by Carmel O'Sullivan, who has charted Boal's political journey. O'Sullivan argues that, unlike Marx and Freire, Boal's emphasis is not on the exploitative and inequitable values of the capitalist system, but on 'corrupt or evil *individuals*' (her italics).[21] She argues that TO is based on examining personal experiences of oppression and, crucially, offering *ideas* which will alter participants' perceptions of the world:

> Whereas Marx recognised that all things are contradictory, and contradiction provides the impulse for activity and change... Boal's techniques inherently deny the 'unity of opposites' in an effort to superficially 'solve' individual oppression.[22]

This implies that people can 'think themselves free', and that social change depends on the creative solutions of imaginative individuals than more collective forms of social action. Or, to put it another way, liberation is created by the idealised spect-actor rather than the inhuman spectator. By individualising social change in this way,

O'Sullivan suggests that Boal fails to take adequate account of the ways in which structures of power are created and sustained. This is particularly significant in terms of Freirean pedagogy. As I pointed out in Chapter 3, Freire recognised that it is the dialectical and dependent relationships between the oppressors and oppressed which maintain unequal systems of power. Breaking these inequitable social patterns involves dismantling the social system on which it is built rather than self-liberation through self-reflection which, according to Freire, supports a culture of conformity. O'Sullivan observes that Boal's use of terminology is indicative of his changing political stance 'from radical social transformation to individual empowerment'.[23] She concludes that Boal is more closely aligned to idealism than the materialism of Freirean praxis.

Although O'Sullivan's analysis of Boal's shifting political position is astute and apposite, she does not take full account of his consistent allegiance to traditional humanism. Boal's optimistic belief in the essential goodness of human nature leads him to accept that individuals are not radically evil but have been corrupted by an iniquitous social system. His theatre has always been explicitly tied to narratives of redemption, placing his faith on the efficacy of creative dialogues between similarly liberated individuals. Boal sees a direct link between freeing the body, freeing the mind and social change, and spect-actors are encouraged to 'know' their bodies as part of this process of liberation, as a way of restoring their lost humanity. In the second edition of *Games for Actors and Non Actors,* Boal not only implies that a synthesis of mind and body is libertarian, but he also recognises the significance of dialogue:

> Life is expansive, it expands inside our own body, growing and developing, and it also expands in territory, physical and psychological, discovering spaces, forms, ideas, meanings, sensations – this should be done as dialogue: receiving from others what others have created, giving them the best of our own creation.[24]

What this redemption narrative misses – or does not accept – is a view of selfhood as discursively or culturally constructed. Boal states clearly that cultural differences are superficial, but in practice his belief in a common humanity can prove to be an obstacle to social change. This is acknowledged in a fascinating interchange between TO practitioners in North America, where Rhonda Payne suggested that in this context one of the limitations of Forum Theatre is its emphasis on individual change at the expense of social change. The discussion offered the example of a play performed by women from Burkina Faso about their conditions at an international conference where 'liberated European' spect-actors stepped in with suggestions which were entirely inappropriate to the African context. The spect-actors' suggestions not only revealed a lack of contextual understanding, but their ill-informed contributions 'had no basis in the reality of the people who were there in the play'.[25] This suggests that the efficacy of TO strategies, particularly Forum Theatre, depends on a degree of shared experience between spect-actors and common understanding of the social situation which is portrayed.

My suggestion is that Boal's work lies between the two theoretical poles of idealism and materialism. It is clear, however, that Boal was neither relativist nor a moderate liberal, and my argument rests on the view that the spirit of his robust commitment to social change has Marxist sympathies, but is actually based on abstract and idealised conceptions of the creative actor. This suggests that an uncritical reading of Boal's theories of creative exchange has the potential to obscure the significance of context to applied theatre. It is left to those who use his techniques, therefore, to consider the political implications of context and to consider how the creative dialogue enabled by TO strategies might illuminate different situations. Practitioners with a range of political perspectives apply Boal's methods to many different situations and problems, and this means that developing a coherent and creative praxis involves recognising that all dramatic dialogues are not only contextually and contingently located but also variously politically situated.

Creative Dialogues

At the end of the last section, I suggested that Boal's techniques and strategies are most successful when the situations presented have immediate concern for all the spect-actors. Without shared knowledge and experience between the participants, as Mady Schutzman rightly points out, there are limitations to a system in which 'the oppressed' is consistently regarded as 'the other' – one of the negative effects of the belief that human nature transcends cultural and social difference.[26] Where there is some degree of homogeneity amongst the spect-actors, however, these problems are potentially sidestepped. In order to tease out these ideas a little further, in this section I shall discuss an example of theatre practice influenced by Boal. I have chosen to focus on the work of the British theatre company 'Cardboard Citizens', which was founded in 1991 by Adrian Jackson, Boal's English translator.

One of the significant aspects of Cardboard Citizens' work is that many of the company members have direct experience of homelessness themselves, which not only lends the company credibility in complex situations, it also suggests that the performers and homeless audiences share an understanding of life on the streets. The company describes itself as 'the only professional company in the UK consistently working with homeless and ex-homeless people, including refugees and asylum seekers as creators, participants and audiences', and the company's work recognises and values their unique experiences.[27] This detailed attention to context demonstrates Jackson's interpretation of Boal's theories, and represents the company's commitment to changing the lives and material circumstances of this particular group of people. The point of this description of practice is to explore the significance of context on creativity, and to examine how the political differences between idealism and materialism are negotiated in a specific performance.

Cardboard Citizens staged a show called *The Man with Size Twelve Feet*, written by Adrian Jackson, during 2002 and early 2003. The play was the company's response to the events of 11 September 2001, and it toured shelters for the homeless as well as more commercial venues. It tells the story of Terry, a man who had been in prison for drug-related offences. Terry's story is told through a series of flashbacks, charting his camaraderie with fellow inmates in prison, his rejection by his daughter on his release, and the destructive effects of drug and alcohol addiction on his life. Thematically, the play explores how world politics impact on ordinary people, with the clear political message that globalisation is exploitative and destructive both in the larger world theatre and on the smaller stage of an individual life. At the end of the play, Terry's sense of personal frustration and despair has become politicised, and his final suicidal gesture is to light the match which will burn down the squat in which he is living. He will take with him his former cell mates, Doug and Abdullah, both of whom had tried, and failed, to find solutions to their problems through religion. In his closing monologue Terry describes himself as a suicide bomber, stating that his act of arson will send a message to all who have exploited him in the past. 'Innocent people', he says, 'have got to die for the truth to come out.' Directly analogous to 9/11, Terry stands for all who fall victim to the destructive effects of globalised power structures.

A few days before Christmas 2002, I arrived with my colleague at a hostel for the homeless in central London to film the performance as part of a research project. It was staged in a cramped basement, and the audience of around sixteen easily filled the space. The Joker, Terry O'Leary, explained to the audience that we would be filming the performance, pointing out that, as residents of the hostel they were used to cameras following their movements (she pointed to a security camera in the corner of the room), and so they had no need to worry about our camcorder in the corner. Although none of the audience seemed concerned by our presence, and the company and the hostel had given us permission to film under clear conditions, were we part of this surveillance? We let the cameras roll, trusting the company's experience and judgement of the situation and on the understanding that we would stop filming at any point if requested. My interest here is in the audience's responses to the play, and in the forum which followed the performance.

The forum which followed the performance followed three distinct stages, facilitated by the Joker's skilful questioning in response to the spect-actors' suggestions. They began by choosing the issue with which they identified most immediately on an emotional and personal level. The forum then moved on to explore the social context in which the protagonist found himself until, finally, there was a discussion of how global forces impact on the lives of individuals. Taken together, this forum mapped a political journey from self-reflection to an exploration of how individuals negotiate societal pressures, and on to an examination of the ways in which material circumstances and global politics shape and determine people's lives. In theoretical terms, there was a negotiation between idealism and materialism throughout this forum.

In the first part of the forum, the spect-actors found what Boal described as 'an imaginary mirror' which enabled them to reflect on their own lives. Much of the play's action revolved around the three male characters, with Terry's daughter as the most rounded female character. From the beginning of the forum it was clear that many of the audience identified with Terry himself, although I was told by company members that when the show was staged in a women's hostel the evening before it was the daughter's situation audience members wanted to explore. This suggests that spect-actors find their own points of entry into the story through identification with individual characters. The Joker began the forum by focusing on the audience's immediate emotional responses to the play, asking them whether they had any sympathy for Terry.

FIRST SPECT-ACTOR: No.

JOKER: You haven't?

SECOND SPECT-ACTOR: No.

JOKER: Why haven't you got any sympathy for Terry?

SECOND SPECT-ACTOR: It's all his own fault, innit, really.

JOKER: It's his own fault? Why?

SECOND SPECT-ACTOR: He should deal with it?

FIRST SPECT-ACTOR: That's it – it's his own fault, innit?

SECOND SPECT-ACTOR: He has to deal with it.

JOKER: Deal with what?

SECOND SPECT-ACTOR: Deal with his drug problem... whatever.

JOKER: Right ... so you think ...

FIRST SPECT-ACTOR: Instead of going into prison, he comes out of prison, whatever ... it ain't like ...

SECOND SPECT-ACTOR: Yeah ... he's clean when he comes out.

JOKER: He's clean when he comes out.

FIRST SPECT-ACTOR: Yeah ... and he do some shit – then, like, basically, it's like all of us. He go in prison – I've been in prison like so many times and I've come out ... I'm still on the gear. Still wrecked. You know what I mean. And it's not as easy as that ...

JOKER: It's not as easy as that. Is it? I mean, like, have you managed to come out of prison and be clean, and then get back on the gear?

FIRST SPECT-ACTOR: About two weeks.

SECOND SPECT-ACTOR: (jokingly) Liar.

This conversation revealed the spect-actors' negative self-images. Contrary to my earlier interpretation of the play, they blamed Terry for his continuing drug problem and, because they identified with his situation, they included themselves in this judgement. The first spect-actor, a man in his late twenties, admitted that the first thing he does when leaving prison is 'score'. He saw addiction as a matter of personal responsibility, arguing that neither childhood nor background should be blamed for drug abuse. In highly individualised terms, he commented that there was 'so much help out there' and that coming off drugs was basically a matter of 'willpower and motivation'. The Joker, however, responded quickly to the spect-actor's comment about the difficulties of overcoming addiction, thereby challenging both the culture of blame and the spect-actor's negative self-image. The style of the conversation was fast and engaged, with participants picking up on each other's contributions and interrupting freely, suggesting that they shared common experiences. Within the first three minutes of the forum, this audience was already using the play to reflect on their own experiences – the combination of the narrative of the play and the facilitation of the forum enabling them to find points of contact between the fictional world of the play and the personal realities of addiction.

The transition moment from individualist interpretations to an examination of societal pressures came when the Joker moved the process forward and encouraged the audience to consider how Terry might have acted differently. Following her prompt, three spect-actors came forward. The dominant suggestion from the audience was that Terry's problems would have been alleviated if he could have avoided peer pressure to take drugs, and that staying with his daughter would have helped this process of rehabilitation. The scene where Terry arrived on his daughter's doorstep asking for accommodation was a good example of a 'forum-able' scene, as it held a clear central debate. The daughter was understandably angry with her father, but at that stage in the play Terry intended to mend his ways. In the script, their relationship deteriorates to the point where Terry insults and threatens the daughter's boyfriend, and is rejected by her. One of the spect-actor's suggestions was that Terry changed the situation by being nicer to his daughter, and he was persuaded to enter the acting area. His intervention was witty, and he asked to see his daughter alone, without her student boyfriend Peter whom he dubbed 'Pete the Plum'. In the scene that followed, in role as Terry he apologised for his past behaviour and tried to convince his daughter that he really intended to stay off the drugs. It was a sensitive scene, and at the moment that she seemed about to soften, the spect-actor playing Terry asked if he could stay with her. At this point, the spect-actor defused the moment of tension by bursting into laughter and leaving the stage. This prompted a discussion amongst other audience members about the difficulty of accepting change, of letting an old life go, even if it was, in the living, very painful. It was an insight which represented a significant shift in thinking from the earlier discussion. Rather than seeing themselves as isolated individuals with sole responsibility for authoring their lives, there was a growing awareness of the significance of social relations in defining a sense of identity and belonging. Seen in this way, breaking old patterns of behaviour is more than a matter of individual choice, willpower or thinking about yourself in new ways. It involves establishing new kinds of relationships with others and, crucially, being accepted and judged differently by others in society.

The final stage in the forum's political journey came almost as the evening was ending. After various attempts to reform Terry's behaviour were suggested, another audience member articulated his response to the play in ways which showed that he recognised the central political theme of the play. Identifying himself as a refugee from an Islamic country, he offered an interpretation which made connections between Terry's inability to change and global politics. This Terry was not a victim of his own self-destructive behaviour, but was caught in a chain of global events which inevitably led him to suicide. This unending chain included 9/11, the US and allies' 'war' on terrorism, and international displacement of the vulnerable – a pattern of events that gave Terry an overwhelming sense of powerlessness. It would not be unreasonable to suppose that this man had been similarly trapped in this web. Like those who stayed in the hostel with him, he was interpreting the play through the lens of his own experiences. But unlike them, he did not think that Terry should learn to overcome his problems, nor that his problems would be resolved when society saw him differently. It was the world that should change, and then his life would be able to change too.

The contrasting interpretations of the dramatic situation offered by the spect-actors not only reflected their own experiences, they also illustrated the differences between idealist principles and materialist politics. Those whose world-view had been influenced by idealist narratives of self-creativity based their suggestions on the assumption that individuals can change their own stories, whereas materialist analyses would expect personal change to follow changes in global politics. What I saw in practice was how these two different perspectives might coexist in the same piece of Forum Theatre. Nothing had been resolved for Terry, of course. But what else has happened in the course of the performance and forum? The audience had entered the fictional world of the play, and for many it confirmed a view that, if they so chose, there is at least the possibility of altering their own life-stories. Others found that the play articulated the social effects of world politics, in which they found themselves caught. The contributions of those who advocated personal change were confessional and emotionally open. The more political interjections were analytical, focused and angry. Somewhere between these two positions there was an interesting negotiation between two world-views which enabled the spect-actors to shift their perspectives and look at the situation differently. The political dynamic of this particular forum, therefore, lay in finding creative ways to think differently *and* act productively in a wider social and global context. Over the years that I have witnessed Cardboard Citizens' work there is a recurring dramatic theme of how people are entrapped and rendered powerless by the social systems they inhabit. It was articulated poetically in

Kate Tempest's 2013 play, *Glasshouse*, where a family experiencing poverty under the UK's coalition government was represented and opened for scrutiny. Cardboard Citizens offer theatre workshops which enable homeless people to develop their artistic creativity, but the dialogue in their Forum Theatre is orientated towards finding ways of living creatively in an uncertain, complex and often dangerous world.

Creative Environments

The work of Cardboard Citizens illustrates the importance of understanding the context in which practice in applied theatre takes place. Because practice in applied theatre is intimately and complexly tied to the contexts in which it takes place, the ways in which space is constructed takes on a particular significance. As Hal Foster has suggested, artists should be 'familiar not only with the structure of each culture well enough to map it, but also with its history well enough to narrate it'.[28] Underpinning debates about creative practice in applied theatre in the twenty-first century is a new interest in the politics of place, and in the environmental implications of creative practice. Sally Mackey's research project 'Challenging Concepts of "Liquid" Place through Performing Practices in Community Contexts', for example, opens important questions about how place is experienced by vulnerable participants.[29] In this section I shall begin to sketch some thoughts about the significance of place and environment in relation to creativity and social intervention.

The renewed concerns about place in applied theatre are mirrored by contemporary theatre-makers' interest in the aesthetics of performance space and site-based performance or theatre in 'found' spaces. This marks a shift in thinking, not only suggesting a change in artistic priorities, but also offers new ways of thinking about creativity as a form of social intervention. The great theatrical symbol of a modernist utopia was the empty space, designed to liberate the soul and the imagination by insulating actors and audiences from the restrictions of history, the regulations of place and the materiality of everyday life. One of the concrete realisations of the ideal of the empty space is the black-box theatre which, as David Wiles has pointed out, 'is also bound up with the modernist goal of transforming society, which may seem paradoxical in view of the way it cuts itself off from any contact with an implicitly corrupt and false social world outside'.[30] Although actually working in a black-box theatre may seem a rare luxury to some practitioners in applied theatre, the symbolism of the empty space as place of creativity and social transformation calls attention to the various ways in which places and spaces are constructed and experienced. The idealisation of the empty space, and the assumption that temporary isolation from other social practices leads to social transformation, rests on the belief that a space which has been stripped of the obvious signs of social interaction is ideologically neutral and without cultural inscription. The idea that participants emerge from an empty space transformed as individuals and ready to transform society is dependent on idealist constructions of the creative imagination, a modernist reinterpretation of Romanticism. It takes the following familiar logic: the imagination is most free when it is least influenced by society, so those whose imaginations are most liberated will create better societies. Although this image appeared appealingly democratic, it ignores the social context in which the drama takes place and the many ways in which spaces are interpreted, experienced and lived.

The idea that any space can exist outside social practice was challenged by the French cultural theorist Henri Lefebvre, whose study *The Production of Space* was first published in 1976 and translated into English in 1991. Lefebvre was critical of idealist conceptions of space, and his central thesis is that space is never empty but always actively socially produced. He furthers an understanding of space as a dynamic social practice which is produced and reproduced through social action and interaction. He contends that space is not simply an abstract concept; it is lived, experienced and embodied physically and is therefore differently interpreted according to culture and history. This means that space is multiply inscribed, and its meanings are continually generated and regenerated as a creative process with 'many aspects and many contributing currents'.[31] This way of thinking about space as a social practice has particular resonance for applied theatre, not least because the work often takes place in environments or institutions (prisons or care homes for the elderly, for example) which already carry very specific meanings. Making what Mihaly Csikszentmihalyi has described as a 'congenial' environment for creativity in such contexts presents particular challenges.[32]

Lefebvre has offered three categorisations of space which, though now well-known, illuminate the different ways in which people relate to space. *Representations of space* are conceived conceptually, usually constructed by professionals as a way of codifying or ordering space according to specific ways of thinking and structures of power. *Representational spaces*, by contrast, are those of everyday life, spaces which are embodied and articulate the complex symbolisations and images of lived experience. *Spatial practices* are the patterns which structure the social world, and relate to people's perceptions of the world and the different social purposes space fulfils. Although, as Wiles has pointed out, theatre would be generally associated with the middle category – representational space – this would not fully explain the complex relationship between participants and space which is evident in applied theatre. Because much applied theatre takes place in very specific contexts and institutional settings, all three categorisations of space Lefebvre outlined – conceived, lived and perceived – are interconnected in its practices.

Applied theatre often engages with creativity in institutional settings, where space is conceived according to structures of disciplinary power, and the rules governing the ways in which space is often used to define relations between people. These spaces are, to use Lefebvre's words, 'informed by effective knowledge and ideology'.[33] This means that work in these contexts is often framed by the ways in which space is used to regulate or order people's movement and behaviour. My visit to the hostel to the homeless to see the work of Cardboard Citizens offers a good example of how representations of space are negotiated and reconstructed in relation to theatre practice. On my arrival at the hostel, the ways in which space was regulated became clear. Gaining admission required me to use the video entry-phone, wait in an entrance hall painted a calming shade of pink whilst my identity was checked, sign in – and only then was I allowed into the performance space, travelling through several locked doors and observed by many surveillance cameras. I have no doubt that my feelings about this experience, and my interpretation of the space, would have been very different from residents of the hostel. A related example is offered by Jenny Hughes, writing about theatre-making in Styal, a women's prison. Hughes's experience of working with the women meant that she was extremely sensitive to the 'double' contexts of the drama workshop and prison life, and she understood that the women would need to 'block out the effects' of the prison culture in order to work creatively on the drama project. As a result, Hughes described one project on which she allowed time at the beginning and end of each day as 'safety valves' – time which enabled the participants to warm up and wind down and discuss any issues which had been raised during the work. Hughes used her knowledge of the potential conflict between the two contexts to support the women in moving into the representational space of the workshop and in easing them back into the more regulated representation of space within the prison environment when the drama was over. In her book *Theatre & Prison*, Caoimhe McAvinchey also comments perceptively that theatre-making and prison life place very different demands on space and time, and their different ways of working can make them incompatible:

> The smooth administration of prison depends on the strict demarcation of time, space and action: particular behaviours happen in specific places for an allocated duration... . In contrast, theatre demands a provocation of ideas of certainty. It invites a playful exploration of time, space and action.[34]

McAvinchey's insight points to the practical implications of working in institutional settings, but she is also alert to the politics of creativity and the disciplinary structures that regulate how places are experienced and embodied.

Transforming highly regulated spaces into creative performance and workshop spaces is not just an interesting artistic challenge, it involves reconstructing how space is conceived and temporarily overlaying its codes with alternative spatial practices. Lefebvre resisted binary oppositions of mind/body, arguing that it is a critical understanding of how spatial practices have been constructed and internalised which makes social intervention possible. More recently, however, new materialist debates in cultural geography and anthropology have prompted further discussion about creative agency. In this conceptualisation creativity is not seen as an internal attribute of the human mind, nor is it understood to be simply responsive to place and material circumstances. The anthropologist Tim Ingold sums up this perspective, in terms that echo many of the ideas that permeate this chapter:

> Attempts to move beyond the modernist polarization of subject and object, or the mental and the material, in terms of a language of agency that remains trapped in these very same categories, are bound to lead to contradiction and confusion.[35]

In place of this bifurcation, Hallam and Ingold suggest a new vocabulary for creative practice that acknowledges that because 'there is no script for social and cultural life', creativity is always durational. Borrowing an insight from Henri Bergson, they suggest that creativity is a process that 'is going on, all the time, in the circulations and fluxes of the materials that surround us and indeed of which we are made – of the earth we stand on, the water that allows it to bear fruit, the air we breathe'.[36] Related to theatre that seeks social intervention, this suggests that practitioners understand how social meanings are inhabited, embodied and reproduced in space and how, reciprocally, the material world inhabits us, both for the duration of the drama and beyond.

Applied theatre is principally concerned with how the aesthetics of drama, theatre and performance might make a difference to the social patterning of everyday life. This way of thinking about creativity environmentally – as integral to everyday, vernacular creativity – provides a basis for discussion about how places are reinterpreted and reproduced over time, where there might be consonance or dissonance between how spaces are conceived institutionally and organisationally, and how they might be experienced and symbolised in the process of making drama. Creative spaces are those in which people are feel safe enough to take risks and to allow themselves and others to experience vulnerability. It is creative moments of transition which enable participants to move out of restricted spaces – literally or symbolically – and beyond identities which are fixed and codified by particular ways of thinking or spatial practices into new forms of social identification and improvisation. This way of thinking about creativity moves the focus of attention away from the inner qualities of the autonomous individual, and understands the significance of responsive, reciprocal and compassionate relationships between participants within the specific context in which the work takes place. It accepts that creativity is an everyday process, formed and broken by habitual actions, which in turn raises ethical questions about how congenial environments of trust might be formed.

7 Human Rights in Performance

Agendas and Advocacy

It has been argued that the language of human rights has filled the vacuum left by the demise of grand political narratives after the Cold War. This view would seem to be borne out by experience and, as the radical students of 1968 start drawing their pensions, idealistic young theatre workers are far more likely to be interested in human rights issues than in starting revolutions. Theatre in search of social change has responded to new world orders, and the successors of mid-twentieth-century theatre activists are more likely to be found working for non-governmental organisations in the developing world than using theatre to mobilise workers in their local factories. This shift from overtly revolutionary politics to more local explorations of injustice is often seen within the wider context of international standards of human rights. Despite the many contradictions and debates about how a human rights agenda might be legitimately furthered, it remains one of the abiding utopian ideas over which there is general international consensus.

As I suggested in the previous chapter, there is a move towards a new political language in socially committed theatre-making in which idealism is tempered by an understanding of the material circumstances of participants and the local and regional conditions in which the work takes place. The balance between abstract idealism and more local expressions of justice appears to be satisfied by recourse to the vocabulary of human rights, taking us beyond the polarisation between universalists and relativists and into more transcultural ideas of morality and humane standards of living. On the surface, the discourse of human rights that has gathered momentum in the post-Cold War era sounds reassuringly principled and humanitarian rather than directly political. Rights-based agendas have claimed a new urgency, and campaigns against torture, discrimination and the effects of poverty, for example, appear entirely uncontroversial. This way of thinking has permeated applied theatre, not least because of the strong alliance between applied theatre and the charitable trusts and human rights organisations which frequently fund practice.[1] In places where human rights are violated, forms of popular theatre which bring together information and entertainment are seen as an effective way of reaching large audiences, particularly where performances are accompanied by discussion or other forms of community participation. Such locally based work, often part of wider regional campaigns, is intended to meet the objectives of an international human rights agenda.

The new global discourse of human rights has legitimised international intervention in the name of universal social justice, but it is not without its dissenters. Although many people associate human rights exclusively with the courageous work of organisations such as Amnesty International who campaign to end human rights violations, it is important to remember that the formal constitution of universal human rights is constructed according to the principles of a liberal democracy which favours capitalism as a political economy. It is based on system of individual rights and civic responsibilities in which society is built on a consensus of abstract political virtues such as freedom of speech, tolerance and the right to self-determination, which are enshrined and protected in law. This notion of rights, enforceable by law, relied on the nation-state for jurisdiction and the broader concept of human rights has been widely promoted by organisations associated particularly with the United Nations General Assembly, which adopted the Universal Declaration of Human Rights in 1948. It has been argued, however, that because contemporary notions of human rights have derived from a very specific history of European liberalism, this has had the effect of normalising Western individualism in ways which are at best insensitive to local cultures and at worst another way in which the hegemonic values of powerful nations are colonised.[2]

Within the field of applied theatre, critics from the developing world have raised questions about who owns the discourse of human rights, and whether this is simply another way in which transnational corporations create local conditions which are favourable to their own globalised work practices. The relationship between universal human rights and political power has also been challenged by a resurgence of regionalism, and there are different interpretations of human rights regimes in, for example, the Asian Pacific Rim, Europe and the Arab world. The tensions between these different conceptions of human rights are exacerbated by the unequal power-relations of global politics, particularly in contexts in which human rights are seen primarily as a Western agenda. Furthermore, the power of the nation-state has eroded in the twenty-first century, and pressing contemporary issues such as climate change and the so called 'war on terror' cannot be contained within national boundaries. In turn, wars in Iraq and Afghanistan have raised urgent questions about whether it is ever morally justifiable to impose human rights by military force. As Rosi Braidotti has commented, '[p]osthuman wars breed new forms of inhumanity'.[3] These are major concerns and, to different degrees, they face practitioners who apply theatre to human rights advocacy. My aim in this chapter is to look at the question of human rights advocacy from a range of different perspectives, and consider how some of the debates about globalisation and human rights impact on practice in applied theatre. The chapter offers no clear-cut answers, but is based on the view that furthering an ethical, rights-based agenda for applied theatre involves understanding and negotiating the tricky terrain within which humanitarian politics are situated.

Human Rights and Globalisation

The idea that human rights are a product of Western liberalism has been subject to particular scrutiny from the political Left, where is has been argued that Enlightenment concepts of universal rights are designed to shore up the interests of possessive individualism within a free-market economy. Susan George, an activist and writer on global poverty, speaking at the Amnesty International lectures in 2003, made the link between human rights and economics explicit. She used her lecture to argue that the standards of ethics set down in the Universal Declaration of Human Rights can only be met in liberal democracies because they do not strive towards complete equality, as might be expected in state socialism for example, but are centrally concerned with the liberal ideals of individual dignity and the right to self-determination.[4] Historically, this has cemented the link between democracy and economics not least, says George, because people vote for parties on the basis of their economic policies. Equally pressingly, debates about the impact of globalisation on the spread of human rights have revealed inconsistencies between the practice of human rights and the humanitarian rhetoric of corporate organisations and governments. If economic interests, human rights and democratic politics are complexly interwoven, it follows that all interventions associated with human rights, including those carried out in applied theatre, are inevitably caught up in this larger conceptual scheme.

Opinion is divided about whether globalisation is an effective means of furthering a human rights agenda, or whether it is incompatible with humanitarian values. On the one hand, global capitalists argue that increasing the global marketplace is one way to extend human rights. Bill Gates, writing in the *Washington Post* in May 2000, argued that China's 'participation in the global community' and 'increased economic and cultural interaction' would enable the West to address the social and human rights issues evident there.[5] Since 2000 the relationship between human rights and multinational industries has deepened, suggesting a major shift in perspective as pressure to comply with Western notions of human rights lies increasingly in the hands of global capitalists who are, arguably equally (or more) powerful than national or federal governments. An attractive picture of globalisation is painted as the means whereby the benefits of the global market are brought to the poorest people in the world through the use of new technologies, a vision that Bill and Melinda Gates now actively promote in their philanthropic work. Yet it remains the case that globalisation, allied to free world trade, appears to unite the principle of universal human rights with an expansion of wealth. This perspective has been vehemently challenged, however, by those who consider it to be more concerned with the spread of capitalism than human happiness. Braidotti argues that, at its most extreme, humanitarianism is used to justify violence on an international scale:

> Many contemporary wars led by Western coalitions under the cover of 'humanitarian aid' are often neo-colonial exercises aimed at protecting mineral extraction and other essential geo-physical resources needed by the global economy.[6]

Noam Chomsky also has made the case that globalisation is incompatible with human rights, and has catalogued an array of practices that reveal how the conduct of the US government falls short of, and contradicts, its libertarian rhetoric. He is particularly critical of the ways in which the doctrine of free trade has been used to further capitalist self-interest, citing the example of tobacco advertising aimed at women and children in Asian countries which was actively promoted by the US and enforced with the threat of economic sanctions. Susan George has argued that globalisation is directly opposed to human rights because it increases divisions in wealth, with power and money continually drifting to the top. The ethical question, she suggests, is 'how can we guarantee the human rights of those that globalisation leaves behind?'[7]

One answer to this question is through philanthropy, and the work of humanitarian agencies and charitable activity, much of which are funded by the affluent West and promoted by high-profile dignitaries and, often, endorsed by celebrities. The complexity of theatre which aims to promote human rights has been thoughtfully analysed by Syed Jamil Ahmed, who has written about theatre for development in his home country of Bangladesh. His work raises questions about the relationship between globalisation and human rights. Ahmed offers an analysis of discourses of development, arguing that international development has been orientated towards 'a bloodless and revolution-free prosperity to the "developing" nations'.[8] He argues that poverty-alleviation schemes, with which theatre for development is often associated, have been funded by aid agencies whose human rights agenda is driven by the economic imperatives of capitalist donors of the West, and this means that the work is inevitably allied to globalisation. In Bangladesh, he observes, issues explored in theatre for development are not chosen by the local people themselves, but by NGOs in collaboration with those in positions of power. His list of topics represented in theatre for development include 'social injustice, dowry, polygamy, *fatwa*, arbitrary violence, gender discrimination, illiteracy, unjust possession of public resources by the power cliques, superstitious health practices, degradation of the environment and its consequences', all of which easily attract foreign donation.[9] On the face of it, all these issues seem entirely acceptable in part, at least, because of their close affinity to an international human rights framework. Ahmed has pointed out that where development workers have not understood the complexities of the local context, however, the issues are frequently presented as crude pieces of agitprop theatre in which obstacles to human rights protection are either ignored or badly oversimplified. Crucially, local people themselves have not been invited to set the agenda for the plays, and although audiences are invited to 'share their opinions', scope for a more robust political (and Freirean) dialogue is limited. The current process does not lead to changing social structures, Ahmed suggests, and this kind of human rights advocacy succeeds only in domesticating villagers rather than liberating them. As a process of domestication, he argues, it serves the needs of globalising capitalists because it creates a docile workforce who are easily exploited as cheap labour. Ahmed's rueful question about theatre for development, therefore, is 'development for whom'?

Ahmed has painted a bleak picture of some of the effects of theatre for development and, no doubt, the motives of the individual theatre practitioners and aid workers are far less cynical. It seems likely that such theatre workers are themselves caught up in structures of power rather than intentionally perpetrating them, and for this reason Foucault's theories of governmentality are apposite. Foucault argued that power is not sustained through fixed systems of domination, but is played out more subtly through a mixture of self regulation and coercion. He claimed that power is seen to be lodged with experts, who possess knowledge which may well be used to support benign intentions – humanitarian reforms of health care, prisons, schools and so on – but the effect of their endeavours is often that individuals are constructed, and construct themselves, according to their perceptions of how they are expected to behave. This process produces what Foucault calls 'docile bodies', people who conform to the disciplinary knowledge of experts without questioning the power base from which it derived, and who regulate their lives accordingly. 'A body which is docile', Foucault argued, 'may be subjugated, used, transformed, improved.'[10] In such a culture of self-improvement, there is no obvious central locus of power which might be opposed. This way of thinking relates closely to Ahmed's account of theatre for development in Bangladesh because it implies that *both* the development workers *and* villagers collude in their own transformation into 'docile bodies'. Seen in this light, the rhetoric of transformation and empowerment so often associated with applied theatre takes on a different meaning. A Foucauldian reading of the situation Ahmed describes would pose the following question: Is theatre is being used to transform Bangladeshi villagers into docile bodies in order that they might be empowered to become effective workers for multinational corporations?

One of the central political questions which Ahmed has identified is concerned with who owns the means of cultural expression in a globalised world. In his utopian 'world without theatre for development', theatre practitioners would not be concerned with 'development' but with 'plain and simple theatre'. His dramatic pedagogy would involve a more equitable process of transcultural collaboration and exchange, with theatre practitioners sharing their knowledge of their own cultural traditions – citing Brecht's and Stanislavski's theatre as areas of interest to Bangladeshi practitioners. Ahmed calls, therefore, for knowledge to be relocated, ensuring that local practitioners have access to both local and international expertise *in theatre* as a form of cultural literacy, a process which would contribute to breaking down the divide between the rural poor and the urban cosmopolitan in Bangladesh.[11] From this point of view, Foucault's deterministic analysis of the power of expert knowledge tells only part of the story. Literacy, as Paulo Freire was well aware, is a cultural practice which enables people to formulate new insights and ideas, to offer social criticism and to develop relationships. If this is extended to the embodied languages of theatre, bodies rendered docile may start to move. This would shift the focus of international development away from message- or issue-based theatre, described by Ahmed as 'top-down', and towards a local and indigenous theatre, where practitioners are able to use their cultural knowledge of different styles of artistic production.

Theatre director Rustom Bharucha commented succinctly that there is a 'policing of human rights by which First World nations legitimate their control of Third World economies on humanitarian grounds'.[12] If applied theatre is to avoid contributing to this cultural policing, practitioners need to be aware of the limits of liberalism and the politics of globalisation, and to understand their place in this process. Bharucha further argues that an intercultural theatre practitioner is always an infiltrator, and not 'a free-floating signifier oscillating in a seemingly permanent state of liminality and in-betweenness'.[13] The problem lies not only in the hypocrisy of governments, but in the foundational link between human rights, global economics and liberal individualism or neoliberalism. This suggests that theatre which is intended to spread human rights necessarily inhabits a contradictory space, in which the tensions between competing values of a world in a permanent state of transition are continually played out. My interest here is not to challenge the general moral aspirations of a human rights framework, but in how we, as theatre practitioners, might exercise continual vigilance over the ethical implications of the interpretation and representation of human rights in different social and cultural contexts.

Representing Human Rights

The tradition of democratic liberalism states that human rights are universals, an assumption that is based on the idealist philosophy that human nature is universally shared and universally good.[14] From an anthropological perspective, it has been pointed out that the individualist vocabularies of human rights are inflexible to local cultures because they are based on European conceptions of human nature developed in the eighteenth and nineteenth centuries, a category described by Richard Wilson as 'one of the more offensive ways of imposing the prejudices of "Western culture"'.[15] The concept of the human subject inscribed in human rights legislation is not, however, a static formation, and it has been redefined many times in the last two hundred years. This philosophical history is always orientated towards improving and extending human rights, and the process of redefining the human subject has led to the explicit inclusion of the rights of women and children in law, for example; it is interesting to note in this context that the only UN member states who have so far (in 2013) failed to ratify the United Nations Convention on the Rights of the Child are the United States of America, Somalia and South Sudan. The Western philosophical tradition claims that the human subject on which the discourse of human rights depends is timeless and universal, but it is actually responsive to specific social struggles.

In his 1995 lecture for Amnesty International, Jacques Derrida made connections between the construction of the human subject, human rights and language. Reminding his audience that the discourse of human rights emerges from a specific philosophical tradition, he argued that neither philosophical concepts of the human subject nor language exist outside the cultures in which they are practised. Language, he suggested, is 'always pretending to be universal', but the use of any specific language inevitably affirms the values, cultural memories and traditions of the nation or groups of nations within which it is used. Language, he argued, carries the imprint of culture and histories. This has particular political consequences for using languages which have become hegemonic, most obviously the English language. If the use of English as a convenient means of international communication has the effect of erasing or denying local languages, it follows that the sense of belonging to a local culture or national identity will be eroded or lost. In looking for a new way of conceptualising language in relation to human rights, Derrida concluded that:

> When you show some respect for the other, you have to respect another's language and to affirm yours. That is the deep experience of translation – it is not only political, but poetic.[16]

Taking Derrida's insight that human rights are affirmed through linguistic practices which are both political and poetic draws attention to the ways in which human rights are represented. This has two specific implications for applied theatre which I should like to explore a little further. The first is concerned with the language of human rights reporting, which raises questions about the impact of narrative in applied theatre. The second is related to the aesthetic languages of theatre and the tools of cultural expression in drama as they are applied to human rights issues.

One of Syed Jamil Ahmed's criticisms of theatre for development is that some Western practitioners have little understanding of the contexts in which the work takes place and that, in the process, theatre workers unwittingly impose their own culturally specific values on the rural poor in Bangladeshi communities. This implies that an uncritical belief in human rights as universal and absolute moral principles is, in fact, prejudicial. From an anthropological perspective, Richard Wilson has explained that one of the difficulties of working towards an understanding of human rights in an international context is precisely because it is built on abstract and legal concepts – freedom of speech, liberty, social justice – and this has meant that human rights issues have tended to be represented in similarly positivist language. He argues that much human rights reporting is couched in legalistic terms, which has the effect of taking stories of abuse out of context. This means that the reports focus on empirical facts, with the consequence that the analysis of the reasons for human rights violation and the motives of the perpetrators is limited. Without a sense of context and narrative, he concludes, questions surrounding the significance of locality and culture are either displaced or erased from official accounts. A more ethical approach, according to Wilson, would not seek to make moral judgements based on universalist abstractions, nor to depersonalise the abusive acts, but to locate the practice or violation of human rights within specific social and community contexts.

> By situating social persons in the communities and contexts, and furnishing thick descriptions of acts of the violent exercise of power, it can be seen how rights themselves are grounded, transformative and inextricably bound to purposive agents rather than being universal abstractions... By embracing a technocratic language, human rights reporting lays itself open to the same critique as could be made of the devalued, dehumanised language of abusive forms of governance.[17]

Chris Brown, an academic who works in international relations, has convincingly argued that this kind of universalism actually impedes the protection of human rights because there is a refusal to admit that its values *are* liberal and Western.[18] Charges of ethnocentrism in these matters are subject to continual debate in non-governmental organisations, where it is acknowledged that the balance between social intervention on an international scale and the imposition of Western political systems is not easily struck.

The debate turns on how human rights become integrated into social practices, and how they shift from the legalistic framework in which they are couched into the vernacular and the everyday. Reciprocally, there are questions about how local practices might influence international human rights debates. Anthropologist Sally Engle Merry has offered an illuminating insight into how 'indigenous peoples' mobilise human rights in order to have 'conversations about justice'. Her study is of Native Hawaiians, where she observed that the people did not accept the imposition of a Western or North American version of human rights, but regarded it as 'an open text' which they might appropriate and redefine according to their own local circumstances.[19] By campaigning for political sovereignty based on Hawaiian cultural practices and languages, the Hawaiians reasserted their local rights by recourse to aspects of international law. In the process, they redefined international human rights law in ways which have influenced discussions about indigenous rights at the United Nations. This suggests, Merry concludes, that it is possible for the global to become localised, and the local to be globalised. In other words, neither human rights nor cultures have fixed, determined, knowable essences or boundaries. They are always and continually in flux, contingent on time and space, and have both porousness and specificity.

Richard Wilson's critique of the a-cultural rhetoric of human rights organisations presents a salutary reminder for workers in applied theatre. It would be easy to suggest that drama is exempt from such concerns because it is necessarily involved in creating narratives and characters which flesh out human rights reports in ways which Wilson appears to be advocating. This warrants further investigation. Drama is used as part of human rights campaigns precisely because it is seen as an effective means of bringing about change. By definition, therefore, any leaning towards what Wilson calls 'soggy relativism where any representation is as good as another' is out of the question.[20] Some rights-based theatre is designed to offer information – about health care or the rights of children, for example – and this means that the drama may contain very precise information. But without working in sustainable partnership with local communities and other agencies, the work is likely to perpetuate the very inequalities which it seeks to erode. None of the commentators invoked in this section would do away with an international framework of human rights, but all acknowledge the limitations of social practices which impose a highly individualised system of rights and 'freedoms' in the name of social progress or development. As Wilson identified, there is a need to recognise that there are multiplicity of narratives inherent in both human rights agendas and their violations, and that a more equitable distribution of power recognises the part local knowledge, cultural languages and personal experiences have to play in the process of redefining and relocating the international discourse of human rights.

Human Rights in Performance

So far, I have argued that theatre which aims to promote human rights needs to be rooted in the cultures in which the work takes place rather than rely on abstract universalism or moral individualism for its efficacy. I am not suggesting, however, that human rights should be entirely locally determined, and I accept that the United Nations charters on human rights represent a compelling system of international social justice. What I am interested in securing are approaches to human rights in theatre that go beyond the rather distracting debates between cultural relativists and universalists. The problem with both these perspectives is that they depend on the outdated view that cultures are fixed, internally coherent and holistic units rather than recognising that societies and cultures change, and are in a continual process of reformulation through local, regional and global dialogues. I am interested in questioning the role theatre might have in facilitating such dialogues about human rights, and how theatre might be used to narrate local and personal experiences.

In terms of applied theatre, this raises a number of questions about how practice might mediate the gap between local and global discourses in relation to human rights advocacy. As it is not unusual for practitioners in applied theatre to seek out situations in which human rights are violated, this has particular implications for our field. In order to interrogate this further, I have chosen to focus on theatre which confronts the rights of women subjected to family violence, in part because as an issue it is fraught with ambiguities and local complexities. Like so many others, I am also aware of its effects at first hand

and witnessing this kind of abuse has given me some insights into how difficult it is for men and women to disclose that it is going on. There is obviously no doubt that family violence is wrong, and that it is a violation of human rights and dignity. But as one experienced NGO in Sri Lanka pointed out to me, to work from the simple premise that women should just not put up with family abuse is not only likely to ignore the complex and powerful emotions at stake, it may also pay scant attention to factors such as the women's economic status or local constructions of honour, duty and family responsibilities. Raising awareness of family violence as a matter of social injustice and as a violation of human rights, rather than primarily as a private or personal problem is, therefore, particularly difficult. As an example of practice, I have chosen campaigns for prevention of violence against women in the family, funded by United Nations Development Fund for Women (UNIFEM). The main focus for this discussion is a project developed in Malawi, but I shall also refer briefly to work undertaken by Philippine Educational Theater Association (PETA). This approach to human rights illuminates different aspects of the negotiation between international standards of human rights and respect for local culture, and they also articulate some solutions to the ethical challenges of humanitarian intervention through theatre.

The project in Malawi was undertaken by Story Workshop Educational Trust, a non-profit-making organisation that 'focuses on supporting Malawians to improve their lives by addressing issue of HIV/AIDS, food security, gender, health, human rights and democracy, and the environment'.[21] Based in Malawi's second city, Blantyre, the organisation has a history of intercultural dialogue about human rights issues which has influenced its work both politically and artistically. In part, this exchange has come about because much of the work is funded by international humanitarian organisations and, although almost everyone working at Story Workshop is Malawian, it is significant that the founder of Story Workshop is American and, during the first decade of the twentieth century, a small number of European theatre practitioners worked with the company, though it is now, appropriately, run entirely by Malawians. There is, of course, a delicate balance to be struck here, and this is reflected in the company's creative output. There is a strong commitment to sustaining Malawi's traditional cultural forms, but the medium of communication is primarily radio, and the main focus of Story Workshop is the production of two radio soap operas which are broadcast across Malawi. This approach is consistent with James Clifford's much quoted observation that contemporary identities:

> [N]o longer presuppose continuous cultures or traditions. Everywhere individuals and groups improvise local performances from (re)collected pasts drawing on foreign media, symbols and languages.[22]

Story Workshop's creative output is similarly inflected by a range of symbolic forms, and they use live theatre, radio drama, comic books and print media, music and a mobile cinema in their work. The two radio soap operas, *Zimachatike* and *Tilitonse*, were started to address issues of rural development and civic education. They were inspired by the long-running BBC radio soap *The Archers*, which was started in the 1950s to provide information for farming communities, and also built on the success of radio dramas produced by the Malawi Broadcasting Corporation in the early 1990s. *Tilitonse* aired from 1999 to 2003, and *Zimachatike* (currently funded by the European Union) still has a huge following: villagers will gather around a radio to catch the latest episodes. Radio is particularly significant form of communication in a country where over 40 per cent of the population are unable to read, and yet 80 per cent have access to a radio. The convention of soaps is that strong and recognisable characters drive a linear plot, and audiences learn to like (and dislike) particular characters and either identify with them, argue with them or empathise with the dramatic situations they portray. In 2013, Story Workshop described the relationship between characters and social issues in the following way:

> The *Zimachitika* characters include well-loved personalities like the grandmother Gogo, the cruel gossip Nabanda, the HIV-positive community activist Zione, and the hardworking young girl Ndaona. They represent typical village types: gossips, troublemakers, peacemakers, tricksters and respected elders. In and around the village, characters animate common barriers to improvement and provide role models for overcoming them. The storylines interweave messages like agroforestry, irrigation, crop diversification, family health, HIV/AIDS prevention and gender messages with the characters' daily lives.[23]

Their wide appeal and commitment to social justice approach means that soaps are particularly well placed to contribute to civic education programmes, as popular characters are able to articulate information in ways which are palatable to audiences. David Kerr, a theatre academic who has worked extensively in Africa, has pointed out that there are similarities between radio drama and the oral traditions of Africa, and the form, as well as the content, account for its popularity.[24]

The success of *Zimachatike* was significant for *Tingathe!*, the theatre project funded by UNIFEM, a play which told the story of family violence against a fictional woman, designed to draw attention to the problems of family violence within a Malawian context. *Tingathe!* was devised as a piece of live theatre by Action Theatre, Story Workshop's community outreach company, and it involved the same performers who appear in the soaps. Radio has made celebrities of these performers, and when they perform live with Action Theatre their popularity not only guarantees large audiences (2000 people is not unusual), they will often also adopt the same role they play in the soap opera. As audiences already know the characters well, the cast are able to take some short-cuts in performance, and this enables the audience to focus quickly on the particular issues the plays seek to explore. It also means that the audiences' perceptions of the celebrity performers and their dramatic roles are interestingly layered. Audiences are often complicit in the illusion that soap characters are 'real people' and this means that performers themselves become intimately connected with the genre. Furthermore, as Frances Harding has observed, audiences for African theatre often perceive the performers' identities in the context of their extended repertoire *as* performers.

> Performers and their acts are judged by spectators at multiple levels: as part of the repertoire of the performer, as part of the performer's whole performance on any one occasion and, in comparison with other like artefacts, as part of a *genre*.[25]

As a genre, soap opera sets up certain expectations of character and familiar patterns of plot which can be both sustained and disrupted in live theatre. Action Theatre have exploited the productive tension between the real and the imaginary which exists in all live theatre, but which is all the more acute in this delicious interpretation of performative identities.

When I visited Story Workshop in 2002, the company was in the process of devising *Tingathe!* Action Theatre perform in Chichewa, the national language most widely spoken in Malawi, and at the time there were two mzungus (white people) working with the cast, Louise Keyworth as director and Kathryn Pugh as her assistant. In the devising process, the significance of this intercultural dialogue became apparent, both in the play's form and content. Story Workshop's policy of including the performative traditions of Malawi within their creative output is regarded as an important educational tool in an increasingly urbanised society, and local songs, proverbs, parables and folk tales are integrated into their live theatre as well as their radio programmes. The Malawi actors had considerable local knowledge of these forms of performance, had extensive ability to improvise both musically and dramatically. They were also able to bring their understanding of how symbolism and metaphor worked in different forms of local performance, which the English directors obviously lacked. The directors, by contrast, had been trained in the tradition of European theatre, and their experiences gave them access to processes of rehearsal and devising which had been unfamiliar to the actors. The combination of these different experiences and cultural backgrounds contributed to a rich melting pot of genres and styles on which the company could draw. Not only was this artistically exciting, the process of collaboration and intercultural dialogue also revealed some of the ways in which dramatic genres imply different ways of thinking about the world.

There was one particular moment in rehearsal which demonstrated to me that the blurring of genres can create new insights into the local and international politics of human rights. The story revolved around a woman, Mrs Mbewe, who had been beaten in her home by her husband, and when I arrived in Malawi the company were at the point in the devising process where they needed to discuss how the plot should develop and, more particularly, what should happen to the abused woman. If she were to leave her husband, she would be ostracised by her community, become economically destitute and homeless. If she stayed, the beatings would doubtless continue as the husband was showing no remorse for his actions and was even justifying them. The actors agreed that this was likely to be the reality of the situation in Malawi, but they were genuinely surprised to hear that family violence is also prevalent in England. In the discussions about her fate, the cast felt that it was important that the audience sympathised with the abused women. This had inevitably given rise to discussions about dramatic form. As director, Louise had suggested that they experimented with naturalism as a form of representation – the subject of this play afforded a good opportunity for these highly skilled professional actors to learn to use Stanislavski's method. As a result of working on the physical and psychological objectives of their roles in different situations, they built characters to whom they hoped the audience would be able to respond emotionally. Contrary to local expectations that live theatre is comic entertainment, this play was intended to be serious and sombre in mood. To this end the cast used three tempos to control the pace and dramatic atmosphere – angry and explosive, heavy and painful, and tense and anxious. It was decided that the mood would be reinforced in performance by the Joker, who would establish a contract with the audience at the beginning of the play. This was a risk, as it was a form of live theatre which was culturally unfamiliar.

The crunch came on the second day I attended rehearsals. The central problem – should Mrs Mbewe leave her husband – had been resolved by a phone call to Pamela Brooke, the American founder and then director of Story Workshop, who strongly advised that she should leave. The company were uncomfortable about this decision and, as an observer in the process, so was I. I was concerned that this decision was based on an Anglo-American feminist answer to family violence and, although I would generally subscribe to this position at home, I feared that in the context of Malawi the resolution did not take full account of how the woman would be treated by her local community if she were to leave her husband. But it was a decision, and the company set about trying to make it work both theatrically and politically. They decided to dramatise the dilemma the woman faced, and invite the audience to discuss her situation after the performance. At the centre of the performance space they constructed a crossroads, which provided a simple theatrical metaphor for the woman's troubled decision. Standing at this powerful central point, the cast improvised a song using the traditional Malawi form of call-and-response which underscored a soliloquy spoken by Mrs Mbewe. It was the meeting point of different theatrical genres, and each had a different dramatic purpose. The soliloquy was designed to elicit audiences' imaginative sympathy for – or empathy with – her emotional turmoil as an individual, and the song suggested a strong collective voice. The soliloquy and song shared the same words, but the aesthetic created a deeper political dialectic. Soliloquy is a theatrical interpretation of the tradition of Western individualism, whereas the call-and-response song invokes the oral and communitarian culture of African performance. In rehearsal this combination of individualism and communitarianism was a powerful and moving way of representing the play's political problem. The cast were aware that audiences would know what would happen to her if she left her violent husband, and they thought it likely that some audience members would be complicit in ostracising someone in her position. But they hoped that, in performance, the sympathy she had gained as a character would make her actions comprehensible. Having left Malawi before the performance took place, I am dependent on Louise Keyworth's description of the event.

The first performance of *Tingathe!* was in a small town outside Blantyre, renowned for its poverty-driven crime. A local man had recently killed and dismembered two women there. We arrived at the open area next to the market. We felt very exposed and the team was apprehensive about performing a controversial piece that was experimental in a part of town we usually all avoided.

Curious, crowds gathered, pushed and shouted as we set up the arena. We dug holes in the ground for the stakes then tied them with rubber to keep the audience out – comprising passers-by and those doing nothing in particular. People asked questions: Is it really their favourite characters Chithope and Nabanda from *Zimachitika*? Are they going to perform? And who are the two white women banging hammers and doing manual work? The atmosphere felt full of aggression. Kat let go of a stretched rubber-band that flew back and knocked her over. The onlookers' laughter was loud and disconcerting.

When we started the arena was surrounded by around a thousand people. Typically in Malawi, audiences laugh when something serious is performed. The Joker challenged the audience directly as Mr Mbewe hit his wife for the first time. It went quiet for two reasons, I think. Firstly, the Joker's words had an effect: 'Why do you laugh my friends? We are not here to make you laugh, see the seriousness…etc.' Secondly, the naturalistic acting style was unfamiliar to most audiences in Malawi. The laughter swapped to tutting and the culturally familiar sound of surprise (a fast, low 'Aah-ahh!'). Their noises became angry and disapproving at the violent moments and verbal abuse. The atmosphere became serious and the previous sense of aggression faded. Women stood alone, thinking, concentrating – different to the usual groups of girlfriends watching something together.

At the end fifteen people entered the arena for the audience-participation session. They were asked if Mrs Mbewe should have left her husband and to stand on the spot that represented their view. The options were 'Yes', 'No' and 'Don't know'. At first most people were equally spilt between Yes and No. One older woman stood at 'Don't know'. The participants hot-seated the characters. The older woman, who was undecided, spoke eloquently and addressed everyone listening. She said the decision was tricky and although violence is wrong Mrs Mbewe's life would be more difficult for cultural reasons. A lively discussion ensued, facilitated by the Joker. At the end of it, participants had the option of moving to a different floor cloth if they'd changed their mind. Twelve moved to 'Don't know' leaving one person on 'Yes' and one on 'No'. The participation at the end of the piece made Mrs Mbewe's choice ambiguous. We all left without resolving the story, deliberately.[26]

This description suggests that the audience's expectations were disrupted by the use of elements of dramatic form which were culturally unfamiliar. The change in the audiences' reactions – from laughter at the husband's beating to an intense silence – implies an empathetic engagement with the play that was profoundly personal, emphasised by the observation that women in the audience moved to watch alone. By showing the emotional effects of family abuse on an individual in the performance, and by presenting an unresolved and unresolvable dilemma in the participatory programme, the audience were invited to respond sympathetically to Mrs Mbewe as an individual, to question their cultural values towards family violence, and examine community responsibilities towards the abused woman. The play had contextualised the human rights 'issue' of family violence, and the ambiguity inherent in the dramatic form recognised its political and cultural complexities. In this instance the intercultural dialogue enabled the company to blur artistic genres, with the effect of making accepted values strange, as if they were viewed from another place.

Tingathe! affords a good opportunity to analyse the political and artistic potential for intercultural dialogue in theatre which seeks to promote human rights. Intercultural dialogue has been described by Rustom Bharucha as a process of 'seeking the familiar in the unfamiliar, the unfamiliar in the familiar'. Such an exchange of cultural capital is not easily equitable and involves not only aesthetic choices but, in Bharucha's words, the ability to 'negotiate different systems of power'.[27] By focusing on the dialogue between European and

FIGURE 2   THE PERFORMANCE OF *TINGATHE!* (PHOTOGRAPHED BY LOUISE KEYWORTH)

Malawian practitioners in this analysis of practice I have, however, given the misleading impression that Malawian culture is homogeneous and internally cohesive, which is very far from the case. As a way of conceptualising the differences within cultures Bharucha has made a useful distinction between *inter*culturalism and *intra*culturalism, terms which he uses to differentiate 'intercultural relations *across* national boundaries, and the intracultural dynamics between and across specific communities and regions *within* the boundaries of the nation-state'.[28] This insight offers a way of analysing how different cultural dynamics found within national boundaries might affect the processes of social change. As no culture is a fixed and stable entity, there are always points of cultural continuity and discontinuity within cultures which means that change takes place. For this process to be productive, Bharucha argues, there needs to be a negotiation of the intracultural space between 'the stabilities of cultural diversity and the indeterminacies of cultural difference'.[29]

The significance of intraculturalism to the process of human rights mobilisation is evident both in the international funding of such projects, but also in the ways in which many cultural NGOs work in partnership with other local organisations. The example that is often offered in this context is Philippine Educational Theater Association (PETA), one of the most experienced and highly respected companies in the world. PETA documented their contribution to a campaign against family violence that took place in 1998–99 called *Breaking Silence*, and this has provide a model for subsequent inter-agency work across the world, including New Zealand's Everyday Theatre.[30] *Breaking Ground* arose from long-term partnerships within the Philippines between PETA, the National Family Violence Prevention Programme (NFVPP) and the Women's Crisis Center. Describing family violence as 'the gravest form of human rights violation' because it turns the safe space of home into a place of danger, the campaigning organisations identified the need for a change in *culture* if women were to be supported in disclosing cases of abuse.[31] Their intention was to use theatre to challenge the attitude that family violence is a private matter by bringing the issue into the public domain and inviting people to talk about it within the safe space of participatory workshops. Research undertaken in advance of the project revealed the nature and extent of family abuse in the Philippines, but significantly it also provided statistical information about the problem on an international scale. Acknowledging that family violence is a global problem placed the attitude found in parts of the Philippines that domestic violence is just 'part of family life' in a wider social context. This research process also provided important information PETA needed to develop a piece of theatre which would both encourage reciprocity and dialogue between audience and performers, and present a clear message that family violence is a matter of public responsibility as a violation of international standards of human rights.[32]

One of the striking aspects of the campaign was that it acknowledged that combating family violence is an extremely complex and multi-layered process because there are different attitudes towards it within any given culture or community. In order to address these intracultural differences, the campaign was structured to offer considerable support and information to women in a variety of ways. PETA worked alongside local and community-based organisations, with NGOs, local government agencies, universities, religious groups and youth organisations in order to address the various and different struggles against family violence experienced across the country. As a direct result of their theatrical intervention, there was an increase in the numbers of abused women seeking help and advice from appropriate agencies. Not only does this multi-agency approach recognise that family violence is not an issue which can be seen in isolation from other cultural values, it also acknowledges that, although theatre is a good form of communication and social mobilisation, on its own it is an incomplete weapon against social injustice.

These projects show that even the most humanitarian interventions are not border-free, but are located on *inter* and *intra* cultural routes of dialogue and exchange. Effective campaigns relate human rights principles to the vernacular and to the everyday practices of life, a process which Richard Wilson has suggested offers the potential to turn the idealistic intentions of an international human rights framework to social action by recognising the cultural contradictions inherent in particular local contexts. Cultures are continually reformulated through creative practice, leading to optimistic encounters between the specificity of local cultures and normative vocabulary of human rights. Theatre has the potential to trouble absolutes and, at best, the aesthetics of production can encourage a reflexivity and a sharing of experience which can contribute to the process of unfixing habitual patterns of thought and behaviour.

Narrating Human Rights

Any perspective on human rights would be disingenuous and incomplete without some serious reflection on its implications at home as well as internationally. I am conscious that all the examples of practice

I have offered so far in this chapter refer to work outside my own British context, for which I might be justly criticised for giving the impression that human rights violations happen 'elsewhere' and that everything in the European garden is rosy. This is not only very far from the actual case, it would also offer a narrow picture of human rights as a collection of social issues rather than, as I have argued, integral to a system of liberal governance. Noam Chomsky rightly points out that powerful nations, including Britain and the US, invoke human rights as justification for military intervention. Writing before the allied forces' war on Iraq, Chomsky cites many cases of human rights violation in the US, such as child poverty, enforced prison labour, and the cases of juvenile offenders sitting on death row.[33] As a conclusion to this chapter, therefore, I should like to take the discussion of the application of theatre to human rights in a slightly different direction. I shall take up Derrida's challenge to construct a poetics of human rights in relation to applied theatre by re-examining some of the recurring themes in this book.

In his lecture entitled 'On Writing Rights', Homi Bhabha described the politics of human rights as a 'process of making connections' between divergent perspectives. Citing Adrienne Rich's poem *Movement,* he argued that constructing an equitable ethic of human rights involves reimagining the construction of human identity not as a series of fixed oppositions (self/other; minority/majority) but as process of movement between different cultural milieux. Not only does Bhabha make a significant point about how the 'human' of human rights is not universal but a cultural category, he also suggests that the process of moving towards equality involves individuals confronting their own demons, desires and motivations. This recognises that individuals inhabit dialogical spaces in which they continually negotiate and renegotiate a sense of who they are and who they might become, in narrative and through conversation. It brings together the ethics of human rights – its legal and formal frameworks – with the aesthetics of self-construction. Describing narrative as 'a moving sign of civic life', he suggests that it is the 'right to narrate' which enables people to re-cognise their own experiences, re-interpret history and change the direction of the future. His words have such resonance with the themes in this book that they are worth quoting at length:

> By the 'right to narrate', I mean to suggest all those forms of creative behaviour that allow us to represent the lives we lead, question the conversations and customs that we inherit, dispute and propagate the ideas and ideals that come to us most naturally, and dare to entertain the most

audacious hopes and fears for the future… Suddenly in painting, dance, or cinema you rediscover your senses, and in that process you discover something profound about yourself, your historical moment, and what gives value to a life in a particular town, at a particular time, in particular social and political conditions.[34]

Bhabha's emphasis on narrative and contextuality is important here, as it shows that human rights are not experienced solely as social 'issues', but are played out in the dialogic space of everyday existence. The practice of the arts enables experiences to be framed and, I am suggesting, practising drama is a process which often involves experiencing life from different perspectives. The interweaving of ethics and aesthetics implies a journey or movement, in which we are asked not only to consider where we are, but to question which way we are going.

Bhabha's concept of the right to narrate locates human rights in the performative practices of everyday life, where an awareness of social justice is articulated in people's behaviour and attitudes towards others. It also draws attention to political questions about the aesthetics of applied theatre, and about who has access to the means of cultural expression and where this right to narrate is denied or suppressed. It is here that the theatre has a particular social and artistic role, both in raising awareness of contemporary concerns and in telling stories from perspectives that may not otherwise be heard. Representing human rights abuses or matters of social injustice has found a particular place in theatre through documentary performance, where 'real' events, told authentically and sometimes in the words of the people involved, can be witnessed. The process of creating such performances is often a mix of archival research and interview, sometimes with people at a vulnerable point in their lives. Janelle Reinelt comments that documentary theatre is often inspired by 'private individuals' who have come to 'public prominence' through the circumstances of their deaths.[35] She cites Matthew Shepherd, Stephen Lawrence, Rachel Corrie and David Kelly, all of whom became the subject of documentary plays. Philip Ralph's play *Deep Cut* adds to this list. First performed at the Edinburgh Festival in 2008, and staged at the Tricycle Theatre in 2008, *Deep Cut* narrates the story of four soldiers whose deaths from gunshot wounds at Deepcut barracks in the UK between 1995 and 2002 remain unexplained. The barracks was known for a culture of bullying and abuse, and although the deaths were considered to be suicide, it has been widely claimed that this verdict contradicts forensic evidence. In an interview with the *Guardian*, the parents of Cheryl James, one of the soldiers who died, were asked if the theatre was the right place to explore such an issue:

> We want people to listen to the story and be concerned, because... this hasn't been resolved. The government has told you that it has, the MOD has told you it has been resolved, but it hasn't been... why are we as a society being forced to look at this situation, and ask these questions on a... on a stage? Is that the correct forum? No of course it isn't. The right forum is a court, where witnesses can be cross-examined, and witnesses can be subpoenaed to answer the judge.[36]

The play allowed audiences to witness the evidence of this case from different perspectives and points of view, and as such, performances hold a powerful role in bringing to a public audience questions of social justice that have been ignored or silenced by official narratives. In her ground-breaking book, *Performance in a Time of Terror: Critical Mimesis and the Age of Uncertainty*, Jenny Hughes comments that 'the critical potential of verbatim theatre resides in its dramatisation and abjection of the voice during a time of crisis, rather than a revitalising contribution to democracy in practice', a perspective that is particularly evident in the interview with Cheryl James's parents.[37]

The case of the Deepcut soldiers resonates with much practice invoked in this book and, in many ways, lies at the heart of applied theatre. The process of narrating and witnessing events is not, in itself, any guarantee of human rights or social justice, and it is here that the political metaphor of the gift remains important. The ambiguity surrounding the gift serves as a reminder that there is no direct elision between theatre and human rights, and that there is a need for constant vigilance about whose concept of 'rights' and 'humanity' are being promoted. There is further potential here to interrogate the limits of linguistic analysis as a frame of reference within a broader ecology of the material world, and to understand that in some ways every social encounter is a performative negotiation of human rights. Derrida's concept of a poetics of human rights might be extended to recognise that there is an affective dimension to ethical social interactions that extend beyond traditional humanist conceptions of the world. Following this line of thought, Rosi Braidotti suggests that what is needed is an 'affirmative politics' that is 'rooted in the micro-practices of everyday life' and 'expresses the multiple ecologies of belonging'.[38] This is, I think, the ethical, intellectual and creative challenge for the twenty-first century, to understand that human *and non-human* rights are practised only when the dialectic between self and other is troubled and the fixed polarity between the human and non-human world is challenged. In this context, therefore, one of the social purposes of theatre becomes to radically reaffirm an assured sense of selfhood within a material and relational world. A poetics of human rights is about taking collective responsibility for the performance of rights, and recognising the creative opportunities afforded by envisioning how social change might be beneficial, and whose interests it serves. This approach to human rights is inherently dramatic and performative because it is affectively engaged, unites the personal with the political, the public with the private, thought and action, and asks all of us to make a daily commitment to redefining human rights for the future.

Part IV
Epilogue

8 The Gift of Theatre

Becoming Ethical

In the opening scene of Rebecca Prichard's play *Yard Gal* the stage directions state that the two characters, Boo and Marie, stare at the floor to avoid looking at the audience as each waits for the other to begin the play. When they do eventually start to speak, it is to goad each other on.

> BOO: Wh' you looking at me for?
> MARIE: Uh?
> BOO: Wha' you looking at me for, man?
> MARIE: Ain't you gonna start it?
> BOO: I ain't starting it start what?
> MARIE: Fuck you man, the play.
> BOO: I ain't tellin' them shit.
> MARIE: What?
> BOO: I ain't telling them shit. If you wanna make a fool of yaself it's up to you. I ain't telling them shit.
> MARIE: You said you's gonna back me up! You said you's gonna back me up tellin' the story.[1]

Yard Gal was written as a result of the playwright's residency at Bulwood Hall women's prison in 1997, and was commissioned by Clean Break Theatre Company as part of their work with women prisoners and ex-offenders. First staged at the Royal Court Theatre Upstairs in London, the play's opening implies a question mark over whether these young women will choose to tell their stories to this audience, whether they will decide to reveal the circumstances which led to Boo's imprisonment to 'them'. This ambiguity was emphasised in the first production by playing the lines with humour; the actors' body language and banter

161

suggested that there was a difference between what the characters actually said – 'I ain't tellin' them shit' – and what they would like to do, which was to enact their stories for a live and captive audience.

I have chosen this theatrical moment to begin this chapter because it raises a number of ethical questions which I should like to revisit and to explore a little further. One of the noticeable qualities of the script is that the characters acknowledge the presence of the audience, introducing themselves in a way which assumes that there are differences between their narratives and experiences and those of the theatre-going audience.

> BOO: We's from Hackney. People talk a lot of shit about Hackney when they ain't never been there, and they talk a lot of shit about yards when they ain't never met none. So me and Maria we come to tell you a story that is FI' REAL.[2]

There is a sense that these characters, though fictional, are putting the record straight about 'real' young women in the criminal justice system by inviting the audience to witness their stories. By referencing the theatricality of the play there is a sense that Prichard is also gesturing towards the context of her residency in which the play was researched. The dialogue acknowledges the understandable ambivalence many feel about revealing their personal narratives so publicly in drama, and the device of re-enacting apparently autobiographical narratives to a live audience also has the effect of honouring the voices of the prisoners who worked with the playwright during her residency. This blurring of fiction and lived experience implies that there are personal and social benefits for both the young women and for the play's audiences. The characters offer a commentary on the stories they enact which demonstrates how reflecting on experience in drama can lead to new insights and ways of thinking. For the audience, the act of witnessing the narratives of struggle and friendship enables them to see 'yard gals' in a different light. Although the yard gals initially view the audience with suspicion, they act generously towards the audience by inviting them into their world through their stories. Taken together, this play raises ethical questions about whose stories are told in drama, about the context and ownership of autobiographical stories, about the power of narrative to effect social change and, by extension, about the relationships of trust and reciprocity between practitioners and participants in applied theatre – all key themes in this book.

Throughout this book I have been concerned with furthering a praxis which, like *Yard Gal*, both bears witness to a plurality of voices and experiences and maintains a commitment to a radical social democracy. Finding a balance (rather than a compromise) between equality and difference is not a matter of moral relativism, where all values are seen to be equally legitimate. Rather, I am interested in developing a praxis which, whilst based on secure principles, does not seek to discriminate against a plurality of perspectives and multiple ways of living. In this respect, the distinction between ethics and morality made by Chantal Mouffe is illuminating. She describes ethics as 'a domain which allows for competing conceptions of the good life' and morality as 'a domain where a strict proceduralism can be implemented and impartiality reached leading to the formulation of universal principles'.[3] Critical of the implication that morality is remote from political concerns, Mouffe's advocacy of a revitalised democracy is based on the view that there needs to be constant vigilance over what constitutes contemporary notions of the 'the good life' if its ethical limits are to be explored and contested. With this in mind, it is the ethics of practice in applied theatre which is the subject of this final chapter. What does it mean to act ethically in contexts where there are 'competing conceptions of the good life' amongst participants and practitioners in applied theatre?

One practical answer to this question might be found in the various guidelines for conduct laid down by professional associations in, for example, dramatherapy and for educational research. These tend to emphasise the need to secure the participants' informed consent to practice and research, and require prescribed levels of confidentiality and competence.[4] The application of drama to community settings is, however, often unregulated and, although standards of professionalism are obviously extremely important, the terms and conditions of codes and contracts are often only invoked when they are seriously transgressed. It is helpful, therefore, to look beyond these standards and for practitioners to consider what is involved in realising ethical partnerships with institutions, social agencies or organisations, with funders and, most importantly, with the participants themselves. These can be difficult sets of negotiations, as there are sometimes conflicting interests at stake, which makes the need for an ethics of praxis all the more acute.

An ethic of praxis which acknowledges and interrogates the 'competing conceptions of the good life' which Mouffe described has been offered by Patti Lather in her article 'Applying Derrida: (Mis)Reading the Work of Mourning in Educational Research' (2003). Lather has critiqued her own assumptions about a praxis based on ideas of 'transformative intellectuals' who work towards 'empowering' or 'emancipating' others, assumptions originally put forward in 1986 and reprinted in her much cited book *Getting Smart* (1991). This easy symmetry between moral action and social transformation, she argues, is no longer compatible with a post-Marxist era in which straightforward equations between 'uncovering [the] hidden forces' of power and social enlightenment have been troubled.[5] Drawing on the ethical preoccupations of Jacques Derrida, Lather offers a way of salvaging many of the political aspirations of Marxism without resorting to the 'dream of cure, salvation and redemption' so often invoked in the rhetoric of theatre practitioners working in community arts.[6] In place of redemption narratives, Lather argues for an ethical praxis that 'disrupts horizons' and, in terms similar to those I identified in Chapter 3, for pedagogies which map 'new possibilities for playing out relations between identity and difference, margins and centres'.[7]

I should like to respond to Lather's challenge to reinscribe praxis, and to Mouffe's call for an ethic of social responsibilities based on a 'never-ending interrogation of the political by the ethical' by returning to the metaphor of the gift. My intention in this final chapter is to draw together some thoughts about the ethics of practice in applied theatre through this theoretical lens. Before I revisit the concept of the gift as a political metaphor that unites the themes of this book, however, I shall attempt to offer a brief summary of some of the distinct arguments in previous chapters as a way of refocusing on the book's core debates.

Becoming Ethical: Revisiting the Scene

The central debate in this book is political. The task I set myself in writing this book was to find ways of conceptualising and articulating practice which maintains and renews the radicalism which has been traditionally associated with community-based theatre, but does not rely on the 'dream of cure, salvation and redemption' which Lather identified as politically limiting in the new world (dis)order. In raising questions about the values of applied theatre, it has not been my intention to suggest that applied theatre is a new discipline with fixed boundaries or predetermined practices. On the contrary, I have suggested that the theories and practices of applied theatre are continually on the move and always renegotiated in relation to changing environments, contexts and material circumstances. Consequently, my attempt to map and narrate the theoretical terrain of applied theatre is based on the premise that, because it involves a process of encounter and engagement, applied theatre is more helpfully conceptualised as a diaspora, rather than disciplinary, space.

In diaspora space, the boundaries which define and confine knowledge, meaning-making and understanding are subject to continual critical scrutiny, and the ways in which power is constructed are closely examined. Rather than seeking a single canonical reference point or a single set of dramatic practices, it is an approach to theatre-making which embraces diverse forms of cultural learning and many different theatre forms. The concept of diaspora space also has the potential to offer ways of thinking about how boundaries are encountered and transgressed, how those on the margins can move to the centre, and how the global asserts itself into the local. As a framework for analysis, this recognises that the process of locating, mapping narrating enables us to more fully appreciate where, temporarily and contingently, the horizons and limits of practice in applied theatre may lie. Aesthetic and performative encounters within diasporic spaces also require the capacity to move around and negotiate different locations, not as the meeting place of fixed identities or positions, but as an open state of becoming. With this in mind, it is worth revisiting the place where I started, and looking at the scene from a different point of view.

The premise with which I began the research for this book was that there are major theoretical concepts that applied theatre calls us to interrogate – community, citizenship, identity, human rights, creativity, the effects and efficacy of narrative – all of which invite us to consider important questions about the wider role and significance of theatre in society. In many ways, the application of theatre to community contexts presses us to confront questions about the ethics of performance which are relevant to all theatre practices but often remain at the level of rhetoric or advocacy elsewhere. I have argued that, at best, the dynamic of live theatre challenges the predictability and sameness of globalisation, and offers creative reinterpretations of what it means to live well and to live ethically. In the period that has intervened since writing the first edition of this book in 2003, I have become increasingly alert to the ways in which practice in applied theatre might (or should) be informed by posthumanist debates in relation to affect, ecology, environmentalism and subjectivity. By raising these issues in this book, I am suggesting that human agency is not only bound up with community and location, but part of also a wider ontology of material and affective engagements with the human and non-human world.

It is not only social participation that has the potential to stretch the ethical imagination but, I contend, calls for a better world which can only be sustained within a wider sensory attentiveness and ethical commitment to the non-human world. My suggestion is that affective engagement in theatre is not simply related to human action and emotions, but invites attentiveness to the ways in which the material world of bodies and objects are complexly intertwined with immaterial ideas and values. What becomes particularly apparent when applied theatre is understood in this way, is that there is always a need to be vigilant about whether the practice is accepted as a generous exercise of care or whether, however well-intentioned, it is regarded as an invasive act or unwelcome intrusion. It is easy for trust to become dependency, for generosity to be interpreted as patronage, for interest in others to be experienced as the gaze of surveillance. As a way of engaging further with this complex debate, I shall return to the metaphor of the gift.

The Metaphor of the Gift

Pierre Bourdieu commented that 'the major characteristic of the experience of the gift is, without doubt, its ambiguity'.[8] Because it is concerned with how values are articulated in diverse social and cultural practices, gift theory also has the potential to offer an ethical alternative to the kind of salvation narratives critiqued by Lather. The application of gift theory to applied theatre is a way of acknowledging the positive attributes of empathy, generosity and care for others which characterises much good practice. Equally significant, however, are the less positive characteristics of the gift, such as self-interest or the system of debts and social obligations which are sometimes associated with the act of giving. It is the ethical problems and uncertainties raised by the metaphor of the gift which makes its application to theatre particularly illuminating. I shall begin by discussing the less positive attributes of the gift, which dominated much early writing in gift theory, before considering the principles of reciprocity and generosity with which it is also associated. As the quotation with which I began this chapter suggests, the experience of the gift is often paradoxical.

The theme of the gift, which has become important to discussions of value in gender studies, economics, philosophy and anthropology and to interdisciplinary debates about ethics, found an early articulation in the work of the French social anthropologist Marcel Mauss. Mauss's essay *The Gift* was first published in 1924 and has formed a touchstone for subsequent discussions. In this essay, Mauss noted that the etymology of *gift* in Germanic languages have given rise to the words both 'present' and 'poison'. He traces this history to gifts of drink offered between ancient Germans and Scandinavians, where the recipients were never quite sure whether their drinks would be poisoned or not. Mauss uses this example to indicate the state of uncertainty associated with the gift, which might be experienced as either pleasure or displeasure. With this in mind, he documented the use and symbolism of gifts in societies he considered archaic, and was amongst the earliest in anthropology to identify the coercive function of gift-giving. In his discussion of the elaborate potlatch ceremonies in communities such as the Kwakiutl in the northwest Pacific, he noted that the aim of gift-giving was to overwhelm rivals with presents which they were both obliged to reciprocate, but which were so 'generous' that they could not possibly repay them. The potlatch symbolised, for Mauss, gift-giving at its most self-interested. His intention in this work was to isolate how aspects of the gift become tied to economic self-interest and thence to a nexus of other social obligations. He described his study of

> presentations which are in theory voluntary, disinterested and spontaneous, but are in fact voluntary and interested. The form usually taken is that of the gift generously offered; but the accompanying behaviour is formal pretence and social deception, while the transaction itself is based on obligation and self-interest.[9]

Despite the many counter-arguments and objections to Mauss's thesis which have since been offered, his observations about the relationship between disinterestedness and self-interest continue to exert a powerful influence on gift theory.

Mauss's legacy has relevance for applied theatre insofar as it problematises the relationship between gift-givers and recipients. It serves as a useful reminder that not all acts of giving are made unconditionally and that, as I pointed out in Chapter 2, self-interest plays a part in many exchanges. This is not necessarily a bad thing; there many rewards associated with working in applied theatre which, I suggest, might be more fully acknowledged by artists, particularly where the balance of power or material wealth between donor and recipient is already uneven. As I have argued throughout this book, the desire for equity and social participation is a major preoccupation for theatre practitioners who apply their craft to different and often complex settings and communities. What a reading of gift theory adds to this debate is a way to question the ethics and motives of the various agencies and individuals which contribute to practice. What do we, as practitioners, expect in return for our labours? Artistic satisfaction? The participants' acquisition of skills or abilities? International travel? Do we ask participants to adopt ways of thinking or different political values that are more closely aligned to our own? Do we expect them to change their behaviour in particular ways? In turn, how far might our own perspectives alter as a result of the work? What about the funders? Do they have expectations of a return? How does the choice of materials and mode of transport impact on the environment? None of these questions can be answered glibly. The paradox of the gift is that, because it can be seen simultaneously as both a present and a poison, it is sometimes worth remembering the unpalatable truth that a gift, however well intentioned, may be thought to be poisonous by those who live in a different context and whose vision of a good life differs from our own.

Although Mauss's analysis of the ethics of gift exchange remains influential, his critics have pointed out that he paid scant attention to forms of giving which are less binding and socially contractual. More recently, concern for an ethic of social welfare has ensured that the more positive attributes of the gift have been well theorised, most conspicuously by the French social theorists and philosophers Hélène Cixous, Jacques Derrida and Pierre Bourdieu. In his work *Given Time* (1992) Derrida challenges the circle of obligation described by Mauss and, in the opening pages, reinscribes the gift as a more open and generous expression of desires and responsibilities. He is interested in developing a new theoretical tradition for the gift which 'interrupts the system as well as the symbol' of debt, counter-giving, credit and the social obligations associated with reciprocal patterns of exchange. He suggests that one of the problems is that as soon as the gift becomes identified as a gift, it has already acquired a symbolism which distorts its value. For Derrida, a gift is made voluntarily and unconditionally, not as an economic exchange, as capitalism invariably requires, but as an ethical alternative to self-interest. He suggests that, when the gift acquires symbolic value, it is already caught up in a chain of exchange:

> For the symbol immediately engages one in resituation. To tell the truth, the gift must not even appear or signify, consciously or unconsciously *as* gift for the donors, whether individual or collective subjects. For the moment the gift would appear as gift... it would be engaged in a symbolic, sacrificial, or economic structure that would annul the gift in the ritual circle of debt.[10]

The gift, for Derrida, is always ethical, but the paradox is that it is inevitably destroyed when it becomes embroiled in cycles of reciprocity.

Because the gift is annulled when it is recognised as a gift, Derrida describes it not as an impossibility, but as 'the impossible'. This means that although it is possible to conceive of the gift in terms which are entirely selfless and generous, the practice of giving always locates it in particular systems of value. Cycles of giving and counter-giving, therefore, are based on common principles of value, where the codes are shared and understood. Derrida suggests that changing the values of society or the dynamics of a relationship requires this symmetry and homogeneity to break, a process that might be achieved if the gift is relocated in the ethical gap between the impossible (a 'pure' gift) and the thinkable (an ethical culture). Such asymmetrical patterns of giving are acts of resistance, challenging those reciprocal relations between donor and recipient which are driven by a political economy based on market exchange. By refusing to reduce the gift to reciprocity, Derrida replaces the homogeneity of a fixed system of economic exchange with the heterogeneity of generosity, in which the gift becomes associated with shifting roles, spontaneity, desire, loss and risk.

In place of the narratives of redemption and salvation, the metaphor of the gift offers a way of examining both the positive qualities of social interaction and those based on less equitable principles. It also points to the political complexities of cultural exchange and the ethical promises and pitfalls associated with social intervention. It is precisely because the gift is unstable, because it has the potential to interrupt established patterns of social interaction and disrupt old certainties, that it provides such a powerful metaphor for the ethics of applied theatre. In following Derridean thought, Lather similarly calls for a praxis based on 'undecidability, incompleteness and dispersion rather than the comforts of transformation and closure'.[11] Applied to theatre, this theoretical reading of the gift relationship acknowledges the risks, contradictions and uncertainties of theatre-making in community settings. It also offers an opportunity to renew a commitment to openness, in which practitioners recognise that their role is not to *give* participants a voice – with all the hierarchical and authoritarian implications that phrase invokes – but to create spaces and places which enable the participants' voices to be heard.

Acts of Giving

As Derrida implies, a significant element of gift-giving practices which is under-emphasised by theories of contractual exchange is the role of the emotions. Gifts are not, of course, always reducible to the political values of the marketplace, and there are many aspects of gift-giving that differ from commercial forms of transaction. Many people enjoy giving and receiving, and although gift-giving practices tell conflicting narratives, there is also a need to recognise that the practice of giving is not always logical, safe and rational but is also (following Derrida) spontaneous, risky and emotional. It is the aspect of the gift which relates to the emotions which has particular relevance for artistic practice, and which I should like to explore a little further in relation to applied theatre.

In her essay on the social and emotional significance of the gift, Lee Anne Fennell suggests that gifts are set apart from ordinary commodities because they are specifically chosen for someone else as part of a process of sustaining and deepening personal relationships. In terms similar to those I discussed in Chapter 4, she uses the phrase 'empathetic dialogue' to describe the most positive aspects of gift-giving in which both donor and recipient gain emotional pleasure. A successful gift, she argues, involves the donor putting herself in the recipients' place and imagining not only what they would like, but also what they would like to receive from this particular person. In turn, recipients imagine the donor's 'empathetic efforts' to find the right gift, and it acquires sentimental value which has little to do with its market value. This form of empathetic dialogue, she suggests, is based on desire.

> The desire to identify with another; the desire to have one's true preferences divined by another (even when those preferences may not even be clear to oneself); the desire to surprise and be surprised.[12]

Giving gifts, she concludes, is part of a 'specialised communication' through which donors are able to express feelings which may not be easily put into words.

Fennell's version of gift-giving is intentionally idealised, and relies on mutual affection between donor and recipients. Her insights into the role of the imagination, positive identification with others and empathy suggest that there is an artfulness about giving and receiving. The parallels between Fennell's optimistic gift relationship and applied theatre are clear – both encourage relationships of empathy and imaginative identification with the lives of others and there are many examples of such positive interactions in this book. It is significant to the ethics of applied theatre, however, that the positive aspects of gift-giving Fennell describes are not solely based on private acts of friendship. Generous gift relationships have wider social and public significance which has been well theorised, particularly by feminist educationalists and philosophers.[13] Writing from a philosophical perspective, Annette Baier has identified the significance of the emotions in the fabric of society. Baier's central thesis is that interpersonal relationships inspire feelings of trust, neediness and interdependency which are central to public life because they provide the bedrock for a society based on an ethic of care. She argues that caring emotions have been effectively privatised and individualised in Western societies, and she questions how far the 'virtues' of independence, autonomy and self-sufficiency have provided an ethical basis for social welfare. In a veiled reference to Mauss, she comments on the inadequacy of theories of the gift which fail to recognise that it symbolises powerful emotional bonds which are socially productive.

> Only those determined to see every proper moral transaction as an exchange will construe every gift as made in exchange for an IOU, and every return gift made in exchange for a receipt.[14]

For Baier, the social significance of the emotions is that feelings of empathy and affection lead to practical action. In this way she links the gift to the practice of citizenship, recognising that emotional involvement with others is generative of a caring ethic which, in turn, has wider social implications. She suggests that one of the consequences of failing to acknowledge the social role of the emotions has been to render caring roles invisible (historically the lot of women). Her ethic of care is intended to relocate the emotions in a political context, and her thesis is orientated towards to redressing this omission.

What I have suggested here is a way of thinking about the gift which takes it out of Mauss's negative cycle of debt, recognises its contextuality, its relationship to desire, its creativity and other positive social and emotional effects. As I have represented this argument, however, it does not entirely satisfy questions about how the gift might be given and received by those with different or competing conceptions of the good life, and it is based on a political economy that takes little account of wider ecological concerns. It is not difficult to imagine, however, how notions of the gift might extend beyond the circularity of human action and emotion to a more inclusive and affective commitment to the wider ecology of the material world. It is here that the work of the political theorist Jane Bennett is particularly apposite. Bennett is concerned to interrogate the motivations for ethical and generous behaviour from within a political commitment to different forms of agency. She calls for a 're-enchantment' with the material world in ways that is both ethical and aesthetic:

> Enchantment is a feeling of being connected to an affirmative way to existence; it is to be under the momentary impression that the natural and cultural worlds *offer gifts* and, in so doing, remind us that it is good to be alive.[15] (italics in the original)

Bennett describes enchantment as a 'weak ontology' that is neither wholly subjective nor 'as dogmatically heavy as a generalizable truth'.[16] Her notion of enchantment is affective, therefore, in the sense that I have used the term in this book; it has a political dynamic because it invites attentiveness in the performative moment to the sensory world that is both human and non-human. In relation to applied theatre, my suggestion is that the metaphor of the gift draws attention to the relationship between motivation and political action, and in particular invites reflection on the ways in which artistic practice is experienced in multiple, and sometimes contradictory, ways.

I have used the metaphor of the gift to indicate some of the fragilities and ambiguities inherent in acts of giving, however generously they may be intended. The analogy between the gift and applied theatre suggests that the ethical principles on which practice is based require continual negotiation and re-evaluation. Throughout this book I have stressed that a sense of belonging is not always shared, that communities are not inevitably homogeneous, that feelings of affection are not always mutual and dramatic experiences can be differently construed and interpreted. Furthermore, because gifts always carry the imprint of those who gave them, their meanings may change over time. When relationships become stale or unhappy this is often reflected in how gifts are given and received and, as people stop taking time to imagine what another would like, and the elements of desire, spontaneity, or surprise is lost. Gifts which were once thought of with hostility or affection may acquire new interpretations, and looking back on experiences in drama may change their meaning and significance. In other words, becoming ethical is an ongoing process; there is a temporality about the feelings attached to gifts which suggests that all meanings are contingent on context and situation. Giving is not always an easy business, and the practice of care can be tough as well as rewarding. This is the paradox of the gift relationship, and there is no easy resolution to this aporia.

The Art of Giving

I have chosen to conclude this discussion of the art of giving with a final example that will, I hope, bring together some thoughts about the relationship between artistic intervention and the politics of the gift. It is a performative protest in London in July 2012 by the activist group Liberate Tate, who presented a wind turbine blade to the Tate Modern art gallery in London as part of its campaign against its sponsorship by BP oil and the environmental damage caused by this multinational oil and gas company. Carefully cleaned and restored, the one-and-a-half-tonne blade was carried by the activists across the Millennium Bridge over the Thames. They made their way into the Tate's Turbine Hall, stating that they were giving the Tate a new work of contemporary art. Entitled 'The Gift', this performative gesture was a creative act of protest that used the concept of the gift as a political weapon. European law has little to say on the subject of gifting; the activists invoked the Museums and Galleries Act 1992 that requires gallery trustees by law to consider all gifts of art-objects made to the nation. The artists and activists pushed past security guards and police, and the gift was installed in the gallery with the precision of a rehearsed performance. Yet despite the activists' sense of victorious achievement and the obvious delight of gallery visitors, the film shows the sense of rising panic amongst the security guards, most of whom were black employees of a privatised security company who are notorious for their short-term contracts and poor employment practices. At one point in the protest a security man lay down in front of the turbine, whilst the arty (mainly white) activists tried to forge ahead. It made the point, but it was an uncomfortable scene that opened one set of injustices but risked ignoring another. It was well named *The Gift*, partly because of the ambivalent reception of the protesters' polished turbine blade, but also because it revealed another layer of inequality within the asymmetry of gift-giving.[17]

My suggestion is that participation in theatre is a gift and, like other gifts, it can be experienced negatively as well as positively. In all its many guises, practice in applied theatre is undertaken by those who want to touch the lives of others, who hope that participants and audiences will extend their perception of how life is, and imagine how it might be different. Although other forms of theatre-making may share these general experiences and aspirations, what is emphasised in applied theatre is its concern to encourage people to use the experience of participating in theatre to move beyond what they already know.

Applied theatre has a tradition of creative and critical questioning, and the process of interpretation and reinterpretation is central to many of its various practices. It also involves sensory engagement, both collectively and individually, that invites creative and affective engagement in the here-and-now of the performative event. Writing about painting, Merleau-Ponty described this dynamic between creativity and perception. He suggests that, in the arts, meanings are never transparent nor easily interpreted, which is why it is important to look beyond the immediate and obvious and into the blanks the painter leaves between the brush-strokes, or the silences between the words.[18] These gaps are expressive; they invite multiple interpretations, and offer an aesthetic space in which meanings are made.

The artistic practices of applied theatre are rich, imaginative and diverse, and the contexts in which it takes place often present very specific challenges. These encounters between art-form and context mean that the ethical boundaries of practice are likely to be constantly challenged. Becoming ethical, therefore, is an ongoing negotiation rather than an encounter of fixed positions, where ideas and values may be altered, revised or reaffirmed through the process of making art. It thrives on the heterogeneity of diverse contexts because it is through the encounter of difference that the ethical limits of citizenship might be recognised and explored. In these ways and in many others, applied theatre can make a contribution to building a more generous and multifaceted world by making a creative space in which fixed and inequitable oppositions between the local and the global, self and other, fiction and reality, identity and difference, human and non-human might be disrupted and challenged. The gift of applied theatre is that it offers an opportunity for an ethical praxis which disrupts horizons, in which new insights are generated and where the familiar might be seen, embodied and represented from alternative perspectives and different points of view. In the words of Merleau-Ponty, describing the 'embodied agency' of the artist's eye, 'this gift is earned by exercise'.[19]

Notes

Notes to Chapter 1: An Introduction to Applied Drama, Theatre and Performance

1. http://stratfordeast.com/poets-manifesto accessed 15 December 2013.
2. Joan Littlewood, *Joan's Book: Joan's Peculiar History as She Tells It* (London: Methuen, 1994), pp. 702–706.
3. Nadine Holdsworth, *Joan Littlewood's Theatre* (Cambridge: Cambridge University Press, 2011), p. 234.
4. Littlewood, p. 740.
5. In her brilliant book, *Joan Littlewood's Theatre*, Nadine Holdsworth analyses the ways in which Littlewood's children's playground articulates notions of citizenship, and she relates this to debates in applied theatre.
6. Shannon Jackson, *Social Works: Performing Art, Supporting Publics* (London: Routledge, 2011).
7. Judith Ackroyd, 'Applied Theatre: Problems and Possibilities', *Applied Theatre Journal*, 1 (2000): http://www.griffith.edu.au/__data/assets/pdf_file/0004/81796/Ackroyd.pdf accessed 15 December 2013.
8. Quoted in Sharon Grady, 'Accidental Marxists? The Challenge of Critical and Feminist Pedagogies for the Practice of Applied Drama', *Youth Theater Journal*, 17:1 (2003), pp. 65–81, at p. 68. http://dx.doi.org/10.1080/08929092.2003.10012553 accessed 15 December 2013.
9. Nicola Shaughnessy, *Applying Performance: Live Art, Socially Engaged Theatre and Affective Practice* (Basingstoke: Palgrave, 2012), p. 13.
10. James Thompson, *Performance Affects: Applied Theatre and the End of Effect* (Basingstoke: Palgrave, 2009), p. 6.
11. Elspeth Probyn, 'Writing Shame', in M. Gregg and G. Seigworth (eds.), *The Affect Theory Reader* (Durham, NC: Duke University Press, 2010), p. 74.
12. Thompson, p. 3.
13. Bjørn Rasmussen, 'Applied Theater and the Power Play – An International Viewpoint', *Applied Theatre Journal*, 1 (2000): http://www.griffith.edu.au/__data/assets/pdf_file/0006/81798/Rasmussen.pdf accessed 15 December 2013.
14. There are many different sources for this discussion. For a sociological analysis see, for example, Pierre Bourdieu, *The Rules of Art*, trans. S. Emanuel (Cambridge: Polity Press, 1996), pp. 135–8; C. Taylor,

Sources of the Self: The Making of the Modern Identity (Cambridge: Cambridge University Press, 1989) offers a reading of how the artist became integrated into the Western consciousness.

15. Jonothan Neelands, *Beginning Drama 11–14* (London: David Fulton, 1998), p. 23.

16. Baz Kershaw, *The Radical in Performance: Between Brecht and Baudrillard* (London: Routledge, 1999), p. 31.

17. Pierre Bourdieu, *Distinction: A Social Critique of the Judgement of Taste*, trans. R. Nice (London: Routledge & Kegan Paul, 1984), p. 34.

18. J. Willett (ed.), *Brecht on Theatre: The Development of an Aesthetic* (London: Methuen, 1964), p. 51.

19. Tony Kushner, 'How Do You Make Social Change?' *Theater*, 31:3 (2001), p. 62.

20. These related and international histories are described in S. Craig (ed.), *Dreams and Deconstructions: Alternative Theatre in Britain* (Ambergate: Amber Lane Press, 1980); T. Shank, *Beyond the Boundaries: American Alternative Theatre* (Ann Arbor: University of Michigan Press, 2002); R. Samuel, E. MacColl and S. Cosgrove, *Theatres of the Left, 1880–1935: Workers' Theatre Movements in Britain and America* (London: Routledge & Kegan Paul, 1985); R. Stourac and K. McCreery, *Theatre as a Weapon: Workers' Theatre in the Soviet Union, Germany and Great Britain, 1917–1934* (London: Routledge & Kegan Paul, 1986); S. Capelin, *Challenging the Centre: Two Decades of Political Theatre* (Brisbane: Playback Press, 1995); K.P. Epskamp, *Theatre in Search of Social Change* (The Hague: Centre for the Study of Education in Developing Countries, 1989). Recent books in applied theatre have offered far more comprehensive histories than I have given here: see Prentki and Preston (2009) and Shaughnessy (2012).

21. See, for example, Jan Cohen Cruz and Mady Schutzman (eds.), *A Boal Companion: Dialogues on Theatre and Cultural Politics* (London: Routledge, 2006).

22. For two contrasting readings of this history in relation to drama education, see D. Hornbook, *Education and Dramatic Art* (Oxford: Basil Backwell, 1989) and G. Bolton, *Acting in Classroom Drama* (Stoke-on-Trent: Trentham Books, 1998). For a more general analysis of the place of the arts in progressive education see J. Donald, *Sentimental Education* (London: Verso, 1992).

23. For analyses and discussion of the history and politics of twentieth-century and contemporary community theatre, see Baz Kershaw, *The Politics of Performance: Radical Theatre as Cultural Intervention* (London: Routledge, 1992); Eugene van Erven, *Community Theatre: Global Perspectives* (London: Routledge, 2001); R. Fotheringham (ed.), *Community Theatre in Australia* (Sydney: Currency Press, 1992); S.C. Haedicke and T. Nellhaus (eds.), *Performing Democracy: International Perspectives*

on Community-Based Performance (Ann Arbor: University of Michigan Press, 2001).

24. Jan Cohen-Cruz, *Local Acts: Community-Based Performance in the United States* (New Brunswick, NJ: Rutgers University Press, 2005).

25. Claire Bishop, *Artificial Hells: Participatory Art and the Politics of Spectatorship* (London: Verso, 2012), p. 18.

26. Adrian Heathfield, 'Going Live' (2003): http://www.thisisliveart.co.uk/projects/adrian-heathfield/ accessed 16 December 2013.

27. Baz Kershaw, *The Radical in Performance*, pp. 6–7; Zygmunt Bauman, *Liquid Times: Living in an Age of Uncertainty* (Cambridge: Polity Press, 2007).

28. Doreen Massey, *For Space* (London: Sage Publications, 2005), p. 61.

29. Victor Turner, *The Anthropology of Performance* (New York: Performing Arts Journal Press, 1986), pp. 72–74.

30. Richard Schechner, 'Performers and Spectators Transported and Transformed', in P. Auslander (ed.), *Performance: Critical Concepts in Literary and Cultural Studies*, vol. 1 (London: Routledge, 2003), p. 270.

31. Tim Etchells, *Certain Fragments* (London: Routledge, 1999), p. 59.

32. Chantal Mouffe, *The Democratic Paradox* (London: Verso, 2000), p. 140.

33. This misreading was evident in Judith Ackroyd's paper, 'Applied Theatre: An Exclusionary Discourse' (2007), in which she suggested that the subtitle of my book, 'The Gift of Theatre', does not consider 'that there may be anything but *good* to arise from the practices' (p. 7). Had she read beyond the book's title, she would have realised her assumptions were unfounded. In Chapter 8 I invoke the long tradition of gift theory, and I point out its ethical and political ambiguities, arguing that in relation to applied theatre a gift can be 'both a present and a poison' (p. 161).

34. Mark Olsteen (ed.), *The Question of the Gift* (London: Routledge, 2002), pp. 9–10.

35. bell hooks, *Teaching to Transgress: Education as the Practice of Freedom* (London: Routledge, 1994), p. 59.

36. Michel Foucault, and Gilles Deleuze, 'Intellectuals and Power', in D.F. Bouchard (ed.), *Language, Counter-Memory, Practice: Selected Essays and Interviews by Michel Foucault* (Ithaca, NY: Cornell University Press, 1977), pp. 205–6.

37. Foucault and Deleuze, p. 207.

Notes to Chapter 2: The Practice of Citizenship

1. Peter Sellars, 'The Question of Culture', in M. Delgado and C. Svich (eds.), *Theatre in Crisis: Performance Manifestos for a New+ Century* (Manchester: Manchester University Press, 2002), p. 142.

2. In *The German Ideology* of 1845, Marx and Engels argued that the citizen of bourgeois theory masked deeper social divisions and inequalities.

3. 'Don't Play Truant to Join Bush Demo, Pupils Warned', *Guardian*, 17 November 2003. For a discussion of how citizenship became absorbed into formal education see J. Beck, *Morality and Citizenship in Education* (London: Continuum, 1998).

4. Chantal Mouffe (ed.), *Dimensions of a Radical Democracy* (London: Verso, 1992), p. 4. She is indebted to the work of Hannah Arendt (1958), who first conceptualised citizenship as political participation, but she is also critical of her rationalist analysis of antagonism.

5. T.H. Marshall and T. Bottomore, *Citizenship and Social Class* (London: Pluto Press, 1992), p. 8.

6. This point is made by Nancy Fraser and Linda Gordon (1994), who observe that although the rhetorical traditions of the United States emphasise civil citizenship, citing 'individual liberties' and 'freedom of speech' as good examples, the idea of collective responsibility for public welfare is largely absent from this aspect of political discourse.

7. Marshall and Bottomore, p. 18.

8. Bryan S. Turner (ed.), *Citizenship and Social Theory* (London; Sage Publications, 1993), p. 2.

9. Mouffe, *Dimensions of a Radical Democracy*, p. 237.

10. See Helen Nicholson, *Theatre, Education and Performance: The Map and the Story* (Palgrave Macmillan, 2011), chapter 8.

11. Alison Jeffers, 'Half-Hearted Promises, or Wrapping Ourselves in the Flag: Two Approaches to the Pedagogy of Citizenship', *Research in Drama Education: The Journal of Applied Theatre and Performance*, 12:3 (2007), pp. 371–381, at p. 373.

12. Stationery Office, *Life in the United Kingdom: A Guide for New Residents*, 3rd edition (London: HMSO, 2013).

13. Chantal Mouffe, *The Democratic Paradox* (London: Verso, 2000), p. 104.

14. Chantal Mouffe, 'Artistic Antagonism and Agonistic Spaces', *Art and Research*, 1:2 (Summer 2007), pp. 1–5: www.artandresearch.org.uk/v1n2/mouffe.html accessed 16 December 2013.

15. I have written elsewhere of the circularity of risk and trust in relation to applied theatre. See Helen Nicholson, 'Drama Education and the Politics of Trust', *Research in Drama Education*, 7:1 (2002), pp. 81–93.

16. Tim Prentki and Jan Selman described popular theatre as motivated by 'an urgent need for change in the society and conditions in which many live' (2000), pp. 9–10.

17. J. Willett (ed.), *Brecht on Theatre: The Development of an Aesthetic* (London: Methuen, 1964), p. 108.

18. Forum theatre is discussed in more detail in Chapter 6.

19. Augusto Boal, *Legislative Theatre* (London: Routledge, 1998), p. 20.

20. Paul Dwyer (2004) traces different versions of Boal's story about the woman in Lima, and concludes that it has been variously inflected to suit Boal's purposes.

21. Claire Bishop, *Artificial Hells: Participatory Art and the Politics of Spectatorship* (London: Verso, 2012), pp. 13–14.

22. Bishop, pp. 19–20.

23. Jonothan Neelands, 'Taming the Political: The Struggle over Recognition in the Politics of Applied Theatre', *Research in Drama Education: The Journal of Applied Theatre and Performance*, 12:3 (2007), p. 315.

24. Mouffe, 'Artistic Antagonism and Agonistic Spaces'.

25. Shannon Jackson, *Social Works: Performing Art, Supporting Publics* (London: Routledge, 2011), p. 74.

26. Neelands, p. 305.

27. For a further discussion of this point see R. Braidotti, *The Posthuman* (Cambridge: Polity Press, 2013).

28. See, for example, B. Shepard and R. Hayduk (eds.), *From ACT UP to the WTO : Urban Protest and Community Building in the Era of Globalisation* (London: Verso, 2002); C. Orenstein, 'Agitational Performance, Now and Then', *Theater*, 31:3 (2002), pp. 139–51; Jan Cohen-Cruz, 'The Motion of the Ocean: The Shifting Face of U.S. Theater for Social Change since the 1960s', *Theater*, 31:3 (2002), pp. 95–107; G. McKay (ed.), *DIY Culture: Party and Protest in Nineties Britain* (London: Verso, 1998).

29. See B. Shepard, *Play, Creativity, and Social Movements: If I Can't Dance, It's Not My Revolution* (London: Routledge, 2011), chapter 5, for a discussion of John Jordan's work.

30. See 'The Arctic Gnome', http://www.edenproject.com/blog/index.php/2012/11/1000-garden-gnomes-descend-on-eden-for-art-installation/ accessed 30 December 2013.

31. See N. Thrift, *Non-Representational Theory: Space/Politics/Affect* (London: Routledge, 2008), p. 271.

32. Baz Kershaw, *The Radical in Performance: Between Brecht and Baudrillard* (London: Routledge, 1999), particularly chapters 1 and 2.

33. S.J. Ahmed, 'When Theatre Practitioners Attempt Changing an Ever-Changing World: A Response to Tim Prentki's "Save the Children? – Change the World", *Research in Drama Education* (8.1)', *Research in Drama Education*, 9:1 (2004), p. 96.

34. Auguste Comte, *The Positive Philosophy of Auguste Comte,* Vol. 11, trans. H. Martineau (London: John Chapman, 1953), p. 479.

35. David Miller, 'Are they *My* Poor? The Problem of Altruism in a World of Strangers', in J. Seglow (ed.), *The Ethics of Altruism* (London: Frank Cass, 2004), p. 109.

36. For an analysis of the beneficial impact of altruism on the giver, see N.K. Badhwar, 'Altruism Versus Self-Interest: Sometimes a False Dichotomy', in

E.F. Paul, D. Miller and J. Paul (eds.), *Altruism* (Cambridge: Cambridge University Press, 1993), pp. 90–117.

37. D. Kerr, 'You Just Made the Blueprint to Suit Yourselves: A Theatre-based Health Project in Lungwena, Malawi', in T. Prentki and S. Preston (eds.), *The Applied Theatre Reader* (London: Routledge, 2009), p. 101.

38. A. Mundrawala, 'Fitting the Bill: Commissioned Theatre Projects on Human Rights in Pakistan: The Work of Karachi-based Theatre Group *Tehrik e Niswan*', *Research in Drama Education: The Journal of Applied Theatre and Performance*, 12:2 (2007), pp. 149–61.

39. S.J. Ahmed, '"Fitting the Bill" for "Helping Them". A Response to "Integrated Popular Theatre Approach in Africa" and "Commissioned Theatre Projects on Human Rights in Pakistan"', *Research in Drama Education: The Journal of Applied Theatre and Performance*, 12:2 (2007), p. 209.

40. A. Tanyi-Tang, 'Theatre for Change: An Analysis of Two Performances by Women in Mundemba Sub-Division', *Research in Drama Education*, 6:1 (2001), 23–38, at p. 35; A. Tanyi-Tang, 'Unpeeling the Onion of Privilege', in J. O'Toole and M. Lepp (eds.), *Drama for Life: Stories of Adult Learning and Empowerment* (Brisbane: Playlab Press, 2000) pp. 67–76.

41. Keith Graham, 'Altruism, Self-Interest and the Indistinctiveness of Persons', in J. Seglow (ed.), *The Ethics of Altruism* (London: Frank Cass, 2004), p. 61.

42. Graham, p. 60.

43. The implications of the relationship between applied theatre and environmentalism were debated by Dee Heddon and Sally Mackey in their editorial, D. Heddon and S. Mackey, 'Environmentalism, Performance and Applications: Uncertainties and Emancipations', *Research in Drama Education: The Journal of Applied Theatre and Performance*, 17:2 (2012), pp. 163–192.

44. Stephen Bottoms, Aaron Franks and Paula Kramer, 'Editorial: On Ecology', *Performance Research: On Ecology*, 17:4 (2012), p. 3.

45. Helen Nicholson, 'Attending to Sites of Learning: London and Pedagogies of Scale', *Performance Research: On Ecology*, 17:4 (2012), pp. 95–105.

46. J.-D. Dewsbury, 'Affective Habit Ecologies: Material Dispositions and Immanent Inhabitations', *Performance Research: On Ecology*, 17:4 (2012), pp. 74–82, at p. 76.

47. Jane Bennett, (2010) *Vibrant Matter: A Political Ecology of Things* (Durham, NC: Duke University Press), p. 118.

48. See James Thompson, *Performance Affects: Applied Theatre and the End of Effect* (Basingstoke: Palgrave, 2009), p. 119 and Nicola Shaughnessy, *Applying Performance: Live Art, Socially Engaged Theatre and Affective Practice* (Basingstoke: Palgrave, 2012).

49. Patricia Ticineto Clough, 'Introduction', in P.T. Clough with J. Halley (eds.), *The Affective Turn: Theorising the Social* (Durham, NC: Duke University Press, 2007), p. 2.

50. Dewsbury, p. 74.
51. B. Anderson and P. Harrison (eds.), *Taking Place: Non Representational Theories and Geography* (Farnham: Ashgate, 2010), p. 9.
52. J. Bennett, *The Enchantment of Modern Life: Attachment, Crossings, and Ethics* (Princeton, NJ: Princeton University Press, 2001), p. 14.

Notes to Chapter 3: Pedagogies, Praxis and Performance

1. Patti Lather, 'Post critical Pedagogies: A Feminist Reading', in C. Luke and J. Gore (eds.), *Feminisms and Critical Pedagogy* (London and New York: Routledge, 1992), p. 121.
2. Patti Lather, *Getting Smart: Feminist Research and Pedagogy with/in the Postmodern* (London: Routledge, 1991), p. 57.
3. Lather, *Getting Smart*, p.11.
4. I am indebted to theatre director and practitioner Fiona Lesley, Director of the Map Consortium, for furthering my understanding of the implications of this metaphor to our field. It is a metaphor I have used more extensively in relation to theatre education (Nicholson, 2011).
5. See H.K. Bhabha, *The Location of Culture* (London: Routledge, 1994) for a postcolonial analysis of this term.
6. See the work of North American critical pedagogues H.A. Giroux (1994); P. McLaren (1995) P. Lather (1992) and C. Doyle (1993), who applied deconstructive thought to education.
7. Dwight Conquergood, 'Performance Studies: Interventions and Radical Research', in H. Bial (ed.), *The Performance Studies Reader* (London: Routledge, 2004), p. 311.
8. Conquergood, p. 312.
9. Conquergood, p. 311.
10. A.M.A. Freire and D. Macedo (eds.), *The Paulo Freire Reader* (London: Continuum, 2001), p. 61.
11. P. Freire, *Cultural Action for Freedom* (Harmondsworth: Penguin Books, 1972), p. 29.
12. Freire, *Cultural Action for Freedom*, pp. 35, 37.
13. This strategy is discussed on the Action Aid website, www.actionaid.org. Resources can be found at www.actionaid.org.uk/doc_lib/189_1_reflect_introduction.pdf accessed 30 December 2013
14. In writing about applied theatre, Philip Taylor attributes the development of the term praxis to Freire himself (2003: 35). This is factually incorrect. It is a term which was popularised by Marx but was derived from the Greek, where *praxis* signified the free action of citizens. Marx's conceptualisation of praxis was based on the idea that the bourgeois consciousness was ideologically limited, and that this was an obstacle to the revolution. Critical of the Enlightenment perception that the ideas of free-thinking intellectuals would change the world, Marx insisted that

thought is the product of material reality, not outside it. In *The German Ideology* Marx and Engels reversed the conventional dialectic between life and consciousness, stating that '[l]ife is not determined by consciousness, but consciousness by life' (1974: 47). If this were the case, it would be possible, therefore, to reshape human consciousness.

15. Freire and Macedo, *The Paulo Freire Reader*, p. 64.
16. S. Grady, 'Accidental Marxists? The Challenge of Critical and Feminist Pedagogies for the Practice of Applied Drama', *Youth Theatre Journal*, 17 (2003), p. 70.
17. H. Foster, *Recodings: Art, Spectacle, Cultural Politics* (Port Townsend: Bay Press, 1985), p. 153.
18. Baz Kershaw, *The Radical in Performance: Between Brecht and Baudrillard* (London: Routledge, 1999), p. 70.
19. Grant Kester, *The One and the Many: Contemporary Collaborative Art in a Global Context* (Durham, NC: Duke University Press, 2011), p. 32.
20. Kester, p. 20.
21. Richard Edwards and Robin Usher, *Globalisation and Pedagogy: Space, Place and Identity* (London: Routledge, 2000), p. 124.
22. Dwight Conquergood, 'Of Caravans and Carnivals: Performance Studies in Motion', *The Drama Review*, 148 (1995), pp. 137–138.
23. See Jon McKenzie, *Perform or Else: From Discipline to Performance* (London: Routledge, 2001), pp. 49–53; Victor Turner, *From Ritual to Theatre: The Human Seriousness of Play* (New York: Performing Arts Journal Publications, 1982).
24. Michael Billig, *Banal Nationalism* (London: Sage Publications, 1995).
25. McKenzie, p. 72. He also includes an analysis of the role of unions, which is not included here.
26. Chantal Mouffe, 'Artistic Antagonism and Agonistic Spaces', *Art and Research*, 1:2 (Summer 2007), p. 1: www.artandresearch.org.uk/v1n2/mouffe.html accessed 16 December 2013.
27. For a fuller discussion, see Michel Foucault, 'Technologies of the Self', in P. Rabinow (ed.), *Ethics: Essential Works of Foucault 1954–1984* (London: Penguin Books, 1994), pp. 223–252.
28. www.personneltoday.com/articles/18/03/2008/44839/drama-based-training-treading-the-training-boards.htm accessed 31 December 2013; see www.purplemonster.co.uk//what-we-do/transformation-change.php accessed 31 December 2013; http://www.stepsdrama.com/our-approach/default.aspx accessed 31 December 2013.
29. M. Hardt and A. Negri, *Empire* (Cambridge, MA: Harvard University Press, 2000), p. 292.
30. Kester, p. 42.
31. Edwards and Usher, p. 132.
32. Claire Bishop, *Artificial Hells: Participatory Art and the Politics of Spectatorship* (London: Verso, 2012), p. 18.

33. Freire, *Cultural Action for Freedom*, pp. 36–37.
34. Ellsworth, E. (1992) 'Why Doesn't This Feel Empowering?', in C. Luke and J. Gore (eds.), *Feminisms and Critical Pedagogy* (London and New York: Routledge) pp. 90–119.
35. Alex Needham, 'Gay Prisoners to Get Jail Tales Shown in Artangel Installation', *The Guardian*, 5 March 2012: www.guardian.co.uk/society/2012/mar/05/gay-prisoners-artangel-installation accessed 31 December 2013.
36. For an analysis of how professional experts have regulated and controlled the lives of those in institutions, see Michel Foucault, *Discipline and Punish*, trans. A. Sheridan (Harmondsworth: Penguin Books, 1991), pp. 170–177.
37. Elizabeth Ellsworth, *Places of Learning* (London: Routledge, 2005), p. 24.
38. James Thompson, *Performance Affects: Applied Theatre and the End of Effect* (Basingstoke: Palgrave, 2009), p. 130.
39. Gilles Deleuze, *Difference and Repetition*, trans. Paul Patton (New York: Columbia University Press, 1994), p. 22.
40. Deleuze, p. 23.
41. J.-D. Dewsbury (2003), 'Witnessing Space: "Knowledge Without Contemplation"', *Environment and Planning A*, 35, p. 1927. I have also developed this argument in Helen Nicholson, 'Attending to Sites of Learning: London and Pedagogies of Scale', *Performance Research: On Ecology*, 17:4 (2012), pp. 95–105.

Notes to Chapter 4: Narrative and the Gift of Storytelling

1. Walter Benjamin, 'The Storyteller', in *Illuminations*, trans. H. Zonn (London: Fontana Collins, 1992), pp. 83–107.
2. Paul Ricoeur, *Oneself as Another*, trans. K. Balmey (Chicago: University of Chicago Press, 1992), p. 170.
3. Kathleen Gallagher, 'Emergent Conceptions in Theatre Pedagogy and Production', in K. Gallagher and D. Booth (eds.), *How Theatre Educates: Convergences and Counterpoints* (Toronto: University of Toronto Press, 2002), p. 12.
4. Avtar Brah, *Cartographies of Diaspora* (London: Routledge, 1996), p. 247.
5. Paul Ricoeur, *The Rule of Metaphor* (London: Routledge, 1977), p. 236. See also Donelan (2004) for the application of this conception of narrative to drama education.
6. Sally Stamp, 'Holding On: Dramatherapy with Offenders', in J. Thompson (ed.), *Prison Theatre: Perspectives and Practices* (London: Jessica Kingsley Publishers, 1998), pp. 89–108.
7. See the British Association of Dramatherapists: http://badth.org.uk/ accessed 1 January 2014.

8. James Thompson, *Applied Theatre: Bewilderment and Beyond* (Oxford: Peter Lang, 2003), p. 183.
9. Sithmparanathan, Keynote Lecture, International Conference on Community Theatre, Batticaloa, Sri Lanka, 26 July 2003.
10. I am grateful to James Thompson for his insights on the longevity of globalisation in this region, and for locating globalisation in relation to its history of colonialism. It is significant in this context that the region was colonised by Westerners bearing gifts of musical instruments.
11. Sigmund Freud, *The Interpretation of Dreams* (Harmondsworth: Penguin Books, 1976), p. 232.
12. Sigmund Freud, 'Group Psychology and the Analysis of the Ego', in *The Complete Psychological Works of Sigmund Freud*, Vol. XVIII (1920–1922) (London: The Hogarth Press, 1950), p. 108.
13. Hélène Cixous and Catherine Clement, *The Newly Born Woman*, trans. B. Wing (Minneapolis: University of Minnesota Press, 1975), p. 148.
14. John Willett (ed.), *Brecht on Theatre: The Development of an Aesthetic* (London: Methuen, 1964), p. 277.
15. Willett, pp. 92–93.
16. Teresa Brennan, 'Introduction', in T. Brennan (ed.), *Between Feminism and Psychoanalysis* (London: Routledge, 1989), p. 10.
17. Fin Kennedy, *'The Urban Girl's Guide to Camping' and Other Plays* (London: Nick Hern Books, 2010), p. ix.
18. Kennedy, p. 101.
19. Alasdair MacIntyre, *After Virtue: A Study in Moral Theory* (London: Duckworth, 1981), p. 216.
20. This point has been particularly well theorised in relation to drama education by Joe Winston (1998).
21. Kennedy, p. 84.
22. Megan Boler, 'The Risks of Empathy: Interrogating Multiculturalism's Gaze', *Cultural Studies* 11 (1997), pp. 253–73, at pp. 261, 263. See also Martha Nussbaum, *Poetic Justice* (Boston: Beacon Press, 1995) for a discussion of the moral authority of sympathy in relation to the practice of reading.
23. Augusto Boal, *Theatre of the Oppressed* (London: Pluto Press, 1979), p. 113.
24. John O'Toole, *The Process of Drama* (London: Routledge, 1992).
25. See Gavin Bolton and Dorothy Heathcote, *So You Want to Use Role Play? A New Approach* (Stoke-on-Trent: Trentham Books, 1999).
26. See, for example, feminist readings of the performance of gender by Judith Butler (1990); readings of performance given by Elin Diamond (1997) and Peggy Phelan (1993); and an analysis of education by Madeleine Grumet (1988).
27. Claire Bishop, *Artificial Hells: Participatory Art and the Politics of Spectatorship* (London: Verso, 2012), p. 25.

28. Peggy Phelan, *Unmarked: The Politics of Performance* (London: Routledge, 1993), p. 163.
29. For an interesting and lively debate on drama and moral education, see the exchange between Brian Edmiston and Joe Winston in *Research in Drama Education*, 5:1 (2000). One of the points of dispute is over Edmiston's claims that participants are transformed in particular ways as a result of working with him in drama.
30. Teresa Brennan, *The Transmission of Affect* (Ithaca, NY and London: Cornell University Press, 2004), p. 3.

Notes to Chapter 5: Narratives of Community and Place

1. Iris Marion Young, 'The Ideal of Community and the Politics of Difference', in L.J. Nicholson (ed.), *Feminism/ Postmodernism* (London: Routledge, 1990), p. 302.
2. See Zygmunt Bauman, *Liquid Life* (Cambridge: Polity Press, 2005).
3. Jan Cohen-Cruz, *Local Acts: Community-Based Performance in the United States* (New Brunswick, NJ: Rutgers University Press, 2005), pp. 97–104.
4. Jean-Luc Nancy, *The Inoperative Community*, trans. Peter Connor (Minneapolis: University of Minnesota Press, 1991), p. 35.
5. Nancy, p. 35.
6. Grant H. Kester, *Conversation Pieces: Community and Communication in Modern Art* (Berkeley: University of California Press, 2004), p. 162.
7. Benedict Anderson, *Imagined Communities* (London: Verso, 1983).
8. Vered Amit, 'An Anthropology without Community?', in V. Amit and N. Rapport, *The Trouble with Community* (London: Pluto Press, 2002), p. 58.
9. Amit, p. 165.
10. Avtar Brah, *Cartographies of Diaspora* (London: Routledge, 1996), p. 93.
11. Brah, pp. 116–118.
12. Lucy Lippard, *The Lure of the Local: Senses of Place in a Multicentered Society* (New York: The New Press, 1997), p. 7.
13. See David Harvey, *Cosmopolitanism and the Geographies of Freedom* (New York: Columbia University Press, 2009); Doreen Massey, *For Space* (London: Sage Publications, 2005); Tim Cresswell, *Place: A Short Introduction* (Oxford: Basil Blackwell, 2004).
14. Elspeth Probyn, 'Travels in the Postmodern: Making Sense of the Local', in L.J. Nicholson (ed.), *Feminism/ Postmodernism* (London: Routledge, 1990), p. 187.
15. Mike Pearson and Michael Shanks, *Theatre/ Archaeology* (London: Routledge, 1991), p. 96; Sally Mackey (2002) has also reflected on the significance of landscape and place to theatre-making and performative practices in applied theatre.

16. Alessandro Portelli, 'What Makes Oral History Different', in R. Perks and A. Thomson (eds.), *The Oral History Reader* (London: Routledge, 1998), p. 69.

17. Personal Narratives Group (eds.), 'Truths', in *Interpreting Women's Lives: Feminist Theory and Personal Narratives* (Bloomington: Indiana University Press, 1998), p. 261.

18. Petra Tait, *Converging Realities* (Sydney: Currency Press, 1994), p. 33.

19. Joan Sangster, 'Telling Our Stories: Feminist Debates and the Use of Oral History', in R. Perks and A. Thomson (eds.), *The Oral History Reader* (London: Routledge, 1998), p. 90.

20. Dee Heddon, *Autobiography and Performance* (Basingstoke: Palgrave, 2008), p. 67.

21. Baz Kershaw, *The Radical in Performance: Between Brecht and Baudrillard* (London: Routledge, 1999), p. 160.

22. Bruce McConachie, 'Approaching the "Structure of Feeling" in Grassroots Theater', in T. Nellhaus and S.C. Haedicke (eds.), *Performing Democracy: International Perspectives on Community-Based Performance* (Ann Arbor: University of Michigan Press, 2001), p. 55.

23. Portelli, p. 66.

24. Carolyn Steedman, *Landscape for a Good Woman* (London: Virago Press, 1986), p. 6.

25. Richard Schechner, 'Performers and Spectators Transported and Transformed', in P. Auslander (ed.), *Performance: Critical Concepts in Literary and Cultural Studies*, Vol. 1 (London: Routledge, 2003), p. 280.

26. Programme notes for *A Woman's Place*, directed by Sarah Sansom.

27. Schechner, p. 270.

28. Schechner, p. 283.

29. Richard Schechner, *Between Theatre and Anthropology* (Philadelphia: University of Pennsylvania Press, 1985), pp. 35–36.

30. Kershaw, p. 173.

31. Michael Balfour and Nina Woodrow, 'On Stitches', in M. Balfour (ed.), *Refugee Performance: Practical Encounters* (Bristol: Intellect, 2013), p. 17.

32. Personal interview, December 2003.

33. Brah, p. 95.

34. Amit, pp. 60–62.

35. Kate Soper, *Troubled Pleasures* (London: Verso, 1990), p. 154.

36. Probyn, p. 187.

37. Augusto Boal, *Games for Actors and Non-Actors*, trans. A. Jackson (London: Routledge, 1992), p. 40.

38. Boal, p. 56. This view is also put forward by Australian theatre director Wesley Enoch (2004), who describes the importance of place and home to his sense of identity.

39. Philip Auslander, *From Acting to Performance* (London: Routledge, 1997), p. 105.
40. Nancy, p. 15.
41. Jean-Luc Nancy, *Being Singular Plural*, trans. R.D. Richardson and A.E. O'Byrne (Redwood City, CA: Stanford University Press, 2000), p. 119.
42. Andrew Dawson, 'The Mining Community and the Ageing Body: Towards a Phenomenology of Community?', in V. Amit (ed.), *Realizing Community* (London: Routledge, 2002), p. 23.
43. Dawson, p. 35.
44. Jean-Luc Nancy, *Listening*, trans. Charlotte Mandell (New York: Fordham University Press, 2007), p. 6.
45. Jeff Friedman, 'Muscle Memory: Performing Embodied Knowledge', in R. Cándida Smith (ed.), *Art and the Performance of Memory* (London: Routledge, 2002), p. 166.
46. Philip Auslander, 'Boal, Blau, Brecht: The Body', in M. Schutzman and J. Cohen-Cruz (eds.), *Playing Boal* (London: Routledge, 1994), pp. 124–133.
47. Michel Foucault, 'Nietzsche, Genealogy, History', in D.F. Bouchard (ed.), *Language, Counter-Memory, Practice: Selected Essays and Interviews by Michel Foucault* (Ithaca, NY: Cornell University Press, 1977), p. 146.
48. Foucault, p.148.
49. Sigmund Freud, 'A Note on the Mystic Writing Pad [1925]', in A. Richards (ed.), *Sigmund Freud: On Metapsychology* (Harmondsworth: Penguin, 1991), p. 429.
50. Jacques Derrida, *Archive Fever*, trans E. Prenowitz (Chicago: University of Chicago Press, 1995), p. 36.
51. Maurice Merleau-Ponty, *The Phenomenology of Perception*, trans. C. Smith (London: Routledge, 2002), pp. 161–162.

Notes to Chapter 6: Creativity and Social Intervention

1. Percy Bysshe Shelley, 'A Defence of Poetry', in A.D.F. Macrae (ed.), *Selected Prose and Poetry of P.B. Shelley* (London: Routledge, 1991), p. 233. Raymond Williams (1993) was an influential critic of Romanticist views of the artist, and the history has been analysed by Marilyn Butler (1981).
2. See, for example, Christine Battersby, *Gender and Genius: Towards a Feminist Aesthetics* (London: The Women's Press, 1989) and Terry Eagleton, *The Ideology of the Aesthetic* (Oxford: Basil Blackwell, 1990).
3. For Gardner's theory of multiple intelligences see Howard Gardner, *Frames of Mind* (New York: Basic Books, 1983).
4. Howard Gardner, *Extraordinary Minds* (London: Weidenfeld Nicolson, 1997), p. 54.

5. See, for example, Ken Robinson, *Out of Our Minds* (Oxford: Capstone Press, 2001), which draws on Gardner's work. Arthur J. Cropley (2001) has outlined a taxonomy of domain-specific forms of creativity which is similar in focus to that of Gardner.

6. Gardner, *Frames of Mind*, pp. 226–229.

7. Bill Roper and David Davis, 'Howard Gardner: Knowledge, Learning and Development in Drama and Arts Education', *Research in Drama Education*, 5:2 (2000), pp. 217–233, at p. 225.

8. Richard Florida, *The Rise of the Creative Class* (New York: Basic Books, 2002).

9. http://www.pz.gse.harvard.edu/good_project.php accessed 8 January 2014.

10. Michael Hardt and Antonio Negri, *Empire* (Cambridge, MA: Harvard University Press, 2000).

11. See Helen Nicholson, *Theatre, Education and Performance: The Map and the Story* (Basingstoke: Palgrave, 2011), chapter 5.

12. Robinson (2002) is particularly interested in the significance of creativity in education, arguing that an education which encourages creativity is essential to economic progress.

13. Alex Callinicos, *The Revolutionary Ideas of Marx* (London: Bookmarks, 1995) offers an analysis of Marx's attitude to the social role of the artist and intellectual.

14. See, for example, Arnold Hauser, *The Sociology of Art*, trans. K. Northcott (London: Routledge, 1982), p. 23; Theodor Adorno, *Aesthetic Theory*, trans. C. Lenhardt (London: Routledge, 1984), p. 245.

15. Augusto Boal, *Theatre of the Oppressed* (London: Pluto Press, 1979), p. 141.

16. Michael Taussig and Richard Schechner, 'Boal in Brazil, France and the USA', in M. Schutzman and J. Cohen-Cruz (eds.), *Playing Boal* (London: Routledge, 2004), pp. 28–30.

17. Jane Milling, and Graham Ley, 'Boal's Theoretical History', in *Modern Theories of Performance* (Basingstoke: Palgrave, 2001), pp. 147–172.

18. Boal, *Theatre of the Oppressed*, p. 155.

19. Augusto Boal, *The Rainbow of Desire*, trans. A. Jackson (London: Routledge, 1995), pp. 13–14.

20. Milling and Ley, pp. 159–169.

21. Carmel O'Sullivan, 'Searching for the Marxist in Boal', *Research in Drama Education*, 6:1 (2001), pp. 85–97, at p. 92.

22. O'Sullivan, p. 90.

23. O'Sullivan, p. 94.

24. Augusto Boal, *Games for Actors and Non-Actors*, trans. A. Jackson, 2nd edition (London: Routledge, 2002), p. 2.

25. Mady Schutzman, 'Canadian Roundtable: An Interview', in M. Schutzman and J. Cohen-Cruz (eds.), *Playing Boal* (London: Routledge, 1994), p. 221.

26. Schutzman, pp. 220–221. Frances Babbage (1995) also acknowledged this risk in her introduction to an issue of *Contemporary Theatre Review* devoted to the work of Boal.
27. Programme notes for Cardboard Citizens, *The Man with Size Twelve Feet*, 2002.
28. Hal Foster, *The Return of the Real* (Cambridge, MA: MIT Press, 1996), pp. 202–203.
29. See www.theatreapplied.org/challenging-place accessed 5 January 2014.
30. David Wiles, *A Short History of Western Performance Space* (Cambridge: Cambridge University Press, 2003), p. 257.
31. Henri Lefebvre, *The Production of Space*, trans. D. Nicholson-Smith (Oxford: Basil Blackwell, 1991), p. 110.
32. Mihaly Csikszentmihalyi, *Creativity: Flow and the Psychology of Discovery and Invention* (New York: Harper Collins, 1996).
33. Lefebvre, p. 42.
34. Caoimhe McAvinchey, *Theatre & Prison* (Basingstoke: Palgrave Macmillan, 2011), pp. 60–61.
35. Elizabeth Hallam and Tim Ingold (eds.), *Creativity and Cultural Improvisation* (Oxford: Berg, 2007), p. 52.
36. Hallam and Ingold, p. 11.

Notes to Chapter 7: Human Rights in Performance

1. See for instance, examples of practice in Richard Boon and Jane Plastow (eds.), *Theatre Matters* (Cambridge: Cambridge University Press, 1998).
2. Noam Chomsky is particularly critical of the ways in which US policy-makers have used human rights as a way of furthering their own power. Noam Chomsky, *The Umbrella of U.S. Power: The Universal Declaration of Human Rights and the Contradictions of U.S. Policy* (New York: Seven Stories Press. 1999).
3. Rosi Braidotti, *The Posthuman* (Cambridge: Polity Press, 2013), p. 122.
4. Susan George, 'Globalizing Rights?', in M.J. Gibney (ed.), *Globalizing Rights* (Oxford: Oxford University Press, 2003), pp. 15–33.
5. Bill Gates, 'Yes, More Trade With China', *Washington Post*, 23 May 2000.
6. Braidotti, p. 123.
7. George, p. 24.
8. Syed Jamil Ahmed, 'Wishing for a World Without "Theatre for Development": Demystifying the Case of Bangladesh', *Research in Drama Education*, 7:2 (2002), pp. 207–219, at p. 208.
9. Ahmed, p. 211.
10. Donald F. Bouchard (ed.), *Language, Counter-memory, Practice: Selected Interviews with Michel Foucault* (Ithaca, NY: Cornell University Press, 1977), p. 136.

11. Ahmed, pp. 217–218.
12. Rustom Bharucha, *The Politics of Cultural Practice: Thinking Through Theatre in an Age of Globalisation* (London: Athlone Press, 2000), p. 21.
13. Bharucha, p. 26.
14. See Richard A. Wilson (ed.), *Human Rights, Culture and Context* (London: Pluto Press, 1997).
15. Wilson, p. 5.
16. Jacques Derrida, *The Amnesty Lectures on Human Rights*, Channel 4 TV, 1995.
17. Wilson, p. 155.
18. Chris Brown, 'Human Rights', in J. Baylis, S. Smith and P. Owens (eds.), *The Globalisation of World Politics* Oxford: Oxford University Press, 2007), pp. 506–521.
19. Sally Engle Merry, 'Legal Pluralism and Transnational Culture', in Wilson, p. 30.
20. Wilson, p. 156.
21. www.storyworkshop.org/ accessed 6 January 2014.
22. Clifford, J. *The Predicament of Culture: Twentieth Century Ethnography* (Cambridge, MA: Harvard University Press, 1988), p. 14
23. www.storyworkshop.org/our_approach/radio/soap_operas/index.html accessed 6 January 2014.
24. David Kerr, *African Popular Theatre: From Pre-Colonial Times to the Present Day* (Oxford: Currey Press, 1995), pp. 177–8.
25. Frances Harding, *The Performance Arts in Africa: A Reader* (London: Routledge, 2002), p. 3.
26. Personal correspondence with Louise Keyworth.
27. Bharucha, pp. 19, 26.
28. Bharucha, p. 6.
29. Bharucha, p. 66.
30. For a more detailed discussion of Everyday Theatre's work on family violence, see Helen Nicholson, 'Dramatising Family Violence: The Domestic Politics of Shame and Blame', *Research in Drama Education: The Journal of Applied Theatre and Performance*, 14:4 (2009), pp. 561–582.
31. Teresita V. Barrameda and Lea L. Espallardo, *Breaking Silence: A Nationwide Informance Tour for the Prevention of Violence against Women in the Family* (Quezon City: PETA, 2000), p. 10.
32. Barrameda and Espellardo, p. 30.
33. Noam Chomsky, '"Recovering Rights": A Crooked Path', in M. J. Gibney (ed.), *Globalizing Rights* (Oxford: Oxford University Press, 2003), pp. 45–80.
34. Homi Bhabha, 'On Writing Rights', in Gibney, pp. 162–183.

35. Janelle Reinelt, 'The Promise of Documentary', in A. Forsyth and C. Megson (eds.), *Get Real: Documentary Theatre Past and Present* (Basingstoke: Palgrave, 2009), p. 18.

36. 'Is the theatre the right place to ask these questions?' *Guardian*, 8 August 2008: http://www.guardian.co.uk/culture/video/2008/aug/08/deepcut. interview accessed 7 January 2014.

37. Jenny Hughes, *Performance in a Time of Terror: Critical Mimesis and the Age of Uncertainty* (Manchester: Manchester University Press, 2011), p. 92.

38. Braidotti, pp. 192–193.

Notes to Chapter 8: The Gift of Theatre

1. Rebecca Prichard, *Yard Gal* (London: Faber, 1998), p. 5.

2. Prichard, p. 6. Hackney is a particularly deprived area of London.

3. Chantal Mouffe, *The Democratic Paradox* (London: Verso, 2000), p. 92.

4. See, for example, the ethical codes of the UK National Association of Drama Therapists at http://badth.org.uk/code accessed 5 January 2014.

5. Patti Lather, 'Applied Derrida: (Mis)Reading the Work of Mourning in Educational Research', *Journal of Philosophy and Education*, 35:3 (2003), pp. 257–270. Reprinted in P. Trifonas and M. Peters (eds.), *Derrida, Deconstruction and Education: Ethics of Pedagogy and Research* (Oxford: Blackwell, 2004), pp. 3–16, at p. 5.

6. A good example of how redemption narratives are applied to community practice is offered in the introduction to Richard Boon and Jane Plastow (eds.), *Theatre and Empowerment: Community Drama on the World Stage* (Cambridge: Cambridge University Press, 2004).

7. Lather, p. 6.

8. Pierre Bourdieu, (1997) 'Marginalia – Some Additional Notes on the Gift', in trans. R.Nice, A.D.Schrift (ed.). *The Logic of the Gift: Towards an Ethic of Generosity* (London: Routledge), p. 231.

9. Marcel Mauss, *The Gift*, trans. I. Cunnison (London: Cohen West, 1954, p. 1.

10. Jacques Derrida, *Given Time: Counterfeit Money*, trans. P. Kamuf (Chicago: University of Chicago Press, 1992), p. 23.

11. Lather, p. 8.

12. Lee Anne Fennell, 'Unpacking the Gift: Illiquid Goods and Empathetic Dialogue', in M. Olsteen (ed.), *The Question of the Gift* (London: Routledge, 2002), p. 86.

13. See, for example, Nel Noddings, *Caring: A Feminine Approach to Ethics and Moral Education* (Berkeley: University of California Press, 1984); Carol Gilligan, *In a Different Voice: Psychological Theory and Women's Development* (Cambridge, MA: Harvard University Press, 1982). For

an analysis of an ethic of care in relation to drama education, see Joe Winston, *Drama, Narrative and Moral Education* (Brighton: Falmer Press, 1978).

14. Annette C. Baier, *Moral Prejudices* (Cambridge, MA: Harvard University Press, 1994), p. 109.

15. Jane Bennett, *The Enchantment of Modern Life: Attachments, Crossings and Ethics* (Princeton, NJ: Princeton University Press, 2001), p. 156.

16. Bennett, p. 161.

17. To see the film of the event, see http://criticallegalthinking.com/2012/07/10/art-as-disobedience-liberate-tates-gift-to-the-nation/ accessed 6 January 2014.

18. Maurice Merleau-Ponty, *The Prose of the World*, trans. J. O'Neill (Evanston, IL: Northwestern University Press, 1973), p. 43.

19. Merleau-Ponty, p. 286.

References

Ackroyd, J., 'Applied Theatre: Problems and Possibilities', *Applied Theatre Journal*, 1 (2000) http://www.griffith.edu.au/__data/assets/pdf_file/0004/81796/Ackroyd.pdf accessed 15 December 2013.

Ackroyd, J., *Applied Theatre: An Exclusionary Discourse* (2007) http://www.griffith.edu.au/__data/assets/pdf_file/0005/52889/01-ackroyd-final.pdf accessed 15 December 2013.

Adorno, T., *Aesthetic Theory*, trans. C. Lenhardt (London: Routledge, 1984).

Ahmed, S.J., 'When Theatre Practitioners Attempt Changing an Ever-Changing World: A Response to Tim Prentki's "Save the Children? – Change the World"', *Research in Drama Education*, 9:1 (2004), pp. 96–100.

Ahmed, S.J., '"Fitting the Bill" for "Helping Them": A Response to "Integrated Popular Theatre Approach in Africa" and "Commissioned Theatre Projects on Human Rights in Pakistan"', *Research in Drama Education: The Journal of Applied Theatre and Performance*, 12:2 (2007), pp. 207–212.

Amit, V., 'An Anthropology without Community?', in V. Amit and N. Rapport, *The Trouble with Community* (London: Pluto Press, 2002), pp. 73–160.

Amit, V. and Rapport, N., *The Trouble with Community* (London: Pluto Press, 2002).

Anderson. B., *Imagined Communities* (London: Verso, 1983).

Anderson, B. and Harrison, P. (eds.), *Taking Place: Non Representational Theories and Geography* (Farnham: Ashgate, 2010).

Arendt, H., *The Human Condition* (Chicago: University of Chicago Press, 1958).

Auslander, P., 'Boal, Blau, Brecht: The Body', in M. Schutzman and J. Cohen-Cruz, *Playing Boal* (London: Routledge, 1994), pp. 124–133.

Auslander, P., *From Acting to Performance* (London: Routledge, 1997).

Babbage, F., 'Introduction to Working without Boal: Digressions and Developments in Theatre of the Oppressed', *Contemporary Theatre Review*, 3:1 (1995), pp. 1–8.

Badhwar, N.K., 'Altruism versus Self-Interest: Sometimes a False Dichotomy', in E.F. Paul, D. Miller and J. Paul (eds.), *Altruism* (Cambridge: Cambridge University Press, 1993), pp. 90–117.

Baier, A.C., *Moral Prejudices* (Cambridge, MA: Harvard University Press, 1994).

Balfour, M. (ed.), *Theatre in Prison* (Bristol: Intellect Books, 2004).

Balfour, M. (ed.), *Refugee Performance: Practical Encounters* (Bristol: Intellect Books, 2013).

Barrameda, T.V. and Espellardo, L., *Breaking Silence: A Nationwide Informance Tour for the Prevention of Violence against women in the family* (Quezon City: PETA, 2002).

Battersby, C., *Gender and Genius: Towards a Feminist Aesthetics* (London: The Women's Press, 1989).

Bauman, Z., *Liquid Life* (Cambridge: Polity Press, 2005).

Bauman, Z., *Liquid Times: Living in an Age of Uncertainty* (Cambridge: Polity Press, 2007).

Beck, J., *Morality and Citizenship in Education* (London: Continuum, 1998).

Benjamin, W., 'The Storyteller', in *Illuminations*, trans. H. Zonn (London: Fontana Collins, 1992), pp. 83–107.

Bennett, J., *The Enchantment of Modern Life: Attachment, Crossings, and Ethics* (Princeton: Princeton University Press, 2001).

Bennett, J., *Vibrant Matter: A Political Ecology of Things* (Durham, NC: Duke University Press, 2010).

Bhabha, H.K., *The Location of Culture* (London: Routledge, 1994).

Bhabha, H.K., 'On Writing Rights', in M.J. Gibney (ed.), *Globalizing Rights* (Oxford: Oxford University Press, 2003), pp. 162–183.

Bharucha, R., *The Politics of Cultural Practice: Thinking Through Theatre in an Age of Globalisation* (London: Athlone Press, 2000).

Billig, M., *Banal Nationalism* (London: Sage Publications, 1995).

Bishop, C., *Artificial Hells: Participatory Art and the Politics of Spectatorship* (London: Verso, 2012).

Boal, A., *Theatre of the Oppressed* (London: Pluto Press, 1979).

Boal, A., *Games for Actors and Non-Actors*, trans. A. Jackson (London: Routledge, 1992).

Boal, A., *The Rainbow of Desire*, trans. A. Jackson (London: Routledge, 1995).

Boal, A., *Legislative Theatre* (London: Routledge, 1998).

Boal, A., *Games for Actors and Non-Actors*, trans. A. Jackson (2nd edition) (London: Routledge, 2002).

Boler, M., 'The Risks of Empathy: Interrogating Multiculturalism's Gaze', *Cultural Studies* 11:2 (1997), pp. 253–273.

Bolton, G., *Acting in Classroom Drama* (Stoke-on-Trent: Trentham Books, 1998).

Bolton, G. and Heathcote, D., *So you Want to Use Role Play? A New Approach* (Stoke-on-Trent: Trentham Books, 1999).

Bond, E., *Saved* (London: Methuen Drama, 1965).

Boon, R. and Plastow, J., *Theatre Matters: Performance and Culture on the World Stage* (Cambridge: Cambridge University Press, 1998).

Boon, R. and Plastow, J., *Theatre and Empowerment: Community Drama on the World Stage* (Cambridge: Cambridge University Press, 2004).

Bottoms, S., Franks. A. and Kramer, P., 'Editorial: On Ecology', *Performance Research: On Ecology*, 17: 4 (2012), pp. 1–4.

Bouchard, D.F. (ed.), *Language, Counter-Memory, Practice: Selected Interviews with Michel Foucault* (Ithaca, NY: Cornell University Press, 1997).

Bourdieu, P., *Distinction: A Social Critique of the Judgement of Taste*, trans. R. Nice (London: Routledge & Kegan Paul, 1984).

Bourdieu, P., *Language and Symbolic Power*, trans. G. Raymond and M. Adamson (Cambridge: Polity Press, 1992).

Bourdieu, P., *The Rules of Art*, trans. S. Emanuel (Cambridge: Polity Press, 1996).

Bourdieu, P., 'Marginalia – Some Additional Notes on the Gift', trans. R.Nice, in A.D. Schrift (ed.), *The Logic of the Gift: Towards an Ethic of Generosity* (London: Routledge, 1997), pp. 231–241.

Brah, A., *Cartographies of Diaspora* (London: Routledge, 1996).

Braidotti, R., *The Posthuman* (Cambridge: Polity Press, 2013).

Brennan, T. (ed.), *Between Feminism and Psychoanalysis* (London: Routledge, 1989).

Brennan, T., *The Transmission of Affect* ((Ithaca, NY: Cornell University Press, 2004).

Brown, C., 'Human Rights', in J. Baylis, S. Smith and P. Owens, (eds.), *The Globalisation of World Politics* (Oxford: Oxford University Press, 2007), pp. 506–521.

Bundy, P., 'Aesthetic Engagement in the Drama Process', *Research in Drama Education*, 8:2 (2003), pp. 171–181.

Butler, J., *Gender Trouble: Feminism and the Subversion of Identity* (London: Routledge, 1990).

Butler, M., *Romantics, Rebels and Revolutionaries* (Oxford: Oxford University Press, 1981).

Callinicos, A., *The Revolutionary Ideas of Marx* (London: Bookmarks, 1995).

Capelin, S., *Challenging the Centre: Two Decades of Political Theatre* (Brisbane: Playback Press, 1995).

Chomsky, N., *The Umbrella of U.S. Power: The Universal Declaration of Human Rights and the Contradictions of U.S. Policy* (New York: Seven Stories Press, 1999).

Chomsky, N., '"Recovering Rights": A Crooked Path', in M.J. Gibney (ed.), *Globalizing Rights* (Oxford: Oxford University Press, 2003), pp. 45–80.

Churchill, C., *Far Away* (London: Nick Hern Books, 2000).

Cixous, H. and Clement, C., *The Newly Born Woman*, trans. B. Wing (Minneapolis: University of Minnesota Press, 1975).

Clifford, J., *The Predicament of Culture: Twentieth Century Ethnography* (Cambridge MA: Harvard University Press, 1988).

Clough, P.T., 'Introduction', in P.T. Clough, with J. Halle (eds.), *The Affective Turn: Theorising the Social* (Durham, NC: Duke University Press, 2007), pp. 1–33.

Cohen-Cruz, J., (ed.), *Radical Street Performance: An International Anthology* (London: Routledge, 1988).

Cohen-Cruz, J., 'The Motion of the Ocean: The Shifting Face of U.S. Theater for Social Change since the 1960s', *Theater*, 31:3 (2002), pp. 95–107.

Cohen-Cruz, J., *Local Acts: Community-Based Performance in the United States* (New Brunswick, NJ: Rutgers University Press, 2005).

Cohen Cruz, J and Schutzman, M. (eds.), *A Boal Companion: Dialogues on Theatre and Cultural Politics* (London: Routledge, 2006).

Coleridge, S.T., *Biographia Literaria* (London: J.M. Dent, 1975).

Comte, A., *The Positive Philosophy of Auguste Comte*, Vol. 11, trans. H. Martineau (London: John Chapman, 1953).

Conquergood, D., 'Of Caravans and Carnivals: Performance Studies in Motion', *The Drama Review,* 148 (1995), pp. 137–141.

Conquergood, D., 'Performance Studies: Interventions and Radical Research', in H.Bial (ed.), *The Performance Studies Reader* (London: Routledge, 2004), pp. 311–322.

Craig, S. (ed.), *Dreams and Deconstructions: Alternative Theatre in Britain* (Ambergate: Amber Lane Press, 1980).

Cresswell, T., *Place: A Short Introduction* (Oxford: Basil Blackwell, 2004).

Cropley, A.J., *Creativity in Education and Learning* (London: Routledge, 2001).

Csikszentmihalyi, M., *Creativity: Flow and the Psychology of Discovery and Invention* (New York: Harper Collins, 1996).

Dawson, A., 'The Mining Community and the Ageing Body: Towards a Phenomenology of Community?', in V. Amit (ed.), *Realizing Community* (London: Routledge, 2002), pp. 21–37.

Deleuze, G., *Difference and Repetition*, trans. Paul Patton (New York: Columbia University Press, 1994).

Derrida, J., *Given Time: Counterfeit Money*, trans. P. Kamuf (Chicago: University of Chicago Press, 1992).

Derrida, J., *The Amnesty Lectures on Human Rights*, Channel 4 TV (1995).

Derrida, J., *Archive Fever*, trans E. Prenowitz (Chicago: University of Chicago Press, 1995).

Dewsbury, J.-D., 'Witnessing Space: 'Knowledge Without Contemplation', *Environment and Planning A*, 35 (2003), pp. 1907–1932.

Dewsbury, J.-D., 'Affective Habit Ecologies: Material Dispositions and Immanent Inhabitations', *Performance Research*: On Ecology, 17:4 (2012), pp. 74–82.

Diamond, E., *Unmaking Mimesis* (London: Routledge, 1997).

Donald, J., *Sentimental Education* (London: Verso, 1992).

Donelan, K., '"Overlapping Spheres" and "Blurred Spaces": Mapping Cultural Interactions in Drama and Theatre with Young People', *Drama Australia*, 28:1 (2004), pp. 15–32.

Doyle, C., *Raising Curtains on Education: Drama as a Site for Critical Pedagogy* (Westport, CT: Bergin & Garvey, 1993).

Dwyer, P., 'Augusto Boal and the Woman in Lima: a Poetic Encounter', *New Theatre Quarterly* (May 2004), pp. 155–163.

Eagleton, T., *The Ideology of the Aesthetic* (Oxford: Basil Blackwell, 1990).

Edmiston, B., 'Drama as Ethical Education', *Research in Drama Education*, 5:1 (2000), pp. 63–84.

Edwards, R. and Usher, R., *Globalisation and Pedagogy: Space, Place and Identity* (London: Routledge, 2000).

Ellsworth, E., 'Why Doesn't This Feel Empowering?', in C. Luke and J. Gore (eds.), *Feminisms and Critical Pedagogy* (London: Routledge, 1992), pp. 90–119.

Ellsworth, E., *Places of Learning* (London: Routledge, 2005).

Enoch, W., 'Home Coming: Points of Reference for Learning and Making Drama', *Drama Australia*, 28:1 (2004), pp. 7–12.

Epskamp, K.P., *Theatre in Search of Social Change* (The Hague: Centre for the Study of Education in Developing Countries, 1989).

Erven, E. van, *Community Theatre: Global Perspectives* (London: Routledge, 2001).

Etchells, T., *Certain Fragments* (London: Routledge, 1999).

Fennell, L.A. 'Unpacking the Gift: Illiquid Goods and Empathetic Dialogue', in M. Olsteen (ed.), *The Question of the Gift* (London: Routledge, 2002), pp. 85–102.

Flax, J., *Disputed Subjects: Essays on Psychoanalysis, Politics and Philosophy* (London: Routledge, 1993).

Florida, R., *The Rise of the Creative Class* (New York: Basic Books, 2002).

Foster, H., *Recodings: Art, Spectacle, Cultural Politics* (Port Townsend: Bay Press, 1985).

Foster, H., *The Return of the Real* (Cambridge, MA: MIT Press, 1996).

Fotheringham, R. (ed.), *Community Theatre in Australia* (Sydney: Currency Press, 1992).

Foucault, M., 'Intellectuals and Power', in D.F. Bouchard (ed.), *Language, Counter-Memory, Practice: Selected Essays and Interviews by Michel Foucault* (Ithaca, NY: Cornell University Press, 1977), pp. 205–206.

Foucault, M., 'Nietzsche, Genealogy, History', in D.F. Bouchard (ed.), *Language, Counter-Memory, Practice: Selected Essays and Interviews by Michel Foucault* (Ithaca, NY: Cornell University Press, 1977), pp. 139–164.

Foucault, M., *Discipline and Punish*, trans. A. Sheridan (Harmondsworth: Penguin Books, 1991).

Foucault, M., 'Technologies of the Self', in P. Rabinow (ed.), *Ethics: Essential Works of Foucault, 1954–1984* (London: Penguin Books, 1994), pp. 223–252.

Fraser, N. and Gordon, L., 'Civil Citizenship against Social Citizenship?', in B. van Steenbergen (ed.), *The Condition of Citizenship* (London: Sage Publications, 1994), pp. 90–107.

Friedman, J., 'Muscle Memory: Performing Embodied Knowledge', in R. Candida Smith (ed.), *Art and the Performance of Memory* (London: Routledge, 2002), pp. 156–180.

Freire, A.M.A. and D. Macedo (eds.), *The Paulo Freire Reader* (London: Continuum, 2001).

Freire, P., *Pedagogy of the Oppressed* (Harmondsworth: Penguin Books, 1970).

Freire, P., *Cultural Action for Freedom* (Harmondsworth: Penguin Books, 1972).

Freud, S., 'Group Psychology and the Analysis of the Ego', in *The Complete Psychological Works of Sigmund Freud*, Vol. XVIII (1920–1922) (London: Hogarth Press, 1955), pp. 67–143.

Freud, S., *The Interpretation of Dreams* (Harmondsworth: Penguin Books, 1976).

Freud, S., 'A Note on the Mystic Writing Pad [1925]', in A. Richards (ed.), *Sigmund Freud: On Metapsychology* (Harmondsworth: Penguin Books, 1991), pp. 427–434.

Gallagher, K., 'Emergent Conceptions in Theatre Pedagogy and Production', in K. Gallagher and D. Booth (eds.), *How Theatre Educates: Convergences and Counterpoints* (Toronto: University of Toronto Press, 2003), pp. 3–13.

Gardner, H., *Frames of Mind* (New York: Basic Books, 1983).

Gardner, H., *Extraordinary Minds* (London: Weidenfeld & Nicolson, 1997).

Gates, B., 'Yes, More Trade With China', *Washington Post*, 23 May 2000.

George, S., 'Globalizing Rights?', in M.J. Gibney (ed.), *Globalizing Rights* (Oxford: Oxford University Press, 2003), pp. 15–33.

Gilligan, C., *In a Different Voice: Psychological Theory and Women's Development* (Cambridge, MA: Harvard University Press, 1982).

Giroux, H.A., *Between Borders: Pedagogy and the Politics of Cultural Studies* (New York: Routledge, 1994).

Giroux, H.A.. *Education and Cultural Studies: Towards a Performative Practice* (New York: Routledge, 1997).

Giroux, H.A., *Pedagogy and the Politics of Hope* (Boulder, CO: Westview Press, 1997).

Goffman, E., *The Presentation of Self in Everyday Life* (London: Penguin Books, 1959).

Grady, S., 'Accidental Marxists?: The Challenge of Critical and Feminist Pedagogies for the Practice of Applied Drama', *Youth Theater Journal*, 17 (2003), pp. 65–81.

Graham, K., 'Altruism, Self-Interest and the Indistinctiveness of Persons', in J. Seglow (ed.), *The Ethics of Altruism* (London: Frank Cass, 2004), pp. 49–67.

green, d.t. *random* (London: Nick Hern Books, 2010).

Gregg, M. and Seigworth, G.J. (eds.), *The Affect Theory Reader* (London: Routledge, 2010).

Grossberg, L., 'The Space of Culture, The Power of Space', in I. Chambers and L. Curti (eds.), *The Post-Colonial Question: Common Skies, Divided Horizons* (London: Routledge, 1996), pp. 169–88.

Grumet, M., *Bitter Milk* (Amherst: University of Massachusetts Press, 1988).

Guardian Editorial, 'Don't Play Truant to Join Bush Demo, Pupils Warned', *Guardian Educational Supplement*, 17 November http://education.guardian. co.uk/schools/story/. accessed 7 January 2014.

Haedicke, S.C. and Nellhaus, T. (eds.), *Performing Democracy: International Perspectives on Community-Based Performance* (Ann Arbor: University of Michigan Press, 2001).

Harding, F. (ed.), *The Performance Arts in Africa: A Reader* (London: Routledge, 2002).

Hardt, M. and Negri, A., *Empire* (Cambridge, MA: Harvard University Press, 2000).

Harvey, D., *Cosmopolitanism and the Geographies of Freedom* (New York: Columbia University Press, 2009).

Hauser, A., *The Sociology of Art*, trans. K. Northcott (London: Routledge, 1982).

Heddon, D., *Autobiography and Performance* (Basingstoke: Palgrave, 2008).

Heddon, D. and Mackey. S., 'Environmentalism, Performance and Applications: Uncertainties and Emancipations', *RiDE. The Journal of Applied Theatre and Performance*, 17:2 (2012), pp. 163–192.

Holdsworth, N., *Joan Littlewood's Theatre* (Cambridge: Cambridge University Press, 2011).

hooks, b., *Teaching to Transgress: Education as the Practice of Freedom* (London: Routledge, 1994).

Hornbrook, D., *Education and Dramatic Art* (Oxford: Basil Backwell, 1989).

Hughes, J., 'Resistance and Expression: Working with Women Prisoners and Drama', in J. Thompson (ed.), *Prison Theatre: Perspectives and Practices* (London: Jessica Kingsley, 1998), pp. 43–64.

Hughes, J., *Performance in a Time of Terror: Critical Mimesis and the Age of Uncertainty* (Manchester: Manchester University Press, 2011).

Ingold, T. and Hallam, E. (eds.), *Creativity and Cultural Improvisation* (Oxford: Berg, 2007).

Jackson, S., *Social Works: Performing Art, Supporting Publics* (London: Routledge, 2011).

Jeffers, A., 'Half-Hearted Promises, Or Wrapping Ourselves In the Flag: Two Approaches To the Pedagogy of Citizenship', *Research in Drama Education: The Journal of Applied Theatre and Performance*, 12:3 (2007), pp. 371–381.

Jeffers, A., *Refugees, Theatre and Crisis* (Basingstoke: Palgrave, 2011).

Jellicoe, A., *Community Plays: How to Put Them On* (London: Methuen, 1987).

Kant, I., *The Critique of Judgement*, trans. J.C. Meredith (Oxford: Clarendon Press, 1952).

Kay, J., *Other Lovers* (Newcastle-upon-Tyne: Bloodaxe Books, 1993).

Kennedy, F., '*The Urban Girl's Guide to Camping*' and Other Plays (London: Nick Hern Books, 2010).

Kerr, D., *African Popular Theatre: From Pre-Colonial Times to the Present Day* (Oxford: Currency Press, 1995).

Kerr, D., 'You Just Made the Blueprint to Suit Yourselves: A Theatre-Based Health Project in Lungwena, Malawi', in T. Prentki and S. Preston, *The Applied Theatre Reader* (London: Routledge, 2009), pp. 100–107.

Kershaw, B., *The Politics of Performance: Radical Theatre as Cultural Intervention* (London: Routledge, 1992).

Kershaw, B., *The Radical in Performance: Between Brecht and Baudrillard* (London: Routledge, 1999).

Kershaw, B., 'Ecoactivist Protest: The Environment as Partner in Protest?', *Drama Review*, 46:1 (2002), pp. 188–130.

Kershaw, B., *Theatre Ecologies: Environments and Performance Events* (Cambridge: Cambridge University Press, 2007).

Kester, G.H. *Conversation Pieces: Community and Communication in Modern Art* (Berkeley: University of California Press, 2004).

Kester, G.H., *The One and the Many: Contemporary Collaborative Art in a Global Context* (Durham, NC: Duke University Press, 2011).

Kushner, T., 'How do you Make Social Change?', *Theater*, 31:3 (2001), pp. 62–93.

Lather, P. *Getting Smart: Feminist Research and Pedagogy with/ in the Postmodern* (London: Routledge, 1991).

Lather, P. 'Post Critical Pedagogies: A Feminist Reading', in C. Luke and J. Gore (eds.), *Feminisms and Critical Pedagogy* (London: Routledge, 1992), pp. 120–137.

Lather, P. 'Applied Derrida: (Mis) reading the work of Mourning in Educational Research', *Journal of Philosophy and Education*, 35:3 (2003), pp. 257–270. Reprinted in P. Trifonas and M. Peters (eds.), *Derrida, Deconstruction and Education: Ethics of Pedagogy and Research* (Oxford: Blackwell, 2004), pp. 3–16.

Lefebvre, H., *The Production of Space*, trans. D. Nicholson-Smith (Oxford: Basil Blackwell, 1991).

Lippard, L., *The Lure of the Local: Senses of Place in a Multicentred Society* (New York: The New Press, 1997).

Littlewood, J., *Joan's Book: Joan's Peculiar History as She Tells It* (London: Methuen, 1994).

Mackey, S., 'Drama, Landscape and Memory: To Be Is To Be In Place', *Research in Drama Education*, 7:1 (2002), pp. 9–26.

Macrae, A.D.F. (ed.), *Selected Prose and Poetry of P.B. Shelley* (London: Routledge, 1991).

Marshall, T.H. and Bottomore, T., *Citizenship and Social Class* (London: Pluto Press, 1992).

Marx, K. and Engels, F., *The German Ideology* (London: Lawrence & Wishart, 1974).

Massey, D., *For Space* (London: Sage Publications, 2005).

Massumi, B. (ed.) *A Shock to Thought: Expression after Deleuze and Guattari* (London: Routledge, 2002).

Mauss, M., *The Gift*, trans. I. Cunnison (London: Cohen & West, 1954).

McAvinchey, C., *Theatre & Prison* (Basingstoke: Palgrave, 2011).

McConachie, B., 'Approaching the "Structure of Feeling" in Grassroots Theater', in T. Nellhaus and S.C. Haedicke, S.C. (eds.), *Performing Democracy: International Perspectives on Community-Based Performance* (Ann Arbor: University of Michigan Press, 2001), pp. 29–57.

McKenzie, J., *Perform or Else: From Discipline to Performance* (London: Routledge, 2001).

McLaren, P., *Critical Pedagogy and Predatory Culture: Oppositional Politics in a Postmodern Era* (London: Routledge, 1995).

McLaren, P.L. and Lankshear, C. (eds.), *Politics of Liberation: Paths from Freire* (London: Routledge, 1994).

Merleau-Ponty, M., *The Prose of the World*, trans. J. O'Neill (Evanston, IL: Northwestern University Press, 1973).

Merleau-Ponty, M., *The Phenomenology of Perception*, trans C. Smith (London: Routledge, 2002).

Merry, S.E., 'Legal Pluralism and Transnational Culture', in R.A. Wilson (ed.), *Human Rights, Culture and Context* (London: Pluto Press, 1997), pp. 28–48.

Miller, D., 'Are they *My* Poor? The Problem of Altruism in a World of Strangers', in J. Seglow (ed.), *The Ethics of Altruism* (London: Frank Cass, 2004), pp. 106–127.

Milling, J. and Ley, G. 'Boal's Theoretical History', *Modern Theories of Performance* (Basingstoke: Palgrave, 2001), pp. 147–172.

Mouffe, C. (ed.), *Dimensions of a Radical Democracy* (London: Verso, 1992).

Mouffe, C., *The Democratic Paradox* (London: Verso, 2000).

Mouffe, C., 'Artistic Antagonism and Agonistic Spaces', *Art and Research*, 1:2 (2007): 1–5 www.artandresearch.org.uk/v1n2/mouffe.html accessed 7 January 2014.

Mundrawala, A., 'Fitting the Bill: Commissioned Theatre Projects on Human Rights in Pakistan: The Work of Karachi-based Theatre Group *Tehrik e Niswan*', *Research in Drama Education: The Journal of Applied Theatre and Performance*, 12:2 (2007), pp. 149–61.

Nancy, J.-L., *The Inoperative Community*, trans. Peter Connor (Minneapolis: University of Minnesota Press, 1991).

Nancy, J.-L., *Being Singular Plural*, trans. Robert D. Richardson and Anne E. O'Byrne (Stanford, CA, Stanford University Press, 2000).

Nancy, J.-L., *Listening*, trans. Charlotte Mandell (New York: Fordham University Press, 2007).

Neelands, J., *Beginning Drama 11–14* (London: David Fulton, 1998).

Neelands, J., 'Taming the Political: The Struggle over Recognition in the Politics of Applied Theatre', *Research in Drama Education: The Journal of Applied Theatre and Performance*, 12:3 (2007), pp. 305–317.

Nicholson, H., 'Aesthetic Values: Drama Education and the Politics of Difference', *Drama Australia*, 23:2 (1999), pp. 81–90.

Nicholson, H., 'Drama Education and the Politics of Trust', *Research in Drama Education*, 7:1 (2002), pp. 81–93.

Nicholson, H., 'The Performance of Memory', *Drama Australia*, 27:2 (2003), pp. 79–92.

Nicholson, H., 'Dramatising Family Violence: The Domestic Politics of Shame and Blame', *Research in Drama Education: The Journal of Applied Theatre and Performance*, 12:3 (2009), pp. 561–582.

Nicholson, H., *Theatre, Performance and Education: The Map and the Story* (Basingstoke: Palgrave, 2011).

Nicholson, H., 'Attending to Sites of Learning: London and Pedagogies of Scale', *Performance Research: On Ecology*, 17:4 (2012), pp. 95–105.

Noddings, N., *Caring: A Feminine Approach to Ethics and Moral Education* (Berkeley: University of California Press, 1984).

Nussbaum, M., *Poetic Justice* (Boston: Beacon Press, 1995).

Orenstein, C., 'Agitational Performance, Now and Then', *Theater*, 31:3 (2002), pp. 139–151.

O'Sullivan, C., 'Searching for the Marxist in Boal', *Research in Drama Education*, 6:1 (2001), pp. 85–98.

Pearson, M. and Shanks, M., *Theatre/ Archaeology* (London: Routledge, 1991).

Personal Narratives Group (eds.), *Interpreting Women's Lives: Feminist Theory and Personal Narratives* (Bloomington: Indiana University Press, 1989).

Phelan, P., *Unmarked: The Politics of Performance* (London: Routledge, 1993).

Popular Memory Group, 'Popular Memory: Theory, Politics, Method', in R. Perks and A. Thomson (eds.), *The Oral History Reader* (London: Routledge, 1998), pp. 75–86.

Portelli, A., 'What Makes Oral History Different', in R. Perks and A. Thomson (eds.), *The Oral History Reader* (London: Routledge, 1998), pp. 63–74.

Prentki, T. and Preston, S., *The Applied Theatre Reader* (London: Routledge, 2009).

Prentki, T. and Selman, J., *Popular Theatre in Political Culture* (Bristol: Intellect Books, 2000).

Prichard, R., *Yard Gal* (London: Faber & Faber, 1998).

Probyn, E., 'Travels in the Postmodern: Making Sense of the Local', in L.J. Nicholson (ed.), *Feminism/ Postmodernism* (London: Routledge, 1990), pp. 176–189.

Probyn, E., 'Writing Shame', in M. Gregg and G. Seigworth (eds.), *The Affect Theory Reader* (Durham, NC: Duke University Press, 2010), pp. 71–90.

Rasmussen, B., 'Applied Theater and the Power Play – An International Viewpoint', *Applied Theatre Journal*, 1 (2000): http://www.griffith.edu.au/__data/assets/pdf_file/0006/81798/Rasmussen.pdf accessed 15 December 2013.

Reinelt, J., 'The Promise of Documentary', in A. Forsyth and C. Megson (eds.), *Get Real: Documentary Theatre Past and Present* (Basingstoke: Palgrave, 2009), pp. 6–23.

Ricoeur, P., *Oneself as Another*, trans. K. Balmey (Chicago: University of Chicago Press, 1992).

Ricoeur, P., *The Rule of Metaphor* (London: Routledge, 1997).

Robinson, K., *Out of Our Minds* (Oxford: Capstone Press, 2001).

Roper, B. and Davies, D., 'Howard Gardner: Knowledge, Learning and Development in Drama and Arts Education', *Research in Drama Education*, 5:2 (2000), pp. 217–234.

Samuel, R., MacColl, E. and Cosgrove, S., *Theatres of the Left 1880–1935: Workers' Theatre Movements in Britain and America* (London: Routledge & Kegan Paul, 1985).

Sangster, J., 'Telling our Stories: Feminist Debates and the Use of Oral History', in R. Perks and A. Thomson (eds.), *The Oral History Reader* (London: Routledge, 1998), pp. 87–100.

Schechner, R., *Between Theatre and Anthropology* (Philadelphia: University of Pennsylvania Press, 1985).

Schechner, R., 'Performers and Spectators Transported and Transformed', in P. Auslander (ed.) *Performance: Critical Concepts in Literary and Cultural Studies*, Vol. 1 (London: Routledge, 2003), pp. 263–290.

Schechner, R. and Chaterjee, S., 'Augusto Boal, City Councillor: Legislative Theatre and the Chamber in the Streets', *Drama Review*, 42:4 (1998), pp. 75–90.

Schutzman, M., 'Canadian Roundtable: An interview', in M. Schutzman and J. Cohen-Cruz (eds.), *Playing Boal* (London: Routledge, 1994), pp. 198–226.

Schweitzer, P., 'Many Happy Retirements', in M. Schutzman and J. Cohen-Cruz (eds.), *Playing Boal* (London: Routledge, 1994), pp. 64–80.

Sellars, P., 'The Question of Culture', in M. Delgado and C. Svich (eds.) *Theatre in Crisis: Performance Manifestos for a New Century* (Manchester: Manchester University Press, 2002), pp. 127–143.

Shank, T., *Beyond the Boundaries: American Alternative Theatre* (Ann Arbor: University of Michigan Press, 2002).

Shaughnessy, N., *Applying Performance: Live Art, Socially Engaged Theatre and Affective Practice* (Basingstoke: Palgrave, 2012).

Shepard, B., *Play, Creativity, and Social Movements: If I Can't Dance, It's Not My Revolution* (London: Routledge, 2011).

Shepard, B. and Hayduk, R. (eds.), *From ACT UP to the WTO: Urban Protest and Community Building in the Era of Globalisation* (London: Verso, 2002).

Soper, K., *Troubled Pleasures* (London: Verso, 1990).

Soper, K., *What is Nature? Culture, Politics and the Non-Human* (Oxford: Basil Blackwell, 1995).

Spivak, G., *In Other Worlds: Essays in Cultural Politics* (London: Methuen, 1987).

Stamp, S. 'Holding On: Dramatherapy with Offenders', in J. Thompson (ed.), *Prison Theatre: Perspectives and Practices* (London: Jessica Kingsley Publishers, 1998), pp. 89–108.

Stationery Office, *Life in the United Kingdom: A Guide for New Residents*, 3rd edition (London: HMSO, 2013).

Steedman, C., *Landscape for a Good Woman* (London: Virago Press, 1986).

Stourac, R. and McCreery, K., *Theatre as a Weapon: Workers' Theatre in the Soviet Union, Germany and Great Britain, 1917–1934* (London: Routledge & Kegan Paul, 1986).

Tait, P., *Converging Realities* (Sydney: Currency Press, 1994).

Tanyi-Tang, A., 'Unpeeling the Onion of Privilege', in J. O'Toole and M. Lepp (eds.), *Drama for Life: Stories of Adult Learning and Empowerment* (Brisbane: Playlab Press, 2000), pp. 67–76.

Tanyi-Tang, A., 'Theatre for Change: an Analysis of Two Performances by Women in Mundemba Sub-Division', *Research in Drama Education*, 6:1(2001), 23–38.

Taussig, M and Schechner, R., 'Boal in Brazil, France and the USA', in M. Schutzman and J. Cohen-Cruz (eds.), *Playing Boal* (London: Routledge, 1994), pp. 17–34.

Taylor, C., *Sources of the Self: The Making of the Modern Identity* (Cambridge: Cambridge University Press, 1989).

Taylor, P., *Applied Theatre: Creating Transformative Encounters in the Community* (Portsmouth, NH: Heinemann, 2003).

Taylor, P., 'Musings on Applied Theatre: Towards a New Theatron', *Drama Magazine*, 10:2 (2003), pp. 37–42.

Thompson, J., 'Ugly, Unglamorous and Dirty: Theatre of Relief/Reconciliation/ Liberation in Places of War', *Research in Drama Education*, 7:1 (2002), pp. 108–113.

Thompson, J., *Applied Theatre: Bewilderment and Beyond* (Oxford: Peter Lang, 2003).

Thompson, J., *Performance Affects: Applied Theatre and the End of Effect* (Basingstoke: Palgrave, 2009).

Thompson, P., *The Voice of the Past: Oral History* (Oxford: Oxford University Press, 1978).

Turner, B.S. (ed.), *Citizenship and Social Theory* (London: Sage Publications, 1993).

Turner, V., *From Ritual to Theatre: The Human Seriousness of Play* (New York: Performing Arts Journal Publications, 1982).

Turner, V., *The Anthropology of Performance* (New York: Performing Arts Journal Publications, 1986).

Wiles, D., *A Short History of Western Performance Space* (Cambridge: Cambridge University Press, 2003).

Willett, J., (ed.), *Brecht on Theatre: The Development of an Aesthetic* (London: Methuen, 1964).

Williams, R., *Culture and Society* (London: Hogarth Press, 1993).

Wilson, R.A. (ed.), *Human Rights, Culture and Context* (London: Pluto Press, 1997).

Winston, J., *Drama, Narrative and Moral Education* (London: Falmer Press, 1998).

Winston, J., 'A Response to Brian Edminston's Article: "Drama as Ethical Education"', *Research in Drama Education*, 5:1 (2000), pp. 112–114.

Wittgenstein, L., *Philosophical Investigations*, trans. G.E.M. Anscombe (Oxford: Basil Blackwell, 1963).

Young, I.M., 'The Ideal of Community and the Politics of Difference', in L.J. Nicholson (ed.), *Feminism/Postmodernism* (London: Routledge, 1990), pp. 300–323.

Index